THE
EXPRESSION WEB
DEVELOPER'S GUIDE
TO ASP.NET 3.5

JIM CHESHIRE

800 East 96th Street
Indianapolis, Indiana 46240

~nts at a Glance

The Expression Web Developer's Guide to ASP.NET

ISBN-13: 978-0-7897-3665-9
ISBN-10: 0-7897-3665-9

Library of Congress Cataloging-in-Publication Data is on file.

Printed in the United States of America

First Printing: November 2007

Trademarks

All terms mentioned in this book that are known to be trademarks or service marks have been appropriately capitalized. Que Publishing cannot attest to the accuracy of this information. Use of a term in this book should not be regarded as affecting the validity of any trademark or service mark.

Warning and Disclaimer

Every effort has been made to make this book as complete and as accurate as possible, but no warranty or fitness is implied. The information provided is on an "as is" basis. The author and the publisher shall have neither liability nor responsibility to any person or entity with respect to any loss or damages arising from the information contained in this book.

Bulk Sales

Que Publishing offers excellent discounts on this book when ordered in quantity for bulk purchases or special sales. For more information, please contact

U.S. Corporate and Government Sales
1-800-382-3419
corpsales@pearsontechgroup.com

For sales outside the United States, please contact

International Sales
international@pearsoned.com

This Book Is Safari Enabled

The Safari® Enabled icon on the cover of your favorite technology book means the book is available through Safari Bookshelf. When you buy this book, you get free access to the online edition for 45 days.

Safari Bookshelf is an electronic reference library that lets you easily search thousands of technical books, find code samples, download chapters, and access technical information whenever and wherever you need it.

To gain 45-day Safari Enabled access to this book:

- Go to http://www.quepublishing.com/safarienabled
- Complete the brief registration form
- Enter the coupon code F6IC-Q6QG-QX5C-AJGI-Z35T

If you have difficulty registering on Safari Bookshelf or accessing the online edition, please email customer-service@safaribooksonline.com.

Associate Publisher
Greg Wiegand

Acquisitions Editors
Stephanie J. McComb
Laura Norman

Development Editor
Laura Norman

Managing Editor
Patrick Kanouse

Senior Project Editor
Tonya Simpson

Copy Editor
Margo Catts

Indexer
Ken Johnson

Proofreader
Linda Seifert

Technical Editor
Jennifer Kettell

Publishing Coordinator
Cindy Teeters

Book Designer
Gary Adair

Page Layout
Bronkella Publishing

Table of Contents

About the Author

Jim Cheshire is the author of several books, including the recently released *Special Edition Using Expression Web*. He has been working with ASP.NET since before its release. Jim works as an escalation engineer on the ASP.NET team at Microsoft, where he specializes in debugging and resolving some of the toughest problems Microsoft sees from users of ASP.NET.

Jim also operates the Jimco Software (www.jimcosoftware.com) and Jimco Books (www.jimcobooks.com) websites, where he distributes software and information for users of both Microsoft FrontPage and Microsoft Expression Web. He has been heavily involved in the web design community for more than a decade and is widely considered an expert in Microsoft's web design technologies.

You can contact Jim via either of his websites.

Dedication

This book is dedicated to Becky, my lovely wife. Thank you for your infinite patience through yet another book. I love you.

Acknowledgments

The cover of this book displays my name, but there are so many people who worked as hard as I did (well, almost) to make this book possible.

My sincerest thanks go to Laura, Stephanie, Jenn, and Margo, and to all the folks at Que Publishing. Your superb work made this book so much more than it would have been without you. Special thanks to Laura for graciously agreeing to help with the book and for helping to ensure I was always headed in the right direction. I'd also like to offer special acknowledgement to Stephanie for sticking with me through three books.

To Mikhail Arkhipov and others on the Visual Web Developer team at Microsoft, thank you for answering my questions and sharing your excitement with me. I hope I did the product justice in this book.

To Mike Coleman, my boss at Microsoft, thank you for supporting my work on this project.

To my family, after two books back to back, I know how tired you must be of hearing me say "I'd like to, but I have to write." Thank you for giving me the time and for being patient with me during those times when I was pushing a tight deadline and not in the best of moods. I love all of you so much.

I'd like to thank my parents for their never-ending confidence in me and for encouraging their friends (who know nothing about technology) to buy my books.

Last, but certainly not least, to my readers; thank you for buying my book and making all the work that went into this book worth something. Without you, all the commitment from those involved in this project would be for naught.

We Want to Hear from You!

As the reader of this book, *you* are our most important critic and commentator. We value your opinion and want to know what we're doing right, what we could do better, what areas you'd like to see us publish in, and any other words of wisdom you're willing to pass our way.

As an associate publisher for Que Publishing, I welcome your comments. You can email or write me directly to let me know what you did or didn't like about this book[md]as well as what we can do to make our books better.

Please note that I cannot help you with technical problems related to the topic of this book. We do have a User Services group, however, where I will forward specific technical questions related to the book.

When you write, please be sure to include this book's title and author as well as your name, email address, and phone number. I will carefully review your comments and share them with the author and editors who worked on the book.

Email: feedback@quepublishing.com

Mail: Greg Wiegand
         Associate Publisher
         Que Publishing
         800 East 96th Street
         Indianapolis, IN 46240 USA

Reader Services

Visit our website and register this book at www.informit.com/title/9780789736659 for convenient access to any updates, downloads, or errata that might be available for this book.

INTRODUCTION

Who Should Read This Book?

Not long ago, I wrote a book on Expression Web called *Special Edition Using Microsoft Expression Web*. Expression Web is a great product that builds on the success of Microsoft FrontPage, and although many web designers (including myself) were excited about Expression Web, many were also disappointed to see the removal of FrontPage web components.

Because Expression Web added support for ASP.NET development, many Expression Web users who were migrating from FrontPage saw ASP.NET as a natural transition from the FrontPage components that they had grown so used to. Unfortunately, they quickly found themselves overwhelmed with ASP.NET. Let's face it: Most FrontPage users migrating to Expression Web are not programmers and don't want to become programmers. Instead, they want to take advantage of the technologies exposed in Expression Web without having to spend months learning how to write code.

If you can relate to the previous two paragraphs, this book is for you! This book is designed to walk you through creating an ASP.NET web application from beginning to end, using Microsoft Visual Web Developer Express Edition, (referred to as simply Visual Web Developer from here on out.) Visual Web Developer has many of the designer features and CSS features that you'll find in Expression Web, but it's much better suited to designing ASP.NET applications.

Here are some of the ASP.NET features this book covers:

- Creating ASP.NET websites
- Creating ASP.NET Web forms and user controls
- Accessing databases with ASP.NET
- Editing database data with ASP.NET
- Using ASP.NET membership to password protect parts of a website
- Sending email with ASP.NET

- Using ASP.NET Ajax 1.0
- Much more...

I'll show you how to implement all these features while writing the least amount of code possible, but when code is necessary, I'll provide samples in both Visual Basic and C#.

How This Book Is Organized

This book is divided into multiple sections so that you can quickly find the information you need. Here is the rundown on all the sections:

- Part I, "Understanding ASP.NET Architecture"—I cover the basics of ASP.NET. You'll learn about ASP.NET code models, compilation models, how ASP.NET page events work, how ASP.NET is configured, and the basics of ASP.NET security.
- Part II, "Creating ASP.NET Applications and Web Forms"—In this section, I cover creating ASP.NET websites and ASP.NET Web forms.
- Part III, "Master Pages and User Controls"—I cover creating Web forms with master pages, a new feature introduced in ASP.NET 2.0. I also cover creating and using reusable ASP.NET components called user controls.
- Part IV, "ASP.NET Membership"—In this section I cover the security features of ASP.NET more closely. You'll create users and roles (ASP.NET groups) and configure their access to the website. You'll also create a login page and other pages to allow users to manage user accounts.
- Part V, "ASP.NET Forms and Validation"— In this section you'll learn how to create custom forms in ASP.NET and how to use the ASP.NET validation controls to configure form validation.
- Part VI, "Styling Web Forms in Visual Web Developer"—In this section you'll learn how to use the powerful CSS toolset that Expression Web brings to Visual Web Developer. I also cover ASP.NET skins and themes.
- Part VII, "Data Access with ASP.NET"—In this section I cover the ASP.NET data controls and how to display, add, edit, and delete data from a database.
- Part VIII, "Sending Email with ASP.NET"—In this section I cover ASP.NET Ajax and web services.
- Part IX, "Debugging and Troubleshooting ASP.NET"—Realizing that things will go terribly wrong when you least expect it, this section covers debugging and troubleshooting ASP.NET applications.
- Part X, "Deploying ASP.NET Applications"—In this section, I cover deploying your ASP.NET application to another web server.

I've also included one appendix that covers all the various options and settings available in Visual Web Developer.

Special Elements

Throughout the book, you'll find some special elements that are designed to make it easy to locate important information or special tips that help you get the most out of Visual Web Developer.

When a special term is used for the first time, it is printed in *italic* and is defined close by. If instructions require you to enter text or values into a dialog, the data you are to enter appears like `this`.

Cross References

This book is designed to be read in order, but you may still find yourself wanting to read up on a specific topic in advance or go back and review a topic covered in a previous chapter. For that reason, I've made sure to cross-reference information where possible.

Notes, Tips, Cautions, and Sidebars

You'll find numerous bits of information in these special elements.

NOTE
> Notes include additional technical information or URLs that you can use to access important information.

TIP
> Tips provide information to make a feature easier to use or information you might not have considered.

CAUTION
> Caution elements are designed to warn you about common pitfalls before you suffer from them.

Read Sidebars for the Big Picture

You won't find sidebars in every chapter. They're designed to give you more insight into a particular topic. If you're the kind of person who wants to know all the details, you'll find sidebars to be extremely valuable.

I've worked hard to make this book the definitive resource on ASP.NET for Expression Web users who don't want to become ASP.NET programmers. I hope this book will excite you about designing ASP.NET applications and adding a whole new realm of possibilities to your web design toolset.

—Jim

PART I

Understanding ASP.NET Architecture

CHAPTER 1

Installing and Configuring ASP.NET

IN THIS CHAPTER

Understanding the .NET Framework and ASP.NET

Computer programming has long been considered the realm of the computer elite. Although many computer users have dabbled in writing code from time to time, few have become competent enough to actually be considered software developers. The reason is simple: Programming technologies are often obscure and complex and becoming proficient in the use of them can involve years of study.

Over the years, several software companies have attempted to make it easier to develop rich applications quickly without having to deal with the complexities of computer architectures. Most of these attempts have met with failure or only limited success.

> **NOTE** Perhaps the most well-known of these is Java, a programming framework released by Sun Microsystems in 1996. Although server-side Java has been relatively successful, Java as a whole has seen limited success and remains a minor force for desktop and web applications.

In 2002 Microsoft released its solution to complex programming, called the .NET Framework. The .NET Framework consists of many technologies that can be leveraged by developers to quickly and easily develop desktop applications and web applications. By providing common libraries for many programming tasks, the .NET Framework makes it easy to build robust applications rapidly. As you progress through this book, you'll get a good idea of just how much power the .NET Framework provides.

> **NOTE** A complete discussion of all the technologies that make up the .NET Framework is outside the scope of this book. Your best resource on in-depth information is the Microsoft Developer Network (MSDN) located at msdn.microsoft.com.

As mentioned previously, the .NET Framework can be used to create Web applications (using ASP.NET) or desktop applications. ASP.NET runs on *Internet Information Services* (IIS), Microsoft's Web server for Windows, and you can run ASP.NET applications on Windows XP, Windows 2000, Windows 2003, and Windows Vista. However, because support for Windows 2000 has been discontinued, I will not discuss it in this book.

> **NOTE** ASP.NET will also be included with Windows Server "Longhorn." However, as of this writing, Longhorn is still in beta and I won't discuss it in this book.

Both Expression Web and Visual Web Developer can use the Microsoft ASP.NET Development Server instead of IIS. I'll discuss that topic in further detail in the next section.

Before we go into the details of developing ASP.NET applications, you'll want to make sure that you have a web server configured to run ASP.NET applications. All operating systems from Windows 2000 up support the use of the ASP.NET Development Server. Table 1.1 shows the web server choices you have in addition to the ASP.NET Development Server for each operating system.

Table 1.1   Available Web Servers

Operating System	Web Server
Windows XP	IIS 5.1
Windows 2003	IIS 6.0
Windows Vista	IIS 7.0

The method of configuring ASP.NET depends upon which web server you are using.

Configuring ASP.NET

The files that are required to run ASP.NET applications are installed when the .NET Framework is installed. However, ASP.NET must be configured on the web server before you can run ASP.NET applications. If you already have your web server installed when you install the .NET Framework, ASP.NET will be automatically configured for you in most cases.

> **N O T E**   If you already have ASP.NET installed, you can skip forward to "Using the ASP.NET Development Server," **p. 15**, in this chapter.

If you have to configure ASP.NET yourself or if you want to change the configuration of ASP.NET, you'll need to follow steps that are specific to the web server you are using. Table 1.2 lists the sections available in this chapter by server version. You can use that information to jump right to the applicable section for your situation.

Table 1.2   Sections in this Chapter Based on Web Server

Web Server	Section	Page
IIS 5.1 or IIS 6	Configuring ASP.NET on IIS 5.1 or IIS 6.0	10
IIS 7	Configuring ASP.NET on IIS 7	12
ASP.NET Development Server	Using the ASP.NET Development Server	15

> **TIP**
>
> If you're not sure whether ASP.NET is configured, it won't hurt anything if you configure it again.

Configuring ASP.NET on IIS 5.1 or IIS 6.0

If you are using IIS 5.1 (on Windows XP Professional) or IIS 6, you configure ASP.NET by using a command-line utility called `aspnet_regiis.exe`. If IIS is installed when the .NET Framework is installed, this happens for you automatically. However, if you install IIS after you've installed the .NET Framework, you need to manually configure ASP.NET.

> **TIP**
>
> The .NET Framework is automatically installed when you install Visual Web Developer.

> **NOTE**
>
> I don't cover the details of managing IIS in this book. If you're interested in thorough coverage of using and managing IIS, read *Microsoft IIS 5 Administration* from Que Publishing for information on IIS 5. For information on IIS 6, read *Microsoft IIS 6 Delta Guide* from Que Publishing. For more information on IIS 7, read *Special Edition Using Microsoft Windows Vista* from Que Publishing.

> **CAUTION**
>
> If ASP.NET 1.1 is already configured in IIS when you install the .NET Framework 3.5, IIS will still use ASP.NET 1.1 after the installation of the new version of the .NET Framework. To use ASP.NET 3.5, you will need to run `aspnet_regiis.exe` as described in this chapter.

The `aspnet_regiis.exe` utility is run from a command line, using command-line parameters. To configure ASP.NET 3.5, you will need to run the `aspnet_regiis.exe` utility from the install directory for the 2.0 version of the .NET Framework because there isn't a new ASP.NET runtime in the .NET Framework version 3.5.

NOTE | The 2.0 version of the .NET Framework is installed in the c:\Windows\ Microsoft.NET\Framework\v2.0.50727 directory.

TIP | The documentation for `aspnet_regiis.exe` uses the term "install" when referring to configuring ASP.NET. I've used that same terminology in Table 1.3 for consistency.

Table 1.3 shows the commonly used command-line parameters. I realize that these commands can be a little confusing at this point, but I feel it is important to provide this content for your reference. You will likely not use many of these parameters.

Table 1.3   `aspnet_regiis.exe` Command Line Parameters

Parameter	Description
`-i`	Installs ASP.NET and upgrades any existing websites with a lower version of ASP.NET to this version.
`-ir`	Registers ASP.NET but does not upgrade any existing websites.
`-enable`	Enables ASP.NET in IIS 6. This option must be used in combination with the `-i`, `-ir`, or `-r` parameter.
`-disable`	Disables ASP.NET in IIS 6. This option must be used in combination with the `-i`, `-ir`, or `-r` parameter.
`-r`	Installs ASP.NET and registers all existing websites with this version, regardless of the existing version.
`-u`	Uninstalls this version of ASP.NET from all websites. The latest existing version of the ASP.NET will be registered in place of this version.
`-ua`	Uninstalls all versions of ASP.NET.
`-lv`	List all versions of ASP.NET that are installed, along with the installation path of each.

To manually configure ASP.NET in IIS 5.1 or IIS 6, follow these steps:

1. Open a command prompt, enter the following command, and press Enter to switch into the c:\Windows\Microsoft.NET\Framework\v2.0.50727 directory:
```
cd \Windows\Microsoft.NET\Framework\v2.0.50727
```

2. Run the following command to uninstall any existing versions:
```
aspnet_regiis -ua
```

TIP | If you're unsure whether any version of ASP.NET is already installed, feel free to run the command in step 2 just to be sure. It won't hurt anything.

3. Run the following command to configure ASP.NET:

Windows 2003

```
aspnet_regiis -i -enable
```

Windows XP

```
aspnet_regiis -i
```

After you've completed these steps, you're ready to run ASP.NET pages in IIS.

Configuring ASP.NET on IIS 7

Configuration of ASP.NET is entirely different in IIS 7 because IIS 7 is entirely different from previous versions of IIS. To use ASP.NET in IIS 7, you first need to make sure that you've installed the proper components in IIS. Specifically, you need to install ASP.NET, and so that you can debug your ASP.NET code, you'll want to install Windows Authentication as well as shown in Figure 1.1.

FIGURE 1.1

To run ASP.NET in IIS 7, check the ASP.NET and the Windows Authentication check boxes in the IIS 7 installation options.

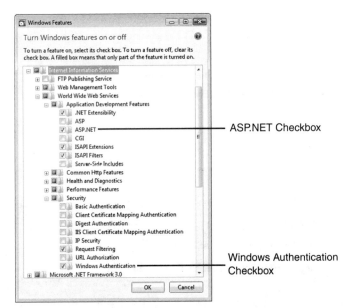

ASP.NET Checkbox

Windows Authentication Checkbox

NOTE If you're familiar with previous versions of IIS, it may seem strange that you would install Windows Authentication. Unlike previous versions, enabling Windows Authentication in IIS 7 involves checking the option during setup. Therefore, you are literally installing Windows Authentication when you enable it in IIS 7.

> **TIP**
> You install IIS 7 by using the Turn Windows Features On and Off link in the Programs and Features applet in the Control Panel.
>
> If you've already installed IIS, you can still add ASP.NET and Windows Authentication by going back through the setup and selecting them from the list of components.

Like IIS 6, IIS 7 uses *application pools* to configure web applications. Each application pool contains its own settings, including which version of ASP.NET it uses and which web applications that are configured to run inside of that specific application pool.

➔ For more information on IIS 7, **see** Microsoft's IIS 7 website at www.iis.net.

IIS 7 creates some application pools automatically when you install it, and at least one of those application pools is configured for ASP.NET 2.0. Even though Microsoft refers to the version of ASP.NET that comes with Visual Web Developer 2008 as ASP.NET 3.5, IIS identifies the version number by the version of the runtime. In the case of ASP.NET 3.5, the runtime version is still 2.0, so make sure that your website is configured to run in one of the application pools that is configured to run ASP.NET 2.0.

To check the application pool settings for your website, follow these steps.

1. Open Internet Information Services (IIS) Manager from Administrative Tools in the Control Panel.

2. The top-level node will show the name of your computer. Expand it.

3. Expand the Web Sites node.

4. Expand the Default Web Site node.

5. Click once on your website to select it, as shown in Figure 1.2.

FIGURE 1.2

To configure settings for your website in IIS 7, select it from the list of web applications.

6. In the Actions pane on the right side of the dialog, click the Basic Settings link as shown in Figure 1.3.

Basic Settings Link

FIGURE 1.3

The Basic Settings link allows you to configure the basic settings (such as the application pool) for the web application.

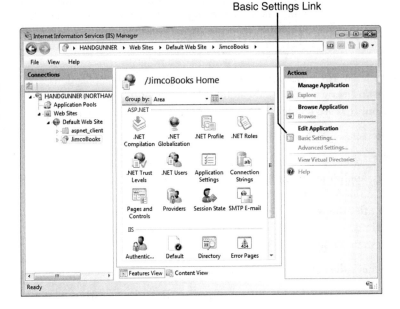

7. In the Edit Application dialog, click the Select button.

8. Make sure the selected application pool is configured for the 2.0 version of the .NET Framework as shown in Figure 1.4. If it is not, select a different application pool from the Application Pool drop-down.

.NET Framework Version

FIGURE 1.4

Check your settings to ensure that your application is configured to run under the 2.0 version of the .NET Framework as shown here.

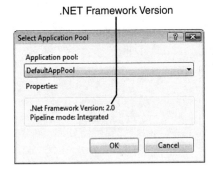

 If there are no application pools configured for the 2.0 version of the .NET Framework, see "No ASP.NET 2.0 Application Pools" in the "Troubleshooting IIS" section of this chapter.

Using the ASP.NET Development Server

The 2.0 version of the .NET Framework introduced a lightweight web server called the ASP.NET Development Server that can be used in lieu of IIS to develop and test ASP.NET websites. If you are using a disk-based path (for example, c:\MyWebSite) for your website, you'll likely be using the ASP.NET Development Server to develop and test your web application.

The ASP.NET Development Server requires no complex configuration. When you run your page in Expression Web or Visual Web Developer, the ASP.NET Development Server starts up and serves the page. However, it is specifically designed for ASP.NET applications, so if you have legacy ASP pages, PHP pages, or pages that use another server-side technology other than ASP.NET, you can't run your application using the ASP.NET Development Server.

There are some drawbacks to using the ASP.NET Development Server. For example, the ASP.NET Development Server always runs using your Windows user information. That means that some parts of your application might work perfectly in the ASP.NET Development Server and then stop working when you move your site to the Internet.

Suppose your application saves information into a database or writes information to a text file. When running under the ASP.NET Development Server, your application is running using your Windows user information. Therefore, your code works fine because you have permission to write to the database or the text file. However, when you move your application to IIS, the application fails because the user under which the application is running changes. You should keep this in mind when developing your application.

There are many other situations in which an application might behave differently in the ASP.NET Development Server than it does in IIS. You therefore should always test your application carefully in IIS before going live.

Now that you've configured ASP.NET, it's time to move on to the fun part; developing and testing ASP.NET applications. Let's get started!

Troubleshooting IIS

In my experience working with ASP.NET and IIS, there are a couple of problems that you might encounter, either one of which will derail you from being able to continue developing the sample website we'll be building throughout the rest of this book. Let's cover those problems and some possible solutions to them.

ASP.NET Tab Missing

I've configured ASP.NET, but when I go to the properties of my website in the Internet Information Services snap-in, there is no ASP.NET tab.

(This troubleshooting note is not applicable to IIS 7.)

There are many possible causes for this. If you are using a 64-bit version of Windows and IIS is running in 32-bit mode, the tab is missing. There's no workaround for that because it's that way by design.

> **NOTE** If you don't know whether you are running IIS in 32-bit mode, it almost certainly means that you aren't. On 64-bit Windows, IIS runs in 64-bit mode unless you explicitly set it not to.

If you are running a 32-bit version of Windows and the tab is missing, you can try to add it manually to the snap-in by following these steps:

1. Click Start and select Run.
2. Enter `mmc` in the Run dialog and click Open.
3. Select File, Add/Remove Snap-in.
4. Click the Add button.
5. Select Internet Information Services and click Add as shown in Figure 1.5.

FIGURE 1.5
The Internet Information Services snap-in can be added manually if required.

6. Click the Close button.
7. Click the Extensions tab.

8. Make sure the ASP.NET Management Extension is checked, as shown in Figure 1.6, and click OK.

FIGURE 1.6

The ASP.NET tab is added to the IIS snap-in, using the ASP.NET Management Extension.

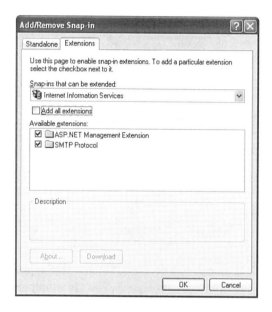

9. Close the MMC and save the new console using any name you choose.

If the ASP.NET tab is still missing after you perform these steps, it means that ASP.NET 2.0 was not properly registered on your system. In that case, you can often correct the problem by running aspnet_regiis -i, as previously described in this chapter.

No ASP.NET 2.0 Application Pools

I have installed IIS 7 and have checked ASP.NET and Windows Integrated Authentication. However, none of the application pools listed in IIS show that they are using ASP.NET 2.0.

(This troubleshooting note is applicable only to IIS 7.)

In some rare cases, you might not have an application pool configured to run ASP.NET 2.0. If you find yourself in that situation, you can easily configure an existing application pool to run ASP.NET by following these steps:

1. Open Internet Information Services from the Administrative Tools applet in Control Panel.

2. Expand the top-level node if it is not already expanded.

3. Click the Application Pools node as shown in Figure 1.7.

FIGURE 1.7

You configure appli-
cation pools by using
the Application Pools
node in the Internet
Information Services
manager.

4. Select the desired application pool from the list of available application pools. Unless you are going to use multiple application pools, you can simply select the `DefaultAppPool` application pool.

5. Click the Basic Settings link in the Edit Application Pool section of the Actions pane shown previously in Figure 1.7.

6. In the Edit Application Pool dialog, select .NET Framework v2.0.50727 from the .NET Framework Version drop-down, as shown in Figure 1.8.

FIGURE 1.8

It's easy to configure
the ASP.NET version
used for a particular
application pool by
using the Edit
Application Pool
dialog.

7. Leave all other settings at the default values and click OK.

You then need to ensure that your website is configured to use the application pool that you configured as described earlier in this chapter.

> **NOTE**
>
> It is not necessary to restart IIS after making application pool settings. Each application pool actually runs inside its own process (called `w3wp.exe`), and when you make configuration changes to an application pool, IIS automatically closes the existing application pool and launches it again with the new settings.

> **NOTE**
>
> I realize that it's confusing to refer to ASP.NET 2.0 and ASP.NET 3.5 as though they are interchangeable. When the .NET Framework 3.5 was in beta, Microsoft intended to not change the ASP.NET version number because the ASP.NET runtime is not updated with the .NET Framework version 3.5.
>
> Shortly after beta 2 of the .NET Framework 3.5, Microsoft decided to call ASP.NET "ASP.NET in the .NET Framework 3.5" and began using the shortened form "ASP.NET 3.5." Unfortunately, because technically there isn't a new version of ASP.NET included with the .NET Framework 3.5, the name "ASP.NET 3.5" causes some confusion. Hopefully this note helps clear up some of that confusion for you.

CHAPTER 2

ASP.NET Code Models

IN THIS CHAPTER

Understanding ASP.NET Web Form Code

Most ASP.NET web pages are made up of two parts: the ASPX page (called a Web form) and server-side code that executes on the web server and adds functionality to the Web form. The code in a Web form is an HTML page with some additional code added that ASP.NET uses to give functionality to the page. That additional code consists of one or more lines of code that tell ASP.NET how to execute the page (called *directives*) and ASP.NET design-time code that defines areas of the page that ASP.NET will replace with HTML when the page is browsed.

> **NOTE**   Even though most ASP.NET pages contain server-side code, having server-side code is not a requirement. As you'll see later in this book, it's possible to per-form complex tasks with ASP.NET without writing any code.
>
> I'll cover server-side code in detail later in this chapter.

→ For more information on exactly what happens when an ASP.NET page executes, **see** "ASP.NET Compilation," **p. 32**.

ASP.NET Directives

ASP.NET directives are lines of code that appear at the top of a Web form and control how ASP.NET handles the page or objects on the page. An ASP.NET directive is always in the following format:

```
<%@ <directive_name> <attribute>="<value>" %>
```

When you create a new Web form, a @ Page directive is added for you automatically. The @ Page directive tells ASP.NET what language the page uses and allows other common prop-erties of the page to be specified. The following code shows a simple @ Page directive speci-fying a language of C#:

```
<%@ Page Language="C#" %>
```

If you choose to place the code in a separate file when creating a new Web form, the @ Page directive might look like the following.

```
<%@ Page Language="C#" AutoEventWireup="true"  CodeFile="Default.aspx.cs"
➥Inherits="_Default" %>
```

Note that the second @ Page directive adds three attributes that are not present in the first: the AutoEventWireup, CodeFile, and Inherits attributes. The AutoEventWireup attribute controls how ASP.NET handles hooking up events for the page, whereas the CodeFile and Inherits attributes specify where the page will look for server-side code.

→ For more information on the AutoEventWireup attribute, **see** "Investigating the Page Lifecycle," **p. 45**.

Some of the most common ASP.NET directives are listed in Table 2.1.

Table 2.1   Common ASP.NET Directives

Directive	Purpose
@ Control	The equivalent of an @ Page directive for a user control.
@ Master	Specifies that the page is an ASP.NET master page and defines attributes for the master page.
@ OutputCache	Defines ASP.NET caching options for the page or user control.
@ Page	Defines attributes for use in a Web form.
@ Register	Maps a custom server control or a user control to a particular tag in a Web form.

➔ For more information on ASP.NET user controls, **see** "Creating a User Control," **p. 164**.

➔ For more information on ASP.NET caching, **see** Chapter 5, "ASP.NET State Management."

➔ For more information on using the @ Register directive, **see** "Adding User Controls to a Page," **p. 166**.

As you progress through the rest of this book, you'll have ample opportunities to work with ASP.NET directives.

ASP.NET Design-Time Code

When you browse an ASP.NET page, the Web form is executed on the web server, where HTML code is generated dynamically and sent to the requesting client. When you are designing a Web form, the code that your design tool generates is quite different from the code that eventually makes its way to the web browser.

ASP.NET functionality is added to a web page via the use of ASP.NET controls. ASP.NET controls can be as simple as a text box or as complex as a feature-rich grid that displays and edits data in a database.

When you add an ASP.NET control to a web page in Visual Web Developer, design-time code is added that determines how the control is displayed in the designer and also how the HTML should be rendered for the page when it is browsed.

The design-time code for an ASP.NET control is in the following format:

```
<prefix:ControlType ID="ControlID" runat="server"></prefix:ControlType>
```

NOTE   All ASP.NET controls will have a runat attribute set to server and an ID attribute set to the ID of the control. Other attributes may be set depending on the type of control and the properties that have been set in Visual Web Developer.

> ➔ For more information on setting properties of ASP.NET, **see** "Creating ASP.NET Web Forms," **p. 130**.

For example, suppose you insert an ASP.NET TextBox control on your page. The code that gets generated in Code view looks similar to the following code:

```
<asp:TextBox ID="TextBox1" runat="server"></asp:TextBox>
```

When ASP.NET renders the page at runtime, the TextBox control renders HTML code as follows:

```
<input name="TextBox1" type="text" id="TextBox1" />
```

> **TIP** Many ASP.NET controls have similar counterparts in regular HTML controls. For example, the Input (Text) HTML control looks like an ASP.NET TextBox control, and both actually render as HTML <input> tags. However, ASP.NET controls have additional functionality specifically designed around ASP.NET.

Server-Side Code Models

As mentioned previously, ASP.NET server-side code is code that runs on the web server and adds functionality to an ASP.NET Web form. Server-side code can be written using one of two models: inline code or code-behind code. Inline code is server-side code that appears inside the Web form itself, whereas code-behind code is added in a separate file that is specified in the @ Page directive.

> ➔ For information on how to choose between inline and code-behind code, **see** "Choosing a Code Model" at the end of this chapter.

Inline Server-Side Code

Inline server-side code is ASP.NET code written in either VB or C# that is added to the Web form itself. Inline code appears inside a <script> block on the page that is explicitly set to run on the server and is added directly above the opening <html> tag.

> **TIP** The inline server-side code will not be displayed in the browser when the page is viewed live. ASP.NET removes it from the page when it sends your page to the browser.

The code in Listing 2.1 shows an example of inline ASP.NET code.

Listing 2.1   Inline Code Example

```
<%@ Page Language="C#" %>

<!DOCTYPE html PUBLIC "-//W3C//DTD XHTML 1.0 Transitional//EN"
➥"http://www.w3.org/TR/xhtml1/DTD/xhtml1-transitional.dtd">

<script runat="server">

    protected void Page_Load(object sender, EventArgs e)
    {
        Response.Write("Welcome to my website.");
    }

</script>

<html xmlns="http://www.w3.org/1999/xhtml" >
<head runat="server">
    <title>Sample Page</title>
</head>
<body>
    <form id="form1" runat="server">
    <div>

    </div>
    </form>
</body>
</html>
```

The code in Listing 2.1 contains code that will display the message "Welcome to my web-site." when the `Page_Load` event for the page is used to browse the ASP.NET page.

NOTE

Don't worry if you don't understand any of the code in Listing 2.1. We'll go into more detail on server-side code as we design an ASP.NET application later in this book.

➜ For more information on events in ASP.NET, **see** "Page Events and the Page Lifecycle," **p. 44**.

TIP

Don't confuse inline ASP.NET code with code that is incorporated into the HTML page using the server-side delimiters <% and %>. You can add ASP.NET code using this legacy method (for example, `<p>It is now <%=Now()%>.</p>`), but it is not recommended because it isn't in keeping with the event-driven nature of ASP.NET.

Code-Behind Server-Side Code

The code-behind model uses server-side code located in a separate file. You configure the connection between the Web form and the code file by using the @ Page directive in the Web form. The following sample @ Page directive illustrates this:

```
<%@ Page Language="C#" CodeFile="Default.aspx.cs" Inherits="_Default" %>
```

In addition to the Language attribute discussed previously in the "ASP.NET Directives" section of this chapter, this @ Page directive includes a CodeFile attribute and an Inherits attribute. These two attributes configure the connection to the server-side code.

The CodeFile attribute defines the name of the file that contains the ASP.NET server-side code. The recommended naming convention for the code-behind file is to use the filename of the Web form with the proper file extension appended: .cs for C# code and .vb for VB code.

When ASP.NET runs your page, it creates a programmatic representation of your page called a *class*. The Inherits attribute tells ASP.NET what the name of that class should be. When you create a new Web form in Visual Web Developer using the code-behind model, Visual Web Developer automatically configures this for you.

NOTE For more information on object-oriented concepts such as inheritance, read *Special Edition Using C#* from Que Publishing if you're using C#, or *Special Edition Using Visual Basic.NET* from Que Publishing if you're using VB.

TIP You can use the Src attribute to connect a code file to a Web form. However, it's not recommended because doing so changes the way that ASP.NET compiles the page at runtime and increases the chance that you may run into problems.

→ For more information on using code-behind files with Web forms, **see** "ASP.NET Compilation," **p. 32**.

Switching Server-Side Code Models

You might find yourself choosing a particular code model only to change your mind later. For example, if you choose inline code and then later add an ASP.NET developer to your team, you might want to break the server-side code and the Web form into separate files to make it easier for everyone to work in a team environment.

Although it's better to choose a model and stick with it, you can switch if necessary. Switching between code models midstream isn't impossible, but it is inconvenient. Let's examine some sample code and how it can be moved between the two code models.

Moving from Code-Behind to Inline Code

Listing 2.2 shows code in a code-behind file in C#. Listing 2.3 shows code in a code-behind file in VB.

Listing 2.2   C# Code

```
using System.Data;

public partial class _Default : System.Web.UI.Page
{
    protected void Page_Load(object sender, EventArgs e)
    {
        Response.Write("Hello.");
    }
}
```

Listing 2.3   VB Code

```
Imports System.Data

Partial Class HomePageVB
    Inherits System.Web.UI.Page

    Protected Sub Page_Load(ByVal sender As Object,
    ➥ByVal e As System.EventArgs) Handles Me.Load
        Response.Write("Hello.")
    End Sub

End Class
```

> **NOTE**   Visual Web Developer adds several using statements in the C# code by default, but it adds no Imports statements to VB code by default. I have added the Imports statement to the VB code and removed several of the using statements from the C# code so that the examples will be the same.

In the C# code the System.Data namespace is imported with the using statement, and in the VB code it is imported with the Imports statement. To move this code to an inline model, you first need to add @ Import directives for the imported namespace. The following code illustrates this:

```
<@ Import Namespace="System.Data" %>
```

Only one namespace can be imported via each @ Import directive, and the syntax is the same whether you are using VB or C#.

After you import all the necessary namespaces, you'll then need to move some of the server-side code into a `<script>` block with a `runat` attribute set to "server" (as discussed previously when we reviewed the details of the inline code model).

The section of code that you want to move is all the code inside of the class declaration. In C#, the class declaration looks like the following code:

```
public partial class _Default : System.Web.UI.Page
```

Directly underneath the class declaration is an opening curly brace. You will copy all the code between that opening brace and the corresponding closing curly brace.

> **TIP**   In Visual Web Developer, you can easily identify the matching closing curly brace by placing the cursor on the same line as the opening curly brace and then pressing Ctrl-] on your keyboard. When you do this, Visual Web Developer highlights both braces, and each press of Ctrl-] toggles you between the two braces.

In VB you will need to copy all the code between the `Partial Class` statement and the `End Class` statement.

Listing 2.4 shows how the code from Listing 2.2 or Listing 2.3 would look after being moved into an inline script block on a page.

Listing 2.4   Code Moved into an Inline Script Block

```
<%@ Page Language="C#" %>
<%@ Import Namespace="System.Data" %>

<script runat="server">

    protected void Page_Load(object sender, EventArgs e)
    {
      Response.Write("Hello.");
    {

</script>
```

> **NOTE**   The opening `<html>` tag for the Web form would appear directly underneath the closing `</script>` tag in Listing 2.4.

Note that the @ `Page` directive has also changed and includes only the `Language` attribute. Other attributes are valid with inline code as well, but both the `CodeFile` and the `Inherits` attributes have been removed because they are not applicable in the inline code model.

Moving from Inline Code to Code-Behind

Moving from inline code to code-behind is simply a matter of reversing the steps you took to move from code-behind to inline code. However, to make the move, you need to add a new code file and connect it to your Web form. You also need to add the necessary framework in your code file.

The easiest way to do that is to create a new Web form in Visual Web Developer and choose the option to place the code in a separate file. You can then make the following modifications to the code-behind file.

- Change the classname to a unique name of your choice.
- Add `using` or `Imports` statements for the necessary namespaces.
- Copy and paste the server-side code from your Web form into the class defined in the new code file.

After you make that change, you need to make the following changes to the Web form code.

- Remove any @ `Import` directives.
- Remove the server-side `<script>` block.
- Add a `CodeFile` attribute to the @ `Page` directive and specify the name of the code file you created.
- Add an `Inherits` attribute to the @ `Page` directive and specify the classname you specified in the code file.

As you can see, it's a lot easier to choose your code model and stick with it. Changing to a new model is possible, but it's a hassle. As the amount of code in your application increases, it becomes more troublesome to change.

Choosing a Code Model

Having two code models to choose from is convenient in that it allows you to choose the best route for your particular development needs, but it also means that there's one more decision you need to make when developing your website.

NOTE | Your choice of code model is going to affect you only during development. After you've finished developing your website and you deploy it to a web server, the code model becomes inconsequential because both inline and code-behind sites are executed by ASP.NET in the same manner.

TIP   If you're an Expression Web user and do all your ASP.NET development in Expression Web, inline code is a good choice. Expression Web does not understand the connection between a Web form and the code file associated with it, so it makes more sense to use the inline model when using Expression Web exclusively. You'll still be able to use Visual Web Developer to edit the file with full IntelliSense support, color-coding, and all the other enhancements provided by that environment.

Code-behind code is often the best choice of code models. The primary reason is that it enables you to separate the server-side code from the design of the website. For example, you could have a designer create graphics and layout in Expression Web at the same time that the implementation of the application is coded in Visual Web Developer.

I've said it before, but it's worth repeating: Whichever code model you choose, you will be best off sticking with it. It's easy to accidentally introduce bugs by changing large portions of code to change code models. Carefully weigh your options before going down the path of making broad changes and do it only if you have no other choice.

CHAPTER 3

ASP.NET Compilation Models

IN THIS CHAPTER

ASP.NET Compilation

In the previous chapter, I covered the basics of ASP.NET code models. In this chapter, we'll discuss the details of how ASP.NET applications are compiled. This information is not vital to your success as an ASP.NET developer, but having an understanding of the architecture of your development environment always makes you a better developer.

ASP.NET is nothing like the legacy ASP with which many developers are familiar. You develop ASP pages by using VBScript or JScript, and they are interpreted, meaning that they are executed just as they are written, directly from the page. ASP.NET is entirely different in that ASP.NET pages are compiled before they are executed.

When you write ASP.NET code, you do so in human-readable text. Before ASP.NET can run your code, it has to convert it into something that the computer can understand and execute. The process of converting code from what a programmer types into what a computer can actually execute is called *compilation*.

Exactly how compilation takes place in ASP.NET depends on the compilation model that you use. Several different compilation models are available to you in ASP.NET 3.5.

The Web Application Compilation Model

The web application compilation model is the same model provided in ASP.NET 1.0 and 1.1. When you use this model, you use the Build menu in Visual Web Developer to compile your application into a single DLL file that is copied to a `bin` folder in the root of your application. When the first request comes into your application, the DLL from the bin folder is copied to the Temporary ASP.NET Files folder, where it is then recompiled into code that the operating system can execute in a process known as *just-in-time (JIT)* compilation. The JIT compilation causes a delay of several seconds on the first request of the application.

NOTE   The web application model is available only in Visual Studio 2008. Visual Web Developer 2008 does not enable you to create ASP.NET applications using the web application model.

NOTE   The Temporary ASP.NET Files folder is located at Windows\Microsoft.NET\ Framework\v2.0.50727\Temporary ASP.NET Files by default.

To create a new ASP.NET web application using the web application compilation model, select File, New Project, and then choose the ASP.NET Web Application template as shown in Figure 3.1.

FIGURE 3.1

Choose the New Project option on the File menu to create a new ASP.NET application that uses the web application compilation model.

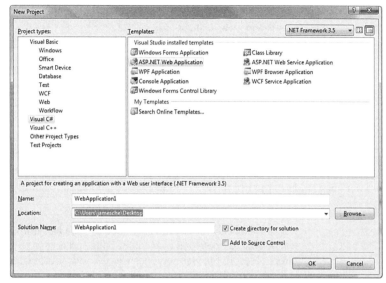

The Website Compilation Model

The website compilation model is the model that developers using Visual Web Developer Express Edition will use because it's the only model available. In this model, all files in the application are copied to the remote web server and are then compiled on the fly by ASP.NET at browse time.

> **NOTE** The website compilation model was the only compilation model available when Visual Studio 2005 (the previous version of Visual Studio) was released. Microsoft added the web application model later as an add-on to Visual Studio 2005, and then incorporated it into Visual Studio 2008.

> **NOTE** You can use the website compilation model whether you are using inline ASP.NET code or code-behind code.

→ For more information on inline code and code-behind code models, **see** "Server-Side Code Models," **p. 24**.

When this compilation model is used, ASP.NET compiles the application into one or more DLLs in the Temporary ASP.NET Files folder when the first page is requested. The DLLs are in a subfolder with a name derived from a special naming convention that allows for dynamic and random directory names. Therefore, a website called MyWebSite might execute from a folder on the server that looks similar to this:

```
C:\Windows\Microsoft.NET\Framework\v2.0.50727\Temporary ASP.NET
➥Files\MyWebSite\650b10f9\e47ff097
```

Inside that folder will be the actual DLLs that contain the compiled code. The naming convention of the DLLs is App_Web_<random_name>.dll.

> **NOTE**
> The compilation of the App_Web DLLs takes place without any explicit action on your part. It's all automatic.

The website compilation model is convenient because developers can open a code file or an ASPX page and make modifications to it on the live server. When those changes are saved, they go into effect immediately. However, using this method requires you to copy all the source code for your application to the live server, and this may be a concern to some developers.

> **CAUTION**
> ASP.NET explicitly forbids the download of code files from a website, so no one will be able to download your source code and access it. However, anyone with direct access to the web server can access your source code when using the website compilation model.

The Precompilation Model

The precompilation model allows you to compile your ASP.NET application into one or more DLLs that can then be copied to the web server in place of any code.

Select Build, Publish Web Site to precompile your website using the Publish Web Site dialog shown in Figure 3.2.

FIGURE 3.2
The Publish Web Site dialog makes precompiling a website simple.

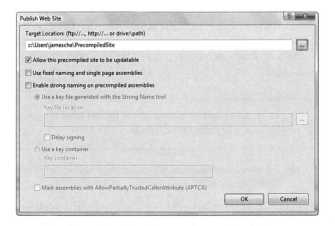

> **NOTE**
> The Publish Web Site menu option is available only in the full Visual Studio version. It is not available in Visual Web Developer Express Edition, but you can add the capability using the steps provided in the "Automating aspnet_compiler.exe in Visual Web Developer Express Edition" section later in this chapter.

If you'd like the option of updating any of your ASPX pages on the live server (for example, making a change to the HTML code), you should check the Allow This Precompiled Site to be Updatable check box. If your site is precompiled with this check box checked, you'll then be able to make modifications to the ASPX pages on the live server if necessary. If it is unchecked, you'll still need to copy the ASPX files to the server, but the precompilation process will remove all the code from them, so you won't be able to change any of them on the live server. We'll talk about that in greater detail a little later in this chapter.

If you are using Visual Web Developer Express Edition, you won't have the option to pre-compile your website within the user interface, but it can still be accomplished if you use the `aspnet_compiler.exe` utility that ships with the .NET Framework.

> **NOTE** The `aspnet_compiler.exe` utility is located in the Windows\Microsoft.NET\ Framework\v2.0.50727 directory.

The `aspnet_compiler.exe` utility runs from a command line. If you have the .NET Framework SDK v2.0 installed, you can select Start, All Programs, Microsoft.NET Framework SDK v2.0 and then click SDK Command Prompt to open a command prompt. This command prompt automatically sets the necessary environment variables to enable you to run `aspnet_compiler.exe` without changing into the v2.0.50727 directory.

> **NOTE** You can download the .NET Framework SDK v2.0 from www.microsoft.com/ downloads/details.aspx?familyid=fe6f2099-b7b4-4f47-a244-c96d69c35dec& displaylang=en. If you'd prefer not to type in that long URL, search on .NET Framework SDK 2.0 and you'll find it.

If you don't have the .NET Framework SDK v2.0 installed, you can still run `aspnet_compiler.exe` from a regular command line, but you need to change into the v2.0.50727 directory first. You can do that by running the following command from a command prompt:

```
cd \windows\microsoft.net\framework\v2.0.50727
```

➔ For information on how to configure a menu item in Visual Web Developer Express Edition that will pre-compile your web application, **see** "Automating `aspnet_compiler.exe` in Visual Web Developer Express Edition," later in this chapter.

Numerous command-line parameters can be used with `aspnet_compiler.exe`. Table 3.1 lists a few that you are likely to use often.

Table 3.1 Frequently Used Parameters for `aspnet_compiler.exe`

Parameter	Description
-?	Prints a description of all parameters.
-v	Specifies the path that follows is a virtual path.
-p	The physical path of the application to compile.
-u	Specifies the compiled application can be updated.
-c	Causes the compiled application to be fully rebuilt, overwriting any existing files.
-d	Creates debug output, making the application easier to debug if a problem arises after it's copied.

Even though there are a lot of parameters for `aspnet_compiler.exe`, the command to pre-compile your ASP.NET application is less complex than you might think. For example, if you have an ASP.NET application located at `c:\myApp` and you want to precompile it and save the result to `c:\compiledApp`, you would run the following command:

```
aspnet_compiler.exe -p "c:\myApp" -v / "c:\compiledApp"
```

The -p parameter is used to point to the location of the application (`c:\myApp` in this case), and the -v parameter points to the virtual location of the application. In a file-based ASP.NET application, the virtual location is always /. That is followed by the path where the compiled files should be written.

If you look in the `c:\compiledApp` directory after this command runs, you can see what looks like the ASPX files for your application, but in fact, these are simply marker files. If you open one of them, you'll see a single line of text in it that says `This is a marker file generated by the precompilation tool, and should not be deleted!` ASP.NET creates this file so that, when the application is browsed on the live server, users won't get an error saying that the file wasn't found.

You'll also see a file called `preCompiledApp.config`. This file contains the version number of the precompilation tool (for ASP.NET 3.5, it is version 2) and specifies whether the site is capable of being updated. If your website has any other configuration files (such as a `web.config` file), it is also in the directory containing the precompiled application, along with any other supporting files and folders such as images and so on.

→ For more information on web.config files, **see** Chapter 6, "ASP.NET Configuration and Performance."

All the code for your application is compiled into a bin directory located at the root of the precompiled site. If you open that directory, you'll see one or more DLLs with names such as App_Web_ekxytkat.dll. All these DLLs start with `App_Web_` and then contain a random group of characters. These DLLs are ASP.NET assemblies, and when your website runs on the live server, it runs from these DLLs.

To publish a precompiled web application to a live web server, simply copy all the files and folders in the directory containing the precompiled website to the live server. When you do, ASP.NET automatically begins using the new files.

Automating `aspnet_compiler.exe` in Visual Web Developer Express Edition

As I pointed out previously, there is a menu option in Visual Studio 2008 that automates the use of the `aspnet_compiler.exe` so that you can easily precompile your applications. That menu option does not exist in Visual Web Developer Express Edition, but you can easily add it to the menu by configuring `aspnet_compiler.exe` as an external tool in Visual Web Developer Express Edition.

To configure menu options for precompiling your web application in Visual Web Developer Express Edition, follow these steps:

1. Launch Visual Web Developer Express Edition.
2. Select Tools, External Tools to access the External Tools dialog.
3. Type **Pre-&Compile (non-updatable)** in the Title text box.

> **TIP** The ampersand in the title means that the character immediately after will be defined as a hotkey for the menu item.

4. Click the browse button next to the Command text box and browse to `aspnet_compiler.exe` in the Windows\Microsoft.NET\Framework\v2.0.50727 directory.
5. Click Open to select the `aspnet_compiler.exe` application.
6. Type **-p** " in the Arguments text box.
7. Click the right-facing arrow button on the right edge of the Arguments text box and select Project Directory, as shown in Figure 3.3.

FIGURE 3.3
You configure the arguments for aspnet_ compiler.exe by using the menu to the right of the Arguments text box.

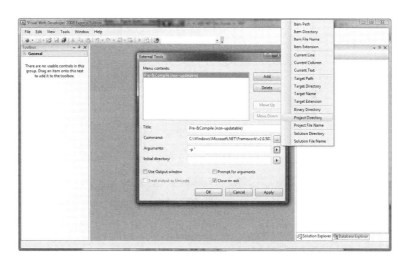

8. Enter a closing quote at the end of the arguments you've entered so far. At this point, the Arguments text box should contain the following text:

    `-p "$(ProjectDir)"`

9. Press the spacebar to add a space at the end of the arguments you've entered so far, and then type **-v / "**.

10. Click the right-facing arrow button at the right edge of the Arguments text box again and select Project Directory.

11. Type **\..\CompiledApp"** after the existing arguments. At this point, the Arguments text box should contain the following text:

    `-p "$(ProjectDir)" -v / "$(ProjectDir)\..\Compiled"`

12. Check the Close on Exit check box.

13. Click OK to add the new external tool to the list.

You now have a new menu option in Visual Web Developer Express Edition (see Figure 3.4) that enables you to precompile your web application as a non-updatable application.

FIGURE 3.4
Adding a menu option in Visual Web Developer Express Edition to automate the aspnet_compiler.exe utility is simple and makes it much more convenient to precompile your applications.

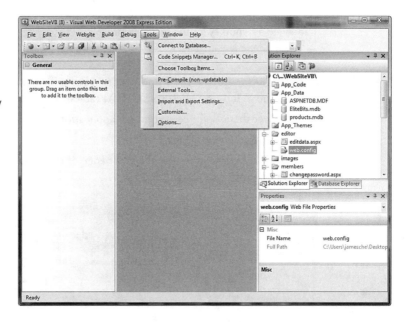

Now let's add a second external tool that precompiles a website and makes it updatable.

1. Select Tools, External Tools to access the External Tools dialog.

2. Click Add to add a new external tool.

3. Enter **Pre-Co&mpile (updatable)** in the Title text box.

4. Configure all other settings as you did before, but this time, add the **-u** argument to the Arguments text box. The arguments text box should contain the following text:

```
-p "$(ProjectDir)" -v / "$(ProjectDir)\..\Compiled" -u
```

When you select one of the new menu items, your ASP.NET application is precompiled into a directory called Compiled. That directory is one level above your ASP.NET application. Therefore, if your ASP.NET application is located at `c:\mysites\myWebApp`, the precompiled website is saved to `c:\mysites\Compiled`.

CHAPTER 4

ASP.NET Events and the Page Lifecycle

IN THIS CHAPTER

An Event-Driven Architecture

Think about the interface for any device you use today, whether it's your car or your MP3 player. They are all based around a cause-and-effect architecture. When you press the gas pedal in your car, it speeds up. When you press the brake, it slows down. When you turn the temperature-control dial counterclockwise, it gets colder. Turn it in the opposite direction and it gets warmer. This same methodology transfers to just about everything we use today.

ASP.NET applications are no different, but in an ASP.NET application, the "effect" is known as an *event*. In an ASP.NET application, everything occurs because of some event. For example, when a page loads, the Load event for the page runs. When a button on the page is clicked, the Click event for that button runs. As a developer, your code is written so that it runs when a particular event runs.

This event-driven architecture makes it much easier to write an ASP.NET application. It enables you to create a user interface (or have someone else create a user interface for you) and then write code that adds functionality to that interface.

Many events in ASP.NET occur because of user interaction. For example, the Click event of a button occurs as a result of a user clicking on that button. However, some events occur automatically, and it's important for you to understand these events and how you can use them in your application.

Application and Session Events

Several events occur in ASP.NET that are not associated with a particular page. These events are known as *application events* and *session events*, and you can hook into these events and run code when they occur by adding a special file to your web application called the global.asax file.

> **TIP**
> The global.asax file does not support the code-behind code model. It always uses inline ASP.NET code.

> **NOTE**
> A thorough discussion of using the global.asax file is outside the scope of this book. If you want comprehensive information on how you can take advantage of the global.asax file, read *Sams Teach Yourself ASP.NET 2.0 in 24 Hours, Complete Starter Kit* from Sams Publishing.

Application Events and the Application Lifecycle

Table 4.1 lists some of the more commonly used application events that might appear in the global.asax file.

Table 4.1   Application Events

Event Name	Description
Start	Occurs when the application starts. If the ASP.NET worker process is restarted this event occurs again when the application restarts.
BeginRequest	Occurs every time a request for the application begins. Code that should run when every page is requested is commonly placed here.
AuthenticateRequest	Occurs after a user has been authenticated to the application.
EndRequest	The last event that occurs when ASP.NET responds to a request for a web application.
End	Occurs when an application is being shut down.
Error	Occurs when an error that is not handled happens in the application.

The following syntax is used to code application events in the global.asax file:

Visual Basic:

```
Sub Application_<Event>(ByVal sender As Object, ByVal e As EventArgs)
    ' Your code goes here.
End Sub
```

C#:

```
void Application_<Event>(object sender, EventArgs e)
{
    // Your code goes here.
}
```

Therefore, if you wanted to write code that runs when an unhandled error occurs, you would write it as follows:

Visual Basic:

```
Sub Application_Error(ByVal sender As Object, ByVal e As EventArgs)
    ' Your code goes here.
End Sub
```

C#:

```
void Application_Error(object sender, EventArgs e)
{
    // Your code goes here.
}
```

→ For more information on handling errors (including the `Application_Error` event) in an ASP.NET application, **see** Chapter 29, "ASP.NET Tracing and Other Troubleshooting Techniques."

Application events occur in a specific order throughout the lifetime of the application. The order of events is called the *application lifecycle*. The events in Table 4.1 are listed in the order in which they occur during the application's lifetime.

> **NOTE** For more details on the application lifecycle, see msdn2.microsoft.com/en-us/library/ms178473.aspx.

Session Events

In addition to the events that apply to the entire application, there are also two events (called Session events) that apply only to a particular user's session. The `Session_Start` event occurs when a new ASP.NET Session is started. The `Session_End` event occurs when an ASP.NET Session is ended.

→ For more information on ASP.NET Sessions and Session events, **see** "Understanding Session Variables," **p. 55**.

Page Events and the Page Lifecycle

As an ASP.NET page executes, a series of page-level events are fired in a particular order. This process is referred to as the *page lifecycle*.

Table 4.2 lists some of the events that occur in a page's lifetime.

Table 4.2   Page Events

Event	Description
Init	Occurs after all the controls on the page have been initialized.
Load	Occurs when ASP.NET is loading the page.
PreRender	Occurs immediately before ASP.NET generates the final code for the page.
Render	Render is not actually an event, but it is automatically called by ASP.NET for each control. This is where the code for the page or control is generated.
Unload	Occurs when ASP.NET has finished generating all code for a page and is unloading it. This event is often used for cleanup code.

> **N O T E** For more information on details of the page lifecycle, see msdn2.microsoft.com/en-us/library/ms178472.aspx.

> **T I P** All the page events shown in Table 4.2 are server-side events. Therefore, before a user sees anything in the browser, the entire page lifecycle is completed.

The Importance of the Lifecycle

At first it might seem that understanding the page lifecycle and the order of events isn't important. However, that couldn't be further from the truth. Many of the code issues with which I help developers deal explicitly with page lifecycle issues.

For example, suppose you have code in the `Init` event that reads in data a user has entered in an ASP.NET form. When your code in the `Init` event runs, you're not actually going to get the value the user entered. Instead, you will get the default value for the data because the data that a user enters into a form is not loaded until the `PreLoad` event. Therefore, if you need to obtain information a user entered in a form, you'll need to do it no earlier than the `Load` event.

This example would be fairly simple to troubleshoot, but there are many issues caused by misconceptions concerning the lifecycle that are much more difficult to track down. It's best to keep a reference to the page lifecycle handy when you're writing code.

> **T I P** A great diagram of the ASP.NET page lifecycle is available at `blog.rioterdecker.net/blogs/avalonboy/archive/2006/06/24/114.aspx`.

Investigating the Page Lifecycle

The easiest way to learn about the page lifecycle is to watch it in action. The easiest way to do that is to create a sample page, add some code to hook up the page events, and see it while it happens.

Let's create a sample page and add some code to intercept events in the page lifecycle.

> **N O T E** You can find the completed website from this section on this book's web page at www.quepublishing.com.

1. Open Visual Web Developer or Visual Studio.

2. Select File, New Web Site and select the ASP.NET Web Site template to create a new website at the location of your choice.

→ For more information on creating websites in Visual Web Developer, **see** Chapter 8, "Creating Websites."

3. Select File, New File.

4. Select Web Form in the list of file types.

> **TIP**   If Web Form is not available as a choice, click Cancel and make sure the project is selected in Solution Explorer. Then select File, New File again and Web Form should be available in the list of templates.

→ For more information on creating ASP.NET Web forms, **see** "Creating ASP.NET Web Forms," **p. 130**.

5. Name the file **default.aspx**, choose either Visual Basic or C#, and check the Place Code in Separate File check box, as shown in Figure 4.1.

FIGURE 4.1
When you create the new Web form, check the box to place the code in a separate file to use the code-behind code model.

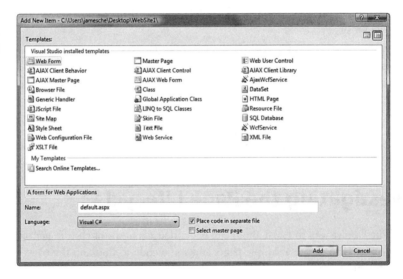

6. Click Add to create the new Web form.

7. Right-click the new Web form in Solution Explorer and select View Code, as shown in Figure 4.2.

FIGURE 4.2

To open the code-behind file, right-click on the Web form and select View Code.

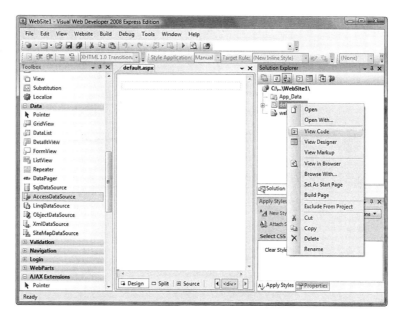

After you've opened the code file, you need to add some code to hook up the page-level events. The location for the new code depends upon the language you are using. If you are using C#, add the code from Listing 4.1 directly under the following code:

```
public partial class _default : System.Web.UI.Page
{
```

If you're using Visual Basic, add the code from Listing 4.2 directly under the following code:

```
Partial Class default
    Inherits System.Web.UI.Page
```

Listing 4.1   C# Code

```
protected void Page_PreInit()
{

}

protected void Page_Init()
{

}

protected void Page_PreLoad()
{

}
protected void Page_Load()
```

continues

Listing 4.1   Continued

```
{

}

protected void Page_PreRender()
{

}
```

Listing 4.2   Visual Basic Code

```
Protected Sub Page_PreInit()

End Sub

Protected Sub Page_Init()

End Sub

Protected Sub Page_PreLoad()

End Sub

Protected Sub Page_Load()

End Sub

Protected Sub Page_PreRender()

End Sub
```

After you've added this code, save your page.

NOTE   In this chapter's sample website, available from download from this book's website, the Visual Basic page is called `DefaultVB` to differentiate it from the C# page.

To see the page lifecycle in action, you need to add some breakpoints to this code. A *breakpoint* is a place in code where a debugger stops when the code executes. To add the necessary breakpoints for this example, right-click on each event and select Breakpoint, Insert Breakpoint as shown in Figure 4.3.

FIGURE 4.3

Insert a breakpoint on each event by right-clicking on the event and selecting Breakpoint, Insert Breakpoint from the menu.

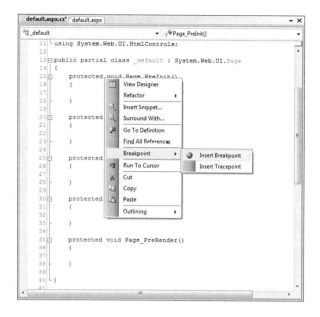

When you insert a breakpoint, you should see a red dot appear in the left margin of that line. If you don't see this red dot, make sure that you are adding the breakpoint to the line of code that defines the event.

If you are using Visual Basic, you need to do one more thing for this code to work. Open the `default.aspx` file and switch to Source view. Change the `AutoEventWireup` attribute in the `@ Page` directive to `true`. The `AutoEventWireup` causes ASP.NET to hook up event handlers automatically when it finds code that matches an event name (such as the code you just added.) This attribute is true by default in C#, so C# developers do not need to change it.

> **TIP** The `AutoEventWireup` attribute is case sensitive. Make sure you set the value to `true` in all lowercase.

Now you're ready to see the page lifecycle as it executes. Press F5 to start debugging. If you are using C#, the first time you debug your application, Visual Web Developer or Visual Studio notifies you that debugging needs to be enabled in the `web.config` file, as shown in Figure 4.4.

FIGURE 4.4

To debug an ASP.NET web application, you must have a `web.config` file with debugging enabled in the root of the application.

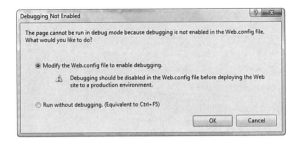

→ For more information on debugging ASP.NET applications, **see** Chapter 27, "Debugging ASP.NET Applications."

→ For more information on using web.config files in an ASP.NET application, **see** "Machine Configuration Files," **p. 66**.

Click OK to configure `web.config` with debugging enabled and you should see your first breakpoint hit on the `PreInit` event. Press F5 and the next breakpoint will be hit and so on. Notice that only after the page's entire lifecycle is completed on the server does the page actually appear in the web browser.

By using the debugger in Visual Web Developer or Visual Studio to examine a page as it progresses through the page lifecycle, you can gain a much better understanding of the lifecycle of an ASP.NET application.

CHAPTER 5

ASP.NET State Management

IN THIS CHAPTER

A Connectionless Environment

I've heard many people describe the communication between a web server and a web browser as akin to a telephone call. A web browser "calls" the web server and a line of communication is opened between the two so that information can be exchanged. In fact, a web application is nothing at all like a telephone conversation. Unlike a telephone call, there is no connection in a web application between the web server and the web browser. The illusion of a connection is created by the network itself.

> **TIP**
>
> In a web application, the web browser machine is called the *client* and the web server machine is called the *server*.

The important thing to remember is that the web server can never send anything to the client without the client explicitly asking it to by making a request. There is no way for the web server to "call" the computer on the other end. A web server strictly responds to requests that the client makes.

Most web pages require state to be maintained between requests. For example, my website used to require that you provide me with your email address to download an add-in. When you clicked a link to download an add-in, a form was displayed asking for your email address. Only after you filled out the form did I allow you to download the add-in. For that to work, I had to save the name of the add-in that you were downloading while you filled out the form and submitted it. The connectionless nature of web applications would make doing this impossible without some mechanism in place to allow for saving information between requests. In ASP.NET, there are three methods of saving information between requests: application variables, Session variables (which is what I used on my site), and the ASP.NET cache.

Understanding Application Variables

Application variables contain information that is not user specific. For example, if you were writing a hit counter for your web application, you would store the number of hits in an application variable. Application variables are often (but not always) set and manipulated in the `global.asax` file.

→ For more information on the `global.asax` file, **see** "Application and Session Events," **p. 42**.

Setting an Application Variable

To set an application variable, you use the following syntax:

for C#:

```
Application["myVariable"] = "someValue";
```

for VB:

```
Application("myVariable") = "someValue"
```

> **TIP** In the sample code, a string is being stored in an application variable. In fact, you can store anything in an application variable, including complex objects with properties, methods, and so on.

The sample code in Listings 5.1 and 5.2 creates a hit counter that increments each time a request is begun for the web application. This code would be included in the global.asax file for the application.

> **NOTE** A completed C# and VB website are included on this book's web page at www.quepublishing.com.

Listing 5.1   C# Hit Counter Code

```
static int numHits;

void Application_BeginRequest(object sender, EventArgs e)
{
    numHits++;
    Application["totalHits"] = numHits;
}
```

Listing 5.2   VB Hit Counter Code

```
Shared numHits As Integer

Protected Sub Application_BeginRequest(ByVal sender As Object, ByVal e As
EventArgs)
    numHits += 1
    Application("totalHits") = numHits
End Sub
```

The first line of this code creates a static (Shared in VB) variable called numHits that is used to increment the total number of hits each time a request comes into the application. By declaring this variable outside any of the events in the global.asax file, you make the variable available for the lifetime of the application. When that variable is static (Shared in VB), it means that all users share a single instance of that variable. If that weren't done, each user would be incrementing a different variable and you wouldn't get an accurate hit count.

In the Application_BeginRequest method, the numHits variable is incremented. The numHits variable is then stored into an application variable named totalHits.

> **NOTE** Because the lifetime of the hit counter variable coincides with the lifetime of the application, a restart of the web server causes the hit counter to reset.

Retrieving an Application Variable

To retrieve the value of an application variable, you use almost the same syntax used to assign a value to the variable. The code that follows demonstrates this:

for C#:

```
someVariable = Application["myAppVariable"];
```

for VB:

```
someVariable = Application("myAppVariable")
```

In the hit counter example, you can display the number of hits to a user by adding the code in Listing 5.3 or Listing 5.4 (depending on your language) to the Page_Load event of a page.

Listing 5.3   C# Code to Display Hits

```
protected void Page_Load(object sender, EventArgs e)
{
    Response.Write("Hits: " + Application["totalHits"].ToString());
}
```

Listing 5.4   VB Code to Display Hits

```
Protected Sub Page_Load(ByVal sender As Object, ByVal e As System.EventArgs)
➥Handles Me.Load
    Response.Write("Hits: " + Application("totalHits").ToString())
End Sub
```

In this case, the Response.Write method is used to write out the number of hits to the page. Note that I've also used the ToString() method in each case to ensure that the application variable is converted into a string suitable for writing out onto the page.

To test this code, run the page. You'll see the number of hits displayed on the page as shown in Figure 5.1. Each time you refresh the page, the number of hits is incremented. If you close the browser window and launch a new browser, the number of hits picks up where it left off.

FIGURE 5.1

The hit counter increments by 1 each time the page is refreshed.

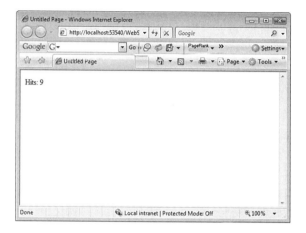

TIP This hit counter is actually not suitable for accurate statistics because it increments on each page refresh. For accurate web stats, it's best to use server logs.

Check with your web host about access to server logs. They'll likely also have (or be able to recommend) a product you can use to analyze the server logs in a nice interface.

Understanding Session Variables

ASP.NET session variables are similar to application variables except that they store information that is specific to a particular user. Each user in an ASP.NET application is associated with a specific ASP.NET Session object. By storing session variables, you can store information that is specific to that user for the lifetime of his or her session.

NOTE Patrick Ng, one of the developers on the ASP.NET team at Microsoft, wrote an excellent FAQ on ASP.NET sessions. You can access it at forums.asp.net/7504/ShowPost.aspx.

ASP.NET identifies a user with a specific session by using a session ID. The session ID is a long string of letters and numbers that is generated on the web server. By default, ASP.NET passes the session ID between the client and server by using a cookie. However, you can change session configuration so that cookieless sessions are used. In cookieless mode, the session ID is passed back and forth in the actual URL. In that case, ASP.NET strips out the session ID when the request first comes in so that the web server doesn't get confused.

> **TIP** A typical session ID might look like edjygf2jqlylkmmbgfcirr45. If cookieless sessions are being used, the session id is passed in the URL. Therefore, the URL for a page might look like www.site.com/ edjygf2jqlylkmmbgfcirr45/page.aspx.

→ For more information on changing session configuration, **see** Chapter 6, "ASP.NET Configuration and Performance."

By default, ASP.NET session variables are stored in memory on the web server. However, you can choose to store session variables in SQL Server or in an ASP.NET State Server as well. The benefit of using SQL Server or State Server is that you can maintain session variables even if the web server is restarted.

An ASP.NET State Server is a special process (`aspnet_state.exe`) that is specifically designed to store session variables for one or more applications. You can run ASP.NET State Server on the same machine as the web server or on a different machine. The benefit of running it on a different machine is that it prevents session variables from being lost if the web server machine has to be rebooted. The drawback to running State Server on another machine is that you then have to pay the cost of moving the session data across a network.

> **NOTE** A thorough discussion of configuring State Server or SQL Server session state is outside the scope of this book. For comprehensive information on configuring ASP.NET session state, see msdn2.microsoft.com/en-us/library/0bb0a3a3-650f 4c47-a0c5-b08b9b591bb4.aspx.

To set a session variable, use the following syntax:

for C#:

```
Session["myVariable"] = "someValue";
```

for Visual Basic:

```
Session("myVariable") = "someValue"
```

To retrieve a variable from session state, use the following syntax:

for C#:

```
someVariable = Session["myVariable"];
```

for Visual Basic:

```
someVariable = Session("myVariable")
```

Just as with application variables, not only can you store strings in session variables, but you can also store complex objects and so forth.

> **NOTE**
>
> If you're new to ASP.NET, I realize that some of this information might be confusing. The easiest way to understand it better is to look at some complete examples of functioning applications.

Using ASP.NET Caching

ASP.NET caching is different than application and server variables in that it is most often used to improve performance. Cache items can be configured to remove themselves (in other words, expire) after a specific interval. In an attempt to free up memory for performance reasons, ASP.NET also forcibly removes cached items in cases where an application is using too much memory.

ASP.NET caching can dramatically improve the performance of an application because it enables you to reuse data that may have been expensive to obtain. Data from a database is a good example. By caching data returned from a query against a database, you can avoid having to go back to the database for the data on each request.

You can use caching in ASP.NET in three ways: page output caching, fragment caching (which is sometimes referred to as partial caching), and the cache application programming interface (API).

> **NOTE**
>
> ASP.NET caching is a complex topic and thorough coverage of it is beyond the scope of this book. For a detailed presentation of caching in ASP.NET, read *Sams Teach Yourself ASP.NET in 21 Days* from Sams Publishing.

Page Output Caching

Page output caching enables you to cache an entire ASP.NET page. You implement it by using the @ OutputCache directive at the top of the Web form. There are numerous attributes to the @ OutputCache directive that define how long the page remains in cache, where the page is cached, and so on.

A typical @ OutputCache directive might look like this:

```
<%@ OutputCache Duration="7200" VaryByParam="county" %>
```

This @ `OutputCache` directive causes the page to be cached for 7200 seconds (2 hours). The `VaryByParam` attribute specifies a parameter name in the URL of the page and a separate version of the page is cached for each unique value of the parameter specified.

For example, suppose your ASP.NET application displays a weather forecast for each county in your state. The weather forecast is updated once every two hours and is stored in a SQL Server database. When the weather page is requested, the URL contains the county for which the weather forecast is desired, like so:

```
www.site.com/weather.aspx?county=tarrant
```

When the web application receives this URL, the ASP.NET code queries the SQL Server database for the weather information for Tarrant County and displays it on the web page.

That database call is expensive because you have to wait on the database server to process the query before the data gets returned. Because the page was cached for 2 hours and a `VaryByParam` attribute of county was used, the first request for a particular county causes that county's weather forecast page to be stored in ASP.NET cache for a period of 2 hours. The next person to request weather for that county within that two-hour period is served the page immediately from ASP.NET's cache and doesn't have to go to the database to get the data.

CAUTION | Be careful that you don't cache data that is too specific to a particular user. Doing so can cause memory usage to increase to the point where your application becomes unstable.

Fragment Caching

Output caching is a great way to improve the performance of your application, but there may be cases where you don't want the entire page to be cached. For example, in the weather page scenario a portion of the page might display severe weather warnings. You wouldn't want that portion of the page to be cached for two hours because that might cause someone to miss vital information about weather dangers in his or her county.

The solution to this dilemma is *fragment caching*, sometimes referred to as *partial page caching*. There are a couple of ways to implement fragment caching: caching of user controls (called control caching) and post-cache substitution.

When you use control caching, user controls are used for content that needs to be cached. In the weather page example, you would display the weather forecast information in a user control and include an @ `OutputCache` directive on the user control. Only the content in the user control would be cached.

→ For more information on user controls, **see** "Creating a User Control," **p. 164.**

Post-cache substitution is the reverse of control caching. When post-cache substitution is used, the entire page is cached, but portions of the page are excluded from that cache. ASP.NET includes a special control for this purpose called the Substitution control. The Substitution control is a placeholder on a page and it gets its content from code that runs and dynamically substitutes the Substitution control with content.

> **N O T E** The details of using the Substitution control can be found in the excellent documentation on the MSDN website, located at msdn2.microsoft.com.

Another control that implements post-cache substitution is the AdRotator control. The AdRotator control is designed to display a rotating series of advertisements. Each time a page is requested, the ad that is displayed changes. If the AdRotator control were cached along with a page, the ad would not change until the cache expired. Therefore, the AdRotator control is designed so that it is never cached regardless of the cache settings for the page on which it is displayed.

> **N O T E** I go into quite a bit of detail on using the AdRotator control in Expression Web in my book, *Special Edition Using Microsoft Expression Web* from Que Publishing.

The Cache API

The cache API (sometimes referred to as programmatic caching) is used when you want to cache something other than a page or a portion of a page. For example, suppose that you created the weather page using an object called `WeatherForecast`. The object has a `County` property, a `TimeCreated` property, and so on. Using the cache API, you can store this `WeatherForecast` object in cache so that you don't have to incur the cost of re-creating it on each request for a particular county's weather.

There are a few ways that you can use the cache API, and all of them use the `Cache` class. You can use a key/value pair, you can use the `Add` method of the `Cache` class, or you can use the `Insert` method of the `Cache` class.

Using a key/value pair is similar to using an application or a session variable. The following code might be used to add an item into cache for a `WeatherForecast` object for Tarrant County:

for C#:

```
Cache["TarrantWeatherForecast"] = myWeatherForecast;
```

for VB:

```
Cache("TarrantWeatherForecast") = myWeatherForecast
```

In this case, `TarrantWeatherForecast` is the key and the `WeatherForecast` object instance called `myWeatherForecast` is the value.

Using the `Add` method of the `Cache` object adds an object to cache and also returns an instance of that object. For example, the following line of code might be used to both store a `WeatherForecast` object in cache and also return it so that it can be used on a page:

for C#:

```
weatherLabel.Text = (string)Cache.Add("TarrantWeatherForecast",
➡ myWeatherForecast.ForecastText);
```

for VB:

```
weatherLabel.Text = CStr(Cache.Add("TarrantWeatherForecast",
➡myWeatherForecast.ForecastText))
```

In this case, you're storing a string in cache, using the key `TarrantWeatherForecast`, and you're also assigning the value to the Text property of a label so that it can be displayed on the page.

CAUTION   If you use the `Add` method to add an item to cache and an item by that name is already in cache, the item already in cache is not replaced.

The `Insert` method is similar to the `Add` method except that it does not return any value, and if you use the `Insert` method to insert an item into the cache and an item already exists by the same name, the existing item is replaced by the new item.

The following code might be used to insert an item into cache with the `Insert` method:

for C#:

```
Cache.Insert("TarrantWeatherForecast", myWeatherForecast.ForecastText);
```

for Visual Basic:

```
Cache.Insert("TarrantWeatherForecast", myWeatherForecast.ForecastText)
```

NOTE   You can specify many options when adding items to the cache. For a full explanation of how to use the ASP.NET cache, see msdn2.microsoft.com/en-us/library/xsbfdd8c.aspx.

Retrieving Items from Cache

Regardless of how items are inserted into cache, items are retrieved from cache by the same method. The following code would retrieve a weather forecast that was previously inserted into cache:

for C#:

```
string strForecast;
strForecast = (string)Cache["TarrantWeatherForecast"];
```

for Visual Basic:

```
Dim strForecast As String
strForecast = CStr(Cache("TarrantWeatherForecast"))
```

> **TIP** Notice that the value that is returned is explicitly converted to a string so that it can be assigned to the strForecast string variable.

There's one extremely important point to keep in mind when working with the cache API. ASP.NET automatically removes items from cache when memory pressure on the application increases, using a process known as *cache scavenging*. Therefore, it's possible that an item you added to cache may no longer be in cache. If that's the case, an error occurs when you try to assign that cached item to a variable. The recommended method of retrieving a value from cache is to first check that the object still exists. If it does, retrieve it. If it doesn't, re-create it. The following code illustrates this concept:

for C#:

```
string strForecast;
strForecast = (string)Cache["TarrantWeatherForecast"];
if (strForecast == null)
{
    strForecast = myWeatherForecast.ForecastText;
    Cache.Insert("TarrantWeatherForecast", strForecast);
}
```

for Visual Basic:

```
Dim strForecast As String
strForecast = CStr(Cache("TarrantWeatherForecast"))
If strForecast Is Nothing Then
    strForecast = myWeatherForecast.ForecastText
    Cache.Insert("TarrantWeatherForecast", strForecast)
End If
```

In this example, the `TarrantWeatherForecast` cached item is assigned to `strForecast`. The `strForecast` string variable is then checked to see whether it actually contains a string. If it doesn't, you know that the `TarrantWeatherForecast` item was previously removed from cache. Therefore, you need to re-create it and then insert it into cache again.

Caching is one of the most effective ways to improve the performance of a web application. However, if used improperly, it's also one of the easiest ways to introduce errors and memory problems. Make sure that you test your application carefully after implementing a cache methodology and you can gain all the benefits without the pain of a poor caching plan.

ASP.NET Viewstate and Control State

In this chapter, we've looked at ways that you as a developer can store information in application variables, session variables, and ASP.NET cache. To complete the illusion of a connected application, ASP.NET uses *viewstate* and *control state* to store information about the state of the controls of a page between two consecutive requests for the same page.

Both viewstate and control state are handled in the same manner by ASP.NET. When ASP.NET builds the code for a Web form, it adds a hidden form field called __VIEWSTATE to the page. That form field contains an encoded string of characters that represents the current state of the control. When you post back the page, that string is sent back to the server and it allows ASP.NET to persist the state of the controls on the page.

For example, suppose you have an ASP.NET `Calendar` control on your page. When the page loads for the first time, the `Calendar` control displays the default date that was set when the page was developed. If a user changes that date and then posts the page back to itself so that the page reloads with new information, ASP.NET uses the data in the __VIEWSTATE form field to make sure that when the page is loaded again the `Calendar` is set to the date the user selected rather than the default date.

> **TIP** Some ASP.NET developers believe that all form fields (such as TextBox controls, RadioButton controls, and so on) use the __VIEWSTATE form field to persist data. In fact, any ASP.NET control that renders as a standard HTML form control persists state using a completely different method than the __VIEWSTATE form field.

In ASP.NET 1.0 and 1.1, all the data in the __VIEWSTATE form field was ASP.NET viewstate. It worked well, but with one major drawback. On a page with a lot of control information, the viewstate could grow to enormous size, and because all the viewstate is carried over the network on each request and response, it had a tendency to slow down the transmission of ASP.NET pages. Many developers therefore simply turned off viewstate.

> **TIP** You can turn off viewstate by setting the `EnableViewState` attribute of the `@` Page directive to `false`. Most controls also have an `EnableViewState` property that can be set to `false` to disable viewstate for that particular control.

In ASP.NET 2.0, the developers of ASP.NET introduced a new technology called control state. Control state is very similar to viewstate, but only information that is critical for the functionality of a control is held in control state. By moving to this architecture, developers can disable viewstate on a page without breaking the functionality of any of the controls on the page.

In most cases, you don't have to bother with viewstate or control state. It's one of those features that works behind the scenes. Even so, it's helpful to have a basic understanding of what's going on under the covers of ASP.NET so that you can have a better idea of how your application works.

> **TIP** As previously mentioned, viewstate and control state are made up of encoded strings. Therefore, they can both be decoded so that you can see just what's in them if you'd like.
>
> Dino Esposito (widely considered one of the best writers on ASP.NET topics) has written an ASP.NET Viewstate Decoder that you can download from www.pluralsight.com/tools.aspx. Make sure that you download the version for the ASP.NET version you are using.

CHAPTER 6

ASP.NET Configuration and Performance

IN THIS CHAPTER

Overview of ASP.NET Configuration

ASP.NET is a highly configurable technology. While many developers will use ASP.NET with the default configuration settings, Microsoft has provided configuration files so that the configuration can be changed easily if desired.

In addition to machine configuration options, there are also options that control how a particular application runs. It's more likely that you'll need to change some of these options because they control such things as whether or not users have to log in to access your website, what happens when an error occurs, and so forth.

ASP.NET Configuration Files

You use XML configuration files to configure both machine configuration options and application configuration options. Machine settings are configured in a file called `machine.config` and application configuration options are configured in a file called `web.config`.

Machine Configuration Files

The configuration of .NET Framework applications is controlled by the `machine.config` file located in the `Windows\Microsoft.NET\Framework\v2.0.50727\Config` directory. This file contains configuration settings that affect all .NET Framework applications running on the machine. In addition to `machine.config`, there are a couple of other similar files in the same directory.

- `machine.config.default`—This file stores the default settings for machine configuration. The settings in it are not read by the .NET Framework. It's purely a reference file.
- `machine.config.comments`—Like the machine.config.default file, this file is not used by the .NET Framework. Instead, it is a reference file that contains many useful comments on the configuration sections located in the `machine.config` file.

> **TIP**
>
> The `machine.config.default` file has explicit permissions set on it so that no one can alter it. You can open it and read the contents, but you cannot change something and save that change unless you first change the permissions on it.
>
> My recommendation is that you don't modify it because then you will have lost your reference on the default settings!

A few configuration settings in the `machine.config` file are of interest to web designers using ASP.NET.

- `<connectionStrings>` element—The `<connectionStrings>` element contains a database connection string that is used by ASP.NET membership, profiles, and roles. By default, it connects to a file-based SQL Server 2005 Express database in the data folder (`App_Data` by default) of the web application.

→ For more information on ASP.NET membership and roles, **see** Chapter 13, "Adding and Managing Users and Groups."

→ For more information on ASP.NET profiles, read *Special Edition Using Microsoft Expression Web* from Que Publishing.

- `<membership>` element—Located in the `<system.web>` section of the `machine.config` file, this element contains settings that configure ASP.NET membership features.

- `<profile>` element—Located in the `<system.web>` section of the `machine.config` file, this element contains settings that configure ASP.NET profiles.

- `<roleManager>` element—Located in the `<system.web>` section of the `machine.config` file, this element contains settings that configure ASP.NET roles.

Application Configuration Files

Application configuration settings are contained in one or more `web.config` files. Settings in the application configuration files affect only ASP.NET applications. The global `web.config` file is located in the `Windows\Microsoft.NET\Framework\v2.0.50727\Config` directory and affects all ASP.NET applications on the machine. In addition the global `web.config` file, the following files also exist in the same folder:

- `web.config.default` file—Contains default settings for ASP.NET configuration.
- `web.config.comments` file—Contains useful comments on the configuration settings available in the application configuration files.

In addition to the global `web.config` file, other `web.config` files can exist within the directory structure of a web application itself. The optional root `web.config` file is located in the root directory of the web application and contains settings that are specific to that application. Other `web.config` files can be located below the root folder, but some configuration settings are allowed only at the root level or in the global `web.config` file.

Here are some of the commonly used configuration elements in the `web.config` file:

- `<authorization>` element—This element controls which users or groups are allowed to access the application. Only requests for ASP.NET files are affected by this setting.

- `<authentication>` element—This element defines how authentication for the site takes place. Valid authentication modes are Windows, Forms, Passport, or None. The default authentication mode is Windows.

→ For more information on ASP.NET authentication methods, **see** "Authentication and Authorization," **p. 98**.

- `<compilation>` element—This element defines how ASP.NET dynamic compilation takes place and whether or not debugging is enabled.

→ For more information on ASP.NET dynamic compilation, **see** Chapter 3, "ASP.NET Compilation Models."

➡ For more information on ASP.NET debugging, **see** Chapter 27, "Debugging ASP.NET Applications."

- `<healthMonitoring>` section—This section contains elements that define how ASP.NET reports errors and application events.

➡ For more information on monitoring the health of ASP.NET applications, **see** "ASP.NET Health Monitoring," **p. 415**.

All these settings are located in the `<system.web>` section of the `web.config` file.

When you open one of the configuration files, it can be overwhelming to see the vast array of configuration options available. Not only is the size of the configuration files intimidating, but they are case-sensitive XML files and a single typo can cause an error in your application. Fortunately, there are easier ways to modify machine and application configuration than editing XML files by hand. The Web Site Administration Tool provides a convenient front end to modifying the configuration of your ASP.NET application.

The Web Site Administration Tool

The Web Site Administration Tool is a browser-based tool for configuring the settings for your application. To access the Web Site Administration Tool, click the ASP.NET Configuration button at the top of the Solution Explorer in Visual Web Developer as shown in Figure 6.1.

ASP.NET Configuration Button

FIGURE 6.1

The ASP.NET Configuration button provides a convenient method of launching the Web Site Administration Tool.

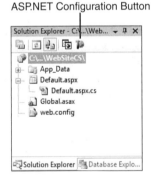

➡ For more information on using the Web Site Administration Tool to configure users and roles, **see** Chapter 13, "Adding and Managing Users and Roles."

NOTE   Users of Expression Web see an Administer Website link when using ASP.NET Login controls in Expression Web. This link does not work from within Expression Web. The Web Site Administration Tool is unavailable from within Expression Web.

The Web Site Administration Tool runs using the ASP.NET Development Server (see Figure 6.2), a lightweight web server that ships with the .NET Framework 2.0.

FIGURE 6.2

The Web Site Administration Tool provides an easy interface for editing the configuration of your ASP.NET application.

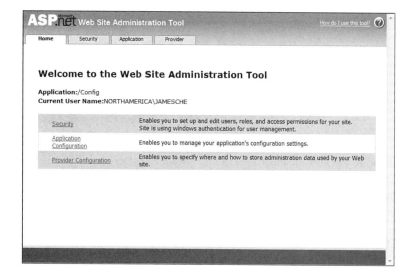

The Home page (shown in Figure 6.2) displays the name of the application and the current user. It also displays links for each of the three areas of the Web Site Administration Tool: Security, Application Configuration, and Provider Configuration.

Security Tab

The Security tab (shown in Figure 6.3) enables you to configure users, roles, and access rules for your application. An area is provided for each of these settings, making it easy to manage your application's security.

FIGURE 6.3
The Security tab pro-
vides access to set-
tings for users, roles,
and access rules for
your application.

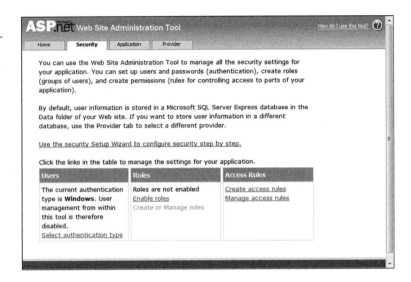

If you're not sure what settings to use for your application, the easiest way to configure security is by using the Security Setup Wizard. A link to the wizard is provided on the Security
page. When you click that link, you'll be walked through a seven-step process of configuring
security.

Step 1—Welcome

Step 1 provides a welcome message explaining the wizard and a link that will take you back
to the page that was displayed when you first clicked the Security tab. To proceed to the next
step in the wizard, click the Next button.

> **TIP** As I previously mentioned, the Web Site Administration Tool has a tendency to
> time out often. Changes that you make in the security Setup Wizard make
> immediate modifications to configuration files, so if the Web Site
> Administration Tool times out while going through the wizard, changes you've
> already made are saved.

Step 2—Select Access Method

In step 2, you choose the access method for your application as shown in Figure 6.4. If your
users will be accessing your application across the Internet and you want to create a login
page for them, choose From the Internet. Otherwise, choose From a Local Area Network.

FIGURE 6.4

You can choose to configure your application for authentication from the Internet or from your local intranet. Your choice here affects the authentication method that is configured for your ASP.NET application.

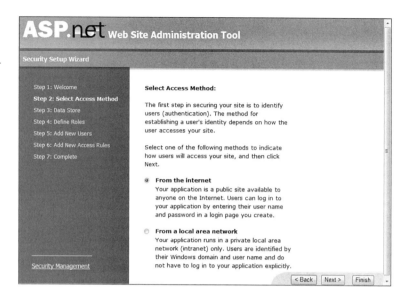

Your choice in this step modifies the `<authentication>` element in the application's `web.config` file. If you choose From the Internet, the following entry is added to the `web.config` file:

```
<authentication mode="Forms" />
```

If you choose From a Local Area Network, the authentication mode is set to Windows. In that case, nothing is added to the `web.config` file because the default authentication mode is Windows.

→ For more information on authentication in ASP.NET, **see** Chapter 7, "Basic ASP.NET Security."

Step 3—Data Store

NOTE   This step is skipped if you choose From a Local Area Network in step 2.

By default, step 3 is an informational step that specifies that you are using advanced provider settings as shown in Figure 6.5. ASP.NET authentication is configured using *providers*. By implementing ASP.NET authentication with the provider model, the developers of ASP.NET made it relatively easy for you to create your own means of authenticating users by creating your own providers if you wish.

FIGURE 6.5

Step 3 is an informational step by default because there is only one provider for Forms-based authentication.

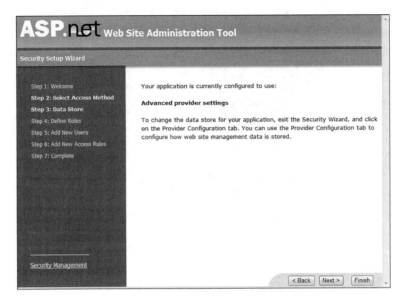

> **NOTE** The provider model is an advanced topic that we won't cover in this book. For details on using the provider model, Microsoft has published an excellent guide that you can download in PDF format by browsing to msdn2.microsoft.com/en-us/library/aa479030.aspx.

Only one provider comes with ASP.NET by default, and that's the `AspNetSqlProvider`, which stores the user and role information in a SQL Server 2005 Express database. That is the data store used for your users by default when you use Forms authentication.

Step 4—Define Roles

> **NOTE** This step is skipped if you choose From a Local Area Network in step 2.

In step 4, you can choose whether or not roles are enabled for your web application. Roles can be granted specific permissions and each user can be assigned to one or more roles. For example, you might have a role called Administrators that is allowed to browse a particular part of the site and another role called Users that is not allowed to access that particular part of the site.

→ For more information on ASP.NET roles, **see** Chapter 7, "Basic ASP.NET Security."

By checking the Enable Roles for this Web Site check box (shown in Figure 6.6) and clicking Next, you can define new roles for your website, as shown in Figure 6.7.

FIGURE 6.6
Roles for a website are enabled by checking the Enable Roles for this Web Site check box.

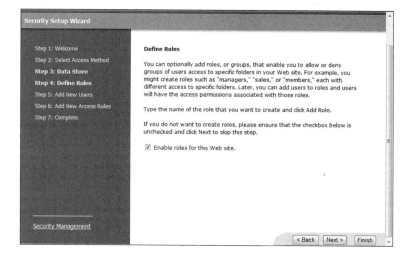

FIGURE 6.7
Adding roles is simple with the interface in step 4. In this case, I've already added a role for Administrators and I'm now adding a new role for Users.

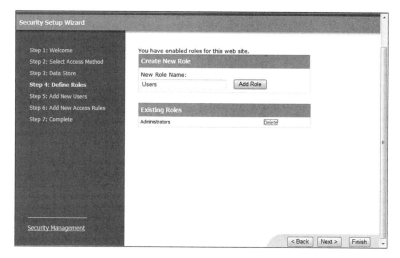

NOTE   By default, ASP.NET uses the `AspNetSqlRoleProvider` provider for roles. If you've changed the provider, you may not be able to add or manage roles in the Web Site Administration Tool.

When roles are enabled, the following line is added to the `web.config` file in the root of your application:

```
<roleManager enabled="true" />
```

Any roles that you create are added to the database that is created in the data folder of your application.

Step 5—Add New Users

> **NOTE** This step is bypassed if you choose From a Local Area Network in step 2.

In this step, you have the option of adding one or more users to your web application as shown in Figure 6.8. By default, users that you add in step 5 are added to the SQL Server 2005 Express database file in the data folder of your web application.

FIGURE 6.8
Users can be added in step 5. If you'd prefer, you can allow users to add themselves to your application by using the CreateUserWizard control.

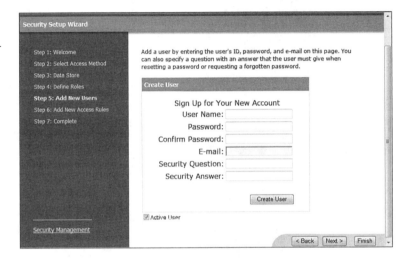

Adding users is not required. If you choose, you can add a CreateUserWizard control to your application to allow users to register themselves with your website.

→ For more information on the CreateUserWizard control, **see** "Creating Accounts Using the CreateUserWizard Control," **p. 202**.

Step 6—Add New Access Rules

In step 6 (see Figure 6.9), you have the option of creating new access rules for your application. Access rules allow you to either allow or disallow a user, users in a particular role, or users browsing the site without logging in (anonymous users) from accessing the entire site or a specified portion of the site.

FIGURE 6.9

In step 6, you configure the access rules for your application.

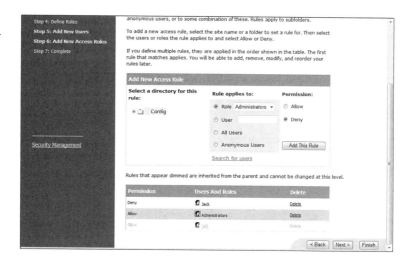

The Web Site Administration Tool does not check to see whether users that you specify actually exist in your user database. Be careful when specifying users because a typo will make your access rule ineffective. If you're in doubt about a user, click the Search for Users link shown in Figure 6.9.

Allowing or denying users or roles will add authorization information to the web.config file. The current authorization rules are listed at the bottom of the page and you can delete one of them by clicking the Delete link shown previously in Figure 6.9.

→ For more information on authorization and web.config files, **see** Chapter 7, "Basic ASP.NET Security."

Access rules need not apply to the entire application. By expanding the list of directories and selecting a specific directory, you can configure access rules for a specific directory.

CAUTION If you add an access rule for a specific directory, the Web Site Administration Tool creates a separate web.config file in that directory. This causes the access rule you configured to affect the directory you selected, as well as all files and folders beneath it, unless a subsequent web.config overrides the rule.

→ For more information on the various entries in a web.config file that control access to a web application, **see** Chapter 7, "Basic ASP.NET Security."

If you choose not to use the Security Setup Wizard, you can access the same functionality by clicking the appropriate link on the Security page.

> **TIP** The pages that allow for the configuration of users and roles use the ASP.NET Login controls for functionality. These are the same controls that you can leverage in your own web application. I'll show you how in Chapter 14.

Application Tab

The Application tab (see Figure 6.10) provides access to application settings for your application. These settings are divided into four sections: Application Settings, SMTP Settings, Application Status, and Debugging and Tracing.

FIGURE 6.10

The Application tab is where you'll find settings that apply to the entire web application.

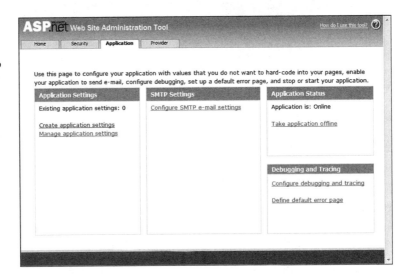

Application Settings

The Application Settings link enables you to easily configure text entries that can be used in your application. These text entries can easily be updated using the Web Site Administration Tool, and all places within the application that use that text are instantly updated.

An application setting can be accessed in code when the name of the setting is used. For example, suppose you create an application setting called BusinessPhone that contains your business phone number. You can assign the value of the application setting to a string variable using the following code:

In C#:

```
string busPhone =
➥System.Configuration.ConfigurationSettings.AppSettings["BusinessPhone"];
```

In Visual Basic:

```
Dim busPhone As String =
➥System.Configuration.ConfigurationSettings.AppSettings("BusinessPhone")
```

When you create a new application setting, it adds or modifies the `<appSettings>` section in the `web.config` file in the root directory of your application. In the preceding example of the `BusinessPhone` application setting, the following XML would be added to the `web.config` file:

```
<appSettings>
        <add key="BusinessPhone" value="212-555-3342" />
</appSettings>
```

You can edit or delete existing application settings by clicking the Manage Application Settings link.

SMTP E-mail Settings

If you use code to send email in your ASP.NET application, you'll want to configure the settings for your outgoing mail server by using the Configure SMTP E-mail Settings link. When you click this link, you are taken to a form where all your SMTP server information can be entered as shown in Figure 6.11.

FIGURE 6.11

SMTP settings enable you to send email easily from your ASP.NET application.

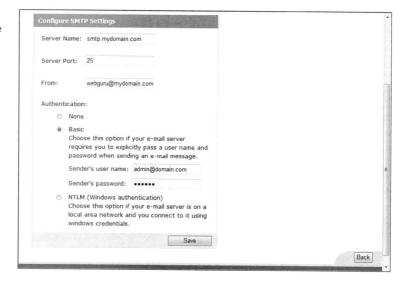

The settings shown in Figure 6.11 save the following XML into the `web.config` file in the root of the application:

```
<system.net>
        <mailSettings>
            <smtp from="webguru@mydomain.com">
```

```
                        <network host="smtp.mydomain.com" password="secret"
                        ➥userName="admin@domain.com" />
                    </smtp>
                </mailSettings>
            </system.net>
```

When you send email programmatically with ASP.NET, these settings are used by ASP.NET to access your outgoing mail server and send the email.

→ For more information on sending email from an ASP.NET application, **see** Chapter 23, "Configuring ASP.NET for Email."

Application Status

If you would like to take your web application offline, thereby making it unavailable to anyone wishing to access it, click the Take Application Offline link shown previously in Figure 6.10.

> **NOTE** It is uncommon to take an application offline, but it might be necessary in a situation where something is wrong with the application and you want to prevent users from accessing it. It's typically an emergency step for a production application.

When you click this link, the link changes to a Take Application Online link, and the following XML is added to the web.config file in the root of your web application:

```
<httpRuntime enable="false" />
```

If you add this line, ASP.NET can no longer process any requests to your application. Users then see the same page that they would see if they requested a non-existent page from the application. Figure 6.12 shows what users see by default when an offline web application is browsed.

To bring the application back online, click the Take Application Online link on the Application tab.

> **TIP** You can also take your application offline by simply adding a file called app_offline.htm to your website. When you use this method, you can add any content you wish to the file so that users see a friendlier message.
>
> Because of the way that Internet Explorer works, it displays a File Not Found message unless your app_offline.htm page is at least 512 bytes long. To prevent this, you can pad your file with HTML comments to reach a file size of at least 512 bytes.

FIGURE 6.12
When an application is taken offline, ASP.NET sends a File Not Found error when any of its pages is browsed.

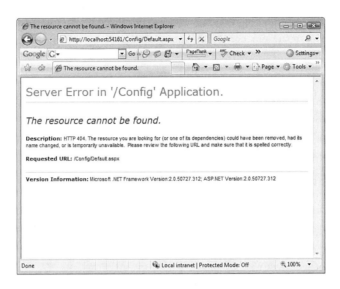

Debugging and Tracing

You can configure debugging and tracing for your application by using the Debugging and Tracing settings available on the Application tab. When you click the Configure Debugging and Tracing link, you are presented with a page enabling you to choose from several options, as shown in Figure 6.13.

FIGURE 6.13
Debugging and tracing settings are easily configurable from the Application tab.

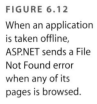

When you enable debugging on your website, the Web Site Administration Tool adds the following XML to the `web.config` file in the root directory of your web application.

```
<compilation debug="true" />
```

This setting alters the way that ASP.NET dynamically compiles your application when it runs. Enabling debugging provides you with information when an error occurs, such as the name of the code file where the error occurred.

→ For more information on ASP.NET compilation, **see** "ASP.NET Compilation," **p. 32**

CAUTION
> Debugging should be used only on your development server and never on a production website. Enabling it has performance and reliability implications for a live site.

Enabling tracing for your application adds a `<trace>` element to your root `web.config` file. ASP.NET tracing is useful for troubleshooting because it provides you with detailed information as a page is executed regarding how long each part of the page lifecycle takes, as well as information such as form field data, cookies, and so on.

→ For more information on ASP.NET debugging and tracing, **see** Chapter 27, "Debugging ASP.NET Applications," and Chapter 29, "ASP.NET Tracing and Other Troubleshooting Techniques."

Default Error Page

By clicking the Define Default Error Page link on the Application tab (shown previously in Figure 6.10), you can specify a custom page to display when unhandled errors occur in your application. By default, ASP.NET displays a generic error page that includes the code that led up to the error and other information that can help you determine the cause of the error. By specifying a custom error page, you can give your users a more attractive and informational page when an error occurs.

Select Specify a URL to Use as the Default Error Page radio button as shown in Figure 6.14, select the page you want to use for your error page, and click Save to apply the changes.

Provider Tab

The Provider tab is an interface for changing providers for ASP.NET membership and roles. By default, both membership and roles use the `AspNetSqlProvider` provider, which means that users and roles are stored in a SQL Server 2005 Express database file in the data folder of your web application.

FIGURE 6.14

A custom error page enables you to display a user-friendly page when an error occurs.

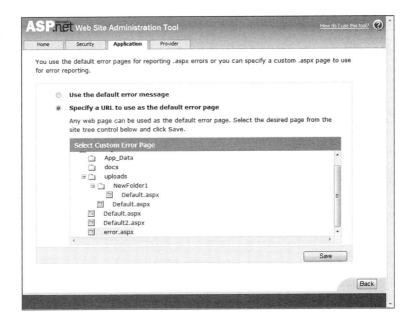

The Provider tab displays two links for configuring providers:

- **Select a Single Provider for All Site Management Data**—When you click this link, you see a list of all providers available. By default, only the AspNetSqlProvider is available.

- **Select a Different Provider for Each Feature (Advanced)**—When this link is clicked, you can select a provider for membership and roles separately, as shown in Figure 6.15.

FIGURE 6.15

You can configure a separate provider for roles and membership in the Provider tab.

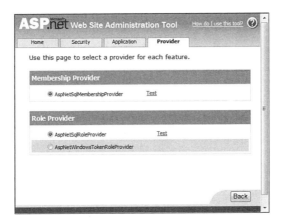

Notice in Figure 6.15 two roles providers are available: the AspNetSqlRoleProvider and the AspNetWindowsTokenRoleProvider. These are the providers that come with ASP.NET 3.5.

> **NOTE** As mentioned previously, a discussion of custom providers is outside the scope of this book. Refer to Microsoft's documentation at msdn2.microsoft.com/en-us/library/aa479030.aspx for more information.

ASP.NET Configuration in IIS

The Internet Information Services MMC in Windows XP and Windows Server 2003 both provide an ASP.NET tab for convenient configuration of ASP.NET applications. IIS 7 in Windows Vista provides similar functionality in the form of numerous screens within the IIS management console. You'll find many of the same configuration options you had in the Web Site Administration Tool in the IIS interface as well.

IIS 5.1 and IIS 6

To access ASP.NET configuration in IIS 5.1 running on Windows XP Professional or IIS 6 running on Windows Server 2003, follow these steps:

1. Open the Internet Information Services snap-in located in Administrative Tools.

2. Select the application you would like to configure, as shown in Figure 6.16.

FIGURE 6.16
You can configure ASP.NET applications with the IIS snap-in. Each application can have different configuration options.

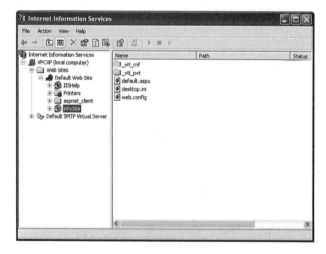

3. Right-click on the application and select Properties.

4. Click the ASP.NET tab, as shown in Figure 6.17.

FIGURE 6.17

ASP.NET configura-
tion is located on the
ASP.NET tab.

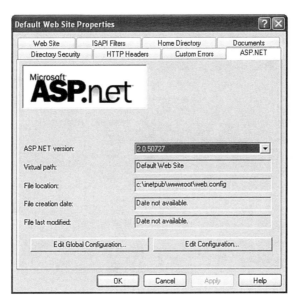

The ASP.NET tab displays the version of ASP.NET under which the application is configured to run. If you have only ASP.NET 2.0 installed, no other versions are listed. However,
if you have other versions of the .NET Framework installed on the machine, you can easily
switch the version of ASP.NET for the application by selecting the desired version in the
ASP.NET Version drop-down.

> **NOTE** Even if you have the .NET Framework 3.5 installed, the lastest version of
> ASP.NET that you'll see in the drop-down on the ASP.NET tab is 2.0.50727.

> **TIP** Note that you can configure the version of ASP.NET only at the application root.
> If you are reviewing the properties of the root folder of your application, but
> the ASP.NET Version drop-down is disabled, it's likely that your application is
> not marked as an application in IIS. Click the Directory tab, and then click the
> Create button to mark the folder as an application.

If you've chosen 2.0.50727 as the ASP.NET version, clicking either the Edit Global
Configuration or Edit Configuration button as shown previously in Figure 6.17 displays a
tabbed dialog as shown in Figure 6.18 where you can edit the configuration of ASP.NET.

> **TIP** The Edit Global Configuration button is available only when you are editing
> properties of the root application of the website. When editing global configu-
> ration, you are actually editing the global web.config file instead of the local
> web.config file.

FIGURE 6.18

The tabbed dialog for editing ASP.NET configuration gives you access to many different configuration options.

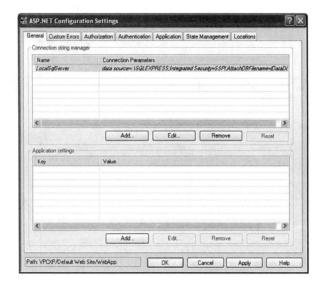

General Tab

The General tab (shown previously in Figure 6.18) provides an interface for managing connection strings and application settings. The items listed in this dialog include all configurations at all levels. The style of the text used to display each item is an indicator of where the item is configured.

The following text styles are used to display items throughout the ASP.NET Configuration Settings dialog. Text styles can be combined (for example, italicized text with strikethrough).

- **Plain Text**—Items displayed in plain text are configured at the current level.
- **Italicized Text**—Items displayed in italic are configured at a level above the current level.
- **Strikethrough Text**—Text that appears with a line through it indicates the setting is configured at a higher level, but is removed at the current level.
- **Bolded Text**—Items displayed in bolded text are configured at the current level, and this setting overrides any setting configured at a higher level.

To get a feel for what this all means, complete these steps:

1. Create a new folder inside the folder for your Default Web Site (located in c:\inetpub\wwwroot by default) called **WebApp**.
2. Open the IIS management console.
3. Expand the Web Sites node.
4. Expand the Default Web Site node and right-click on the WebApp folder you just created.
5. Select Properties.

6. On the Directory tab, click the Create button to mark the folder as an application.

7. Click the ASP.NET tab.

8. Click the Edit Configuration button.

9. Select the LocalSqlServer connection string and click Edit.

10. Change any character in the connection string (it doesn't matter what change you make) and click OK. Note that the connection string now appears in bolded text, indicating you have overridden a setting from a higher level.

11. Select the connection string and click Remove.

Note that the connection string now appears as italicized text with a line through it as shown in Figure 6.19. This indicates the setting is configured at a higher level but has been removed at this level.

FIGURE 6.19

This setting appears as italicized text with a line through it. This means it was defined at a higher level and is removed at the current level.

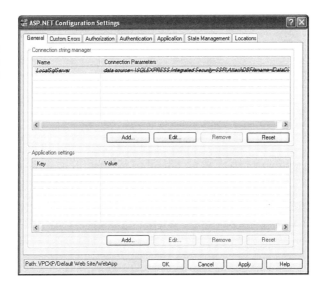

When you click Remove, you'll notice that the item doesn't get removed from the list. This happens because you may decide at some point to use one of the items configured at a higher level that is available to you. Because the item is still in the list and displayed with a line through it, it remains available to you for use at a later time if desired.

> **TIP** You can reset things to the default by clicking the Reset button shown previously in Figure 6.19.

→ For more information on configuring connection strings in ASP.NET, **see** Chapter 21, "Displaying Data from a Database."

Custom Errors Tab

The Custom Errors tab (shown in Figure 6.20) enables you to configure custom pages for different errors that may occur in your application based on HTTP status codes and a catch-all custom error page as well.

FIGURE 6.20

You can configure custom error pages based on HTTP status codes on the Custom Errors tab.

To configure a custom error page as a catch-all page that will be displayed when any unhandled error occurs, enter the relative URL for the page in the Default Redirect URL textbox.

To configure custom error pages for particular HTTP status codes, click the Add button. Enter the status code and a URL for the desired error page relative to the root of the website as shown in Figure 6.21.

FIGURE 6.21

To configure an HTTP status error page, enter the HTTP status code and a URL relative to the root of the application.

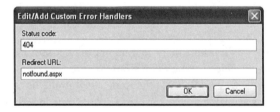

> **TIP** The list of inherited custom errors cannot be edited. It is there only for informational purposes. Any local entries override inherited entries.

NOTE
For a complete listing of HTTP status codes, see support.microsoft.com/kb/318380.

The Custom Error Mode drop-down controls when custom errors configured in this dialog are displayed. The following three settings are available:

- **RemoteOnly**—This is the default setting. When it is selected, custom errors are displayed only when the site is being browsed from a remote machine.
- **Off**—When this setting is selected, custom error pages are never displayed.
- **On**—When this setting is selected, custom error pages are always displayed regardless of whether the site is being browsed remotely.

Authorization Tab

The Authorization tab (see Figure 6.22) provides a convenient means of creating authorization rules for your application.

FIGURE 6.22
Authorization rules are easily configured in the Authorization tab.

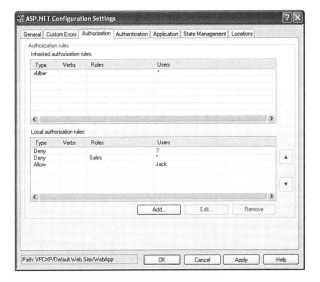

TIP
The list of inherited authorization rules is not editable and is provided for informational purposes. Any locally created authorization rules override inherited rules.

→ For more information on creating authorization rules with the ASP.NET Configuration Settings dialog, **see** "Configuring Authorization with the ASP.NET Configuration Settings Dialog (IIS 5 and 6 Only)," **p. 108**.

Authentication Tab

The Authentication tab (shown in Figure 6.23) is where you'll configure the type of authentication that your website uses.

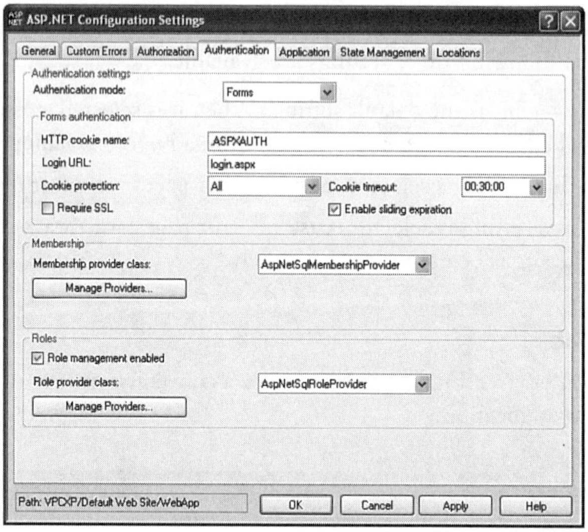

FIGURE 6.23

Configuring the authentication method for your website is accomplished on the Authentication tab.

To configure the authentication mode for the application, use the Authentication Mode drop-down. The following modes are available:

- **Windows**—This is the default authentication mode. In this mode, users are identified by their Windows logins when anonymous access is disabled.

- **Forms**—Forms authentication is a feature built in to ASP.NET that uses a cookie to determine whether users have logged in. If they haven't, they are presented with a login page that you create. The ASP.NET login controls are commonly used with Forms authentication.

- **Passport**—Passport authentication enables you to use Microsoft's .NET Passport system to authenticate users. Doing so requires a fair amount of custom code. This is the most complex authentication mode, and it's rarely used.

- **None**—When None is selected, users are never authenticated. If everyone is allowed to browse your site anonymously, this is the preferred method because it gives you a slight performance boost.

The details of configuring authentication methods are covered in Chapter 7.

Application Tab

The Application tab (shown in Figure 6.24) contains settings for configuring runtime and compilation options.

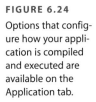

FIGURE 6.24
Options that configure how your application is compiled and executed are available on the Application tab.

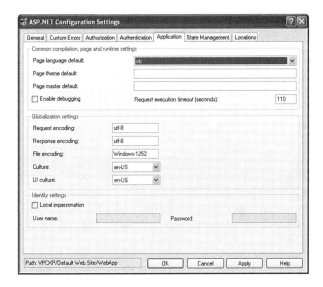

There are three sections on the Application tab. The first contains compilation, page, and runtime settings. The following settings are available in this section:

- **Page Language Default**—When an ASP.NET application executes, it automatically compiles files that are used for the application. The page language default specifies what language is used to generate these files. Visual Basic is the default.

- **Page Theme Default**—This setting specifies an ASP.NET theme that is applied to all pages in the application unless a different theme is applied at the page level.

→ For more information on ASP.NET themes, **see** "Introduction to ASP.NET Themes," **p. 270**.

- **Page Master Default**—This setting specifies an ASP.NET master page that is applied to pages in the website. This can be overridden by a master page specified in the @ Page directive or programmatically.

→ For more information on ASP.NET master pages, **see** Chapter 10, "Creating and Using Master Pages."

- **Enable Debugging**—When this box is checked, ASP.NET compiles your application with debugging enabled. Doing so provides you with more detailed error messages.

CAUTION

> You should always disable debugging in a production website. Not doing so can cause performance and memory problems.

- **Request Execution Timeout**—Specifies the amount of time that an ASP.NET request waits for a response before timing out.

Globalization settings can also be configured on the Application tab. There are settings for request and response encoding, page encoding, and culture.

> **NOTE** Globalization is a complex topic and outside of the scope of this book. For details on globalization and localization in ASP.NET, see msdn2.microsoft.com/en-us/library/c6zyy3s9.aspx.

The third section of the Application tab provides settings for impersonation. By default, your ASP.NET application runs under the identity of the ASP.NET worker process. In IIS 5, ASP.NET runs under the local ASPNET account on a member server and the IWAM account on a domain controller. In IIS 6, it runs under the NETWORK SERVICE account by default. By enabling impersonation, you can specify that your application should run under a different context.

If you check the Local Impersonation check box and don't enter a username and password, each page executes under the identity of the user who is authenticated to the web server. If someone is browsing anonymously, it runs under the context of the anonymous user, `IUSR_<machine_name>` in IIS by default. If you check the Local Impersonation check box and enter a username and password, each page executes under the identity of the user you specify.

Impersonation is especially useful in cases where your application needs to access an external resource, write to the file system, and so on. Suppose, for example, that your ASP.NET application accesses a remote SQL Server database and you have different permissions configured in SQL Server for each user. If you enable impersonation and don't specify a username and password, your page runs under the identity of the user who is authenticated to the web server. Therefore, you can easily authenticate the specific user to the SQL Server database.

> **NOTE** The concept of impersonation and identities in ASP.NET can be confusing. For more information on impersonation, a good resource is the InformIT website at www.informit.com.

State Management

The State Management tab (shown in Figure 6.25) configures the settings for ASP.NET Session state.

FIGURE 6.25

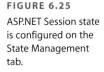

ASP.NET Session state is configured on the State Management tab.

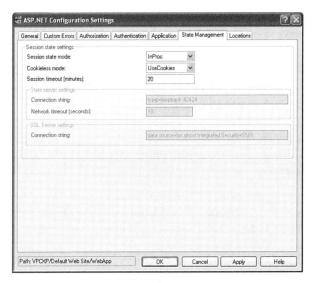

Four Session state modes are available:

- **InProc**—This is the default Session state mode. In this mode, Session information is stored in memory on the web server.

- **StateServer**—In this mode, Session information is stored in memory, but in a separate process called `aspnet_state.exe` that is specifically designed to store ASP.NET Session state. The State Server process can run on the web server or on a different machine. Configuration for State Server is provided in the State Server Settings section of the State Management tab.

- **SQLServer**—In this mode, Session information is stored on SQL Server. This is the most reliable Session state mode, but it's also the slowest. Configuration for SQL Server Session state is provided in the SQL Server Settings section of the State Management tab.

- **Custom**—In this mode, ASP.NET assumes that you have written your own state management system.

→ For more information on ASP.NET Session state, **see** Chapter 5, "ASP.NET State Management."

The Cookieless Mode drop-down enables you to configure how ASP.NET passes the Session ID between the client and the web server. Four options are available.

- **UseUri**—In this mode, the Session ID is passed in the URI (URL) on each request.

- **UseCookies**—This is the default setting. When this setting is used, a cookie is used to pass the Session ID.

- **AutoDetect**—When this setting is used, ASP.NET detects whether the requesting device supports cookies. If it does, cookies are used. If it does not, the Session ID is passed in the URL.
- **UseDeviceProfile**—When this setting is used, ASP.NET uses the user-agent string to determine whether the requesting device supports cookies. If it does, cookies are used. If not, the Session ID is passed in the URL.

The Session Timeout specifies how long an ASP.NET Session remains active in minutes. ASP.NET uses a sliding expiration, which means that when each request is issued, the timeout countdown is reset.

ASP.NET Sessions are still valid if a user browses away from the website and then back to it. However, if the user closes the browser and launches a new browser, a new ASP.NET Session is started even if the timeout time has not elapsed on the first Session.

Locations Tab

The Locations tab enables you to create a separate configuration for a particular file or folder. To add a new location, click the Add button as shown in Figure 6.26. Specify a location, using a path relative to the root of the application. You can specify a path to a directory or to a specific file.

FIGURE 6.26

The Locations tab makes it easy to have separate configurations for specific files and/or directories.

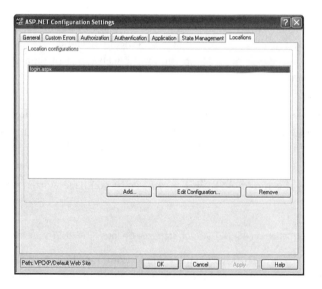

After you've added a location, you can edit the configuration for that location by selecting it in the list and clicking the Edit Configuration button. When you do, a new ASP.NET Configuration Settings dialog is opened. Any changes made in the new dialog affect only the location you specified.

IIS 7

Configuration in IIS 7 is also accomplished with the Internet Information Services Manager, but the layout is quite a bit different. As shown in Figure 6.27, ASP.NET settings are configured with a series of icons in an ASP.NET area.

FIGURE 6.27

Configuration of ASP.NET in IIS 7 is accomplished through a series of icons for each configuration area.

IIS 7 is currently available only in Windows Vista. The server version of IIS 7 will be available on Windows Longhorn Server. Configuration settings are the same as they are in IIS 5 and IIS 6, and full, context-sensitive documentation is provided. Therefore, I won't go into all the details of configuring ASP.NET on IIS 7 in this chapter. Check the web page for this book at www.quepublishing.com for more information as it becomes available.

Encrypting Information in the Configuration Files

As you've seen in this chapter, the ASP.NET configuration files contain many sections that provide vital information regarding how your application runs. You might have noticed that some of these configuration sections can contain sensitive data, and because they are in XML format, anyone with access to the web server can plainly see that data.

> **TIP**
> ASP.NET explicitly prevents browsing directly to any file with a `.config` file extension. Therefore, no one can browse to your configuration files from a remote machine.

Fortunately, ASP.NET makes it possible to encrypt the data in the configuration files. This prevents prying eyes from accessing things such as passwords that appear in your configuration files. The easiest way to encrypt configuration sections is to use the `aspnet_regiis.exe` tool.

> **NOTE** Almost all configuration sections can be encrypted with `aspnet_regiis.exe`. However, some cannot. For information on what sections cannot be encrypted with `aspnet_regiis.exe` and alternate methods of encrypting those sections, see msdn2.microsoft.com/en-us/library/ms998280.aspx.

→ For more information on using the `aspnet_regiis.exe` tool, **see** "Configuring ASP.NET on IIS 5.1 or IIS 6.0," **p. 10**.

Listing 6.1 shows a typical `<connectionStrings>` section in a `web.config` file.

Listing 6.1 The Unencrypted Configuration Section

```
<connectionStrings>
    <add name="HRSQLServer1" connectionString="Data Source=HRSS22;Initial
    ➥Catalog=EmployeeData;User Id=ssUserHR2;Password=VitcaHonor6;" />
</connectionStrings>
```

Notice that this section contains a username and password for accessing the HRSS22 SQL Server that contains employee data. To encrypt the `<connectionStrings>` section of this configuration file, run the following command:

```
aspnet_regiis -pe "connectionStrings" -app "/WebApp"
```

The `-pe` parameter specifies the configuration section to encrypt and the `-app` parameter points to the application path relative to the root of the website. If you need to use an absolute disk path to the application, you can use the following syntax instead:

```
aspnet_regiis -pef "connectionStrings" "c:\myWebSites\WebApp"
```

> **TIP** The `-pef` parameter is especially useful when you are encrypting a configuration file for a disk-based web application.

After you run this command, the `<connectionStrings>` section is changed to what you see in Listing 6.2.

Listing 6.2   The Encrypted Configuration Section

```xml
<connectionStrings configProtectionProvider="RsaProtectedConfigurationProvider">
        <EncryptedData Type="http://www.w3.org/2001/04/xmlenc#Element"
            xmlns="http://www.w3.org/2001/04/xmlenc#">
            <EncryptionMethod Algorithm=
            ➥"http://www.w3.org/2001/04/xmlenc#tripledes-cbc" />
            <KeyInfo xmlns="http://www.w3.org/2000/09/xmldsig#">
                <EncryptedKey xmlns="http://www.w3.org/2001/04/xmlenc#">
                    <EncryptionMethod Algorithm=
                    ➥"http://www.w3.org/2001/04/xmlenc#rsa-1_5" />
                    <KeyInfo xmlns="http://www.w3.org/2000/09/xmldsig#">
                        <KeyName>Rsa Key</KeyName>
                    </KeyInfo>
                    <CipherData>

<CipherValue>dUv/5F/WI0sFTtp8+ZKSIrtIVCiLx/RIOVZYtkOOxUHODGOmImW+XCMSv3y148
➥HyZUZe/l+7a55QgEzxHdB+5WJOrX84CV4HfLwHokiNcWcbkhUuowZ78D8AqKcMCg1LC
➥MV6Fgk1u513QjZ6Pxzdi6wWId1mZwGIFiq9TeKnP8M=</CipherValue>
                    </CipherData>
                </EncryptedKey>
            </KeyInfo>
            <CipherData>

<CipherValue>bl7mp5UdlIeTpc0HdHnQNgI/Da8iEwKRZvHZ2N15gr3aMBnLb7nthoyewJJ40e
➥s67qlCNvxPyHc/9kxrBI+5F5vNsHiV+C76jgnnlWDQtydnTjNBpxGkWXsKlqfAN+cUz
➥NqRS2dR8m5pLMPC34ahXxOt6IZiQiAyPks2En8wOzgGMRTsZRdsMKw3DX+ElBtaFWOb
➥iLzkmKWWdS3zCSqHOAETtVZ7LscaS6X+bIDFAM6lBvnoS4GJ8n00z5XtkF6d
➥</CipherValue>
            </CipherData>
        </EncryptedData>
    </connectionStrings>
```

There's now quite a bit of new XML code, but the important parts of this are the `<CipherData>` sections. These contain the encrypted connection string information.

To decrypt the `<connectionStrings>` section back to human-readable data, use the following command line:

```
aspnet_regiis -pd "connectionStrings" -app "/WebApp"
```

or

```
aspnet_regiis -pdf "connectionStrings" "c:\myWebSites\WebApp"
```

After this command runs, the configuration file is restored to what you saw in Listing 6.1.

It's always a good idea to encrypt any data in your configuration file that contains passwords or other sensitive data. The `aspnet_regiis` tool makes it so easy that there's really no excuse for not keeping your sensitive data secure.

CHAPTER 7

Basic ASP.NET Security

IN THIS CHAPTER

Authentication and Authorization

In the previous chapter, we glazed over some of the configuration options available for ASP.NET security. In this chapter, we'll dig deeper into security concepts and how to configure authentication and authorization options in ASP.NET.

Before we go into the details of ASP.NET security, it's important to understand essentially two steps are involved: authentication and authorization. *Authentication* is the process by which a user's identity is determined, and *authorization* is the process of determining whether an identified user should be allowed to access a particular resource.

ASP.NET uses the <authentication> section of the configuration file for authentication settings and the <authorization> section for authorization settings.

The <authentication> section of the configuration file determines the mode of authentication and any particular options associated with the selected mode. The <authentication> section is valid only inside the global web.config file or the web.config file in the root of the application.

→ For more information on the global web.config file and other configuration files, **see** "ASP.NET Configuration Files," **p. 66**.

The default authentication mode in an ASP.NET application is Windows authentication. However, you can also choose from Forms authentication, Passport authentication, or no authentication at all. We'll discuss Windows and Forms authentication in detail later in this chapter.

> **TIP**
>
> If your application is a typical Internet website that doesn't ever require users to log in, you might want to choose None as your authentication method. Doing this reduces the amount of code that ASP.NET runs "under the hood" when your pages are served. You won't notice a difference in speed in most cases, but you will see a small performance gain that can make a big difference if your application is subjected to high load.

The options that you typically specify in the <authentication> section differ depending on which authentication mode you've chosen. We'll go into the details of these options as we discuss specific authentication modes later in this chapter.

The <authorization> section is where you specify who does and does not have access to browse the application or certain resources within the application. You have granular control over access to all ASP.NET resources.

CAUTION
If you are using the ASP.NET Development Server, the `<authorization>` section applies to all resources in your web application. However, when running in IIS, the `<authorization>` section applies to only ASP.NET resources. HTML pages, images, scripts, and so on are not affected by authorization rules.

Using the `<authorization>` section, you can control whether specific users or users in a particular role can access your application. Access can be controlled at the file and folder level as well, and you can specify particular HTTP verbs that are allowed or denied. For example, you could specify that users in a specific role are not allowed to use the `OPTIONS` verb for your web application.

Authorization rules are evaluated in the order in which they appear in the configuration file. Therefore, the order you use can mean the difference between effective and ineffective settings. We'll look at this in more detail as we progress through this chapter.

Configuring Windows Authentication

Windows authentication is enabled by default in the global `web.config` file. If you create a new `web.config` file, Windows authentication is explicitly enabled in that `web.config` file as well.

The following line in your `web.config` file enables Windows authentication:

```
<authentication mode="Windows" />
```

When Windows authentication mode is used, users are identified by their Windows logins, but only if anonymous browsing is disabled. You can disable anonymous browsing in IIS (which affects all requests, ASP.NET and otherwise) or you can disable anonymous browsing for just ASP.NET requests. We'll cover how to disable anonymous for ASP.NET-only requests in the "ASP.NET Authorization" section later in this chapter.

Disabling Anonymous Browsing in IIS 5 and 6

If you want to disable anonymous browsing for all files and folders in IIS 5 or 6, follow these steps:

1. Open the Internet Information Services manager in Administrative Tools.
2. Expand the website in which your application resides until you can see the root of your application.
3. Right-click on the root of your application and choose Properties.
4. Click the Directory Security tab.
5. Click the Edit button as shown in Figure 7.1.

FIGURE 7.1
The Edit button enables you to edit the directory security options in IIS.

6. Uncheck the Anonymous Access check box. Make sure at least one other authentication method is selected, as shown in Figure 7.2.

FIGURE 7.2
You must have at least one method of authentication enabled in IIS. If you uncheck Anonymous Access, make sure that you check at least one other method.

7. Click OK to exit the Authentication Properties dialog and OK again to exit the properties of the web application.

After this change is made, users have to authenticate to the website to access it.

> **NOTE** Keep in mind that after you disable anonymous browsing in IIS, you have disabled it for all requests, whether ASP.NET or not.

Disabling Anonymous Browsing in IIS 7 (Windows Vista)

If you're using IIS 7 on Windows Vista, follow these steps to disable anonymous browsing:

1. Open the Internet Information Services (IIS) Manager from Administrative Tools.
2. Expand the websites until you get to the root of your application.
3. Click once on the root of your application to select it.
4. Double-click on the Authentication icon in the IIS area as shown in Figure 7.3.

FIGURE 7.3

In IIS 7, authentication is configured with the Authentication icon.

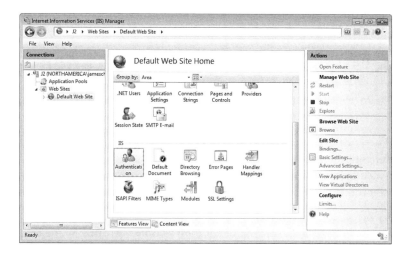

5. Click once on the entry for Anonymous Authentication.
6. Either right-click on Anonymous Authentication and select Disable or click the Disable link in the Action pane shown in Figure 7.4.
7. Make sure that at least one other authentication method is enabled.

> **NOTE** The ASP.NET Configuration Settings dialog places the check box to enable ASP.NET roles on the Authentication tab. However, a discussion of roles is more appropriate in the section on Authorization, so we'll cover that topic there.

FIGURE 7.4

The available authentication options and the current status of each are available after you double-click the Authentication icon.

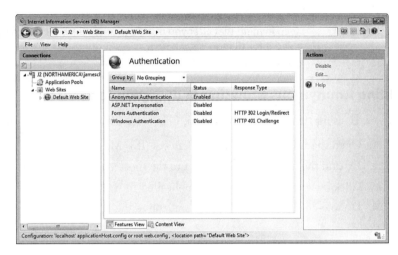

Understanding Forms Authentication

Before we get into the details of how Forms authentication is configured, let's briefly go over how Forms authentication works.

When ASP.NET Forms authentication is enabled, ASP.NET checks for a special Forms authentication cookie when each request comes into the application. If the request is accompanied by a valid Forms authentication cookie, the user is allowed to access the requested resource. If there is no Forms authentication cookie or if the cookie is invalid or expired, the user is automatically redirected to a login page so that he or she can log into the website.

The login page in a Forms authentication website is created by the developer. You can use the ASP.NET Login controls on the page if you want to take advantage of ASP.NET's membership features. However, you can also use your own controls and your own provider rather than rely on the built-in ASP.NET features.

NOTE

We will not cover the topic of creating custom providers in this book. Instead, we will use the membership features that are provided by ASP.NET.

When ASP.NET redirects the user to the login page, it adds a query string to the URL that includes the relative URL of the originally requested page. Therefore, the URL that ASP.NET uses to automatically redirect a user to the login page might look like this:

```
http://www.site.com/login.aspx?ReturnURL=%2fRecords%2femployeeRecords.aspx
```

TIP The ReturnURL query string that ASP.NET uses is always URL encoded. Therefore, in the example URL shown here, the slashes in the URL are displayed as %2f.

After the user successfully logs in to the web application, a Forms authentication cookie is sent to the user. This cookie is valid for only a certain amount of time (30 minutes by default.) If the user does not make a request within that 30-minute timeframe, the cookie expires and any subsequent requests require the user to log in again.

All this happens without you having to write a single line of code because the ASP.NET membership features take care of all the work for you.

Configuring Forms Authentication

ASP.NET applications that are accessed via the Internet are well suited for Forms authentication because Forms authentication doesn't rely on any particular network infrastructure. When you use Forms authentication, users log in to your website using a login web page that you create and ASP.NET takes care of all the plumbing for you.

Configuring Forms Authentication with the ASP.NET Web Site Administration Tool

You can enable Forms authentication by using the ASP.NET Web Site Administration Tool. Click the Security tab, and then click the Select Authentication Type link. When the next screen appears, select the From the Internet radio button to enable Forms authentication, as shown in Figure 7.5.

FIGURE 7.5
To enable Forms authentication in the Web Site Administration Tool, select the From the Internet radio button.

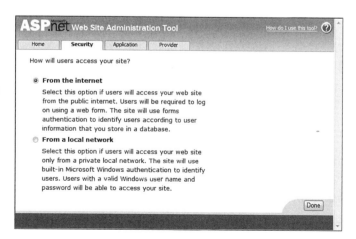

→ For more information on configuring a website for Forms authentication, **see** "Configuring Authentication," **p. 186**.

Unfortunately, you cannot configure any Forms authentication settings with the Web Site Administration Tool. To do that, you need to use either the ASP.NET Configuration Settings dialog (IIS 5 or 6) or use the IIS Manager in IIS 7.

Configuring Forms Authentication with the ASP.NET Configuration Settings Dialog (IIS 5 or 6 Only)

To configure Forms authentication in the ASP.NET Configuration Settings dialog, open the IIS manager from Administrative Tools and navigate to the root of your web application. Right-click on the root folder and select Properties. Then click the ASP.NET tab and the Edit Configuration button to access the ASP.NET Configuration Settings dialog.

Authentication modes are configured on the Authentication tab. Select Forms in the Authentication Mode drop-down, as shown in Figure 7.6.

FIGURE 7.6

Forms authentication can be configured easily in the ASP.NET Configuration Settings dialog.

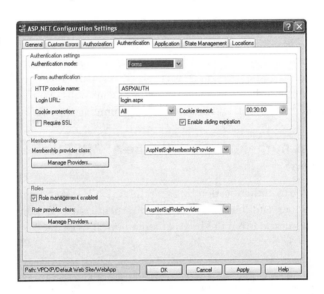

Configuring Forms Authentication with the IIS Manager (IIS 7 Only)

If you are using IIS 7 on Windows Vista, configuration of Forms authentication is accomplished with the IIS Manager.

IIS 7 is actually based on ASP.NET. Therefore, some of the configuration options that you might be used to setting separately from IIS settings are now integrated into IIS.

To enable Forms authentication on IIS 7, follow these steps:

1. Open the Internet Information Services (IIS) Manager from the Administrative Tools.

2. In the Connection pane, select the root folder of your web application.

3. Double-click on the Authentication icon, as shown in Figure 7.7.

FIGURE 7.7

In IIS 7, Forms authentication is enabled with the Authentication settings in IIS itself.

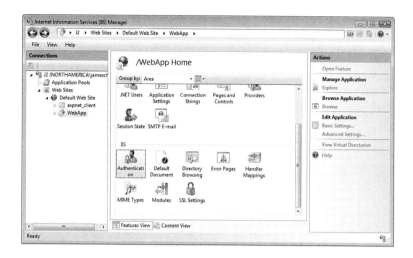

4. In the Authentication screen, right-click on Anonymous Authentication and select Disable.

5. Right-click on Forms Authentication and select Enable as shown in Figure 7.8.

FIGURE 7.8

Anonymous authentication is disabled and Forms authentication is enabled in the same dialog in the IIS Manager.

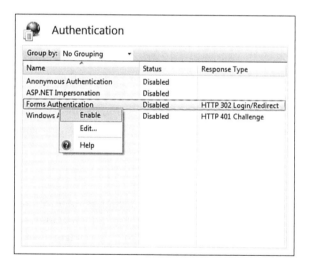

After you've enabled Forms authentication, you can configure it by right-clicking on it and selecting Edit from the menu. Doing so reveals the Edit Forms Authentication Settings dialog shown in Figure 7.9.

FIGURE 7.9

Editing Forms authentication settings in IIS 7 is accomplished with the Edit Forms Authentication Settings dialog.

Other Forms Authentication Settings

After you've enabled Forms authentication, several other options are available to you.

- **HTTP Cookie Name**—The HTTP cookie name defaults to `.ASPXAUTH`. There's usually no need to change it, but if you are using Forms authentication on several applications running on the same box, you might want to use unique cookie names simply for the sake of clarity if, for example, you need to troubleshoot authentication.

- **Login URL**—The login URL is the URL of the login page relative to the root of the web application. If you don't specify a value, ASP.NET uses `login.aspx` in the root of the web application. If that page doesn't exist, users receive a File Not Found error when attempting to log in.

- **Cookie Protection**—By default, cookie protection is set to All, which means that ASP.NET both validates and encrypts the Forms authentication cookie to prevent tampering with it. If you choose, you can select to only validate or only encrypt the cookie. You can also choose to neither validate nor encrypt it. The recommended value is All for security reasons.

- **Cookie Timeout**—When ASP.NET creates the Forms authentication cookie, it configures it to expire after a certain number of minutes have elapsed. You can control the timeout value of the cookie by using the Cookie Timeout setting. It defaults to 30 minutes.

- **Require SSL**—If this check box is checked, ASP.NET requires that you use SSL (HTTPS) for the website. If this option is enabled and you don't use SSL, you receive an error, as shown in Figure 7.10.

FIGURE 7.10

If Require SSL is checked and you don't use SSL, ASP.NET generates an error when you attempt to use the website.

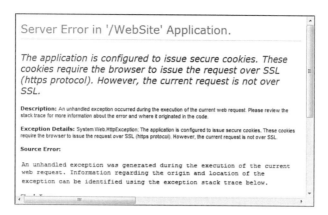

> Server Error in '/WebSite' Application.
>
> *The application is configured to issue secure cookies. These cookies require the browser to issue the request over SSL (https protocol). However, the current request is not over SSL.*
>
> **Description:** An unhandled exception occurred during the execution of the current web request. Please review the stack trace for more information about the error and where it originated in the code.
>
> **Exception Details:** System.Web.HttpException: The application is configured to issue secure cookies. These cookies require the browser to issue the request over SSL (https protocol). However, the current request is not over SSL.
>
> **Source Error:**
>
> An unhandled exception was generated during the execution of the current web request. Information regarding the origin and location of the exception can be identified using the exception stack trace below.

- **Enable Sliding Expiration**—When this check box is checked, the timeout clock is reset each time a user makes a new request. If the box is unchecked, the timeout value is absolute regardless of when the last request was made by a particular user.

> **TIP**
>
> It's recommended that you disable sliding expiration when using Forms authentication. Otherwise, you may end up with a large number of active Forms authentication sessions even though the users are no longer using the site.

One configuration option for Forms authentication that's missing in the user-interface of the ASP.NET Configuration Settings dialog is the option of using cookieless authentication. ASP.NET 2.0 introduced a new `cookieless` attribute for Forms authentication so that you can use Forms authentication without using cookies.

The sample `web.config` code in Listing 7.1 shows an example of using the `cookieless` attribute.

Listing 7.1   Using the `cookieless` Attribute

```
<authentication mode="Forms">
        <forms loginUrl="login.aspx"
                name=".ASPXAUTH"
                protection="All"
                cookieless="AutoDetect" />
</authentication>
```

The following values are available for the `cookieless` attribute:

- **UseCookies**—When this value is used, cookies are always used.
- **UseUri**—When this value is used, cookies are never used. Instead, the Forms authentication information is added to the URL.

- **AutoDetect**—When this value is used, ASP.NET automatically detects whether the requesting device supports cookies. If it does, cookies are be used. Otherwise, the Forms authentication information is added to the URL.

- **UseDeviceProfile**—When this value is used, ASP.NET uses the user agent string to identify the requesting device. If that device supports cookies, cookies are used. If not, the Forms authentication information is added to the URL. This is the default value.

The difference between `AutoDetect` and `UseDeviceProfile` is that ASP.NET checks to see whether cookies are enabled on the device if AutoDetect is used. It does not check to see whether cookies are enabled if `UseDeviceProfile` is used. If the device supports cookies (whether or not they are enabled), ASP.NET uses them.

ASP.NET Authorization

So far, we've covered the details of ASP.NET authentication. As I said previously, authentication is the means by which a user's identity is determined. After a user's identity is known, the next step is to determine whether the user should be allowed the requested access requesting. That process is called *authorization*.

ASP.NET enables you to perform authorization based on the username or on a role to which the user belongs. You can restrict or allow access to files, folders, or for specific HTTP verbs.

Configuring Authorization with the ASP.NET Configuration Settings Dialog (IIS 5 and 6 Only)

To configure authorization using the ASP.NET Configuration Settings dialog, follow these steps:

1. Open the Properties dialog for the root folder of your web application as previously described.
2. Click the ASP.NET tab and then click the Edit Configuration button.
3. Click the Authorization tab.
4. Click the Add button to add a new authorization rule.
5. Select the Allow or Deny radio button for the rule type as shown in Figure 7.11.
6. Select All Verbs for this rule to apply to all HTTP verbs or select Specific Verbs and enter the verb(s) to which this rule should apply. Separate multiple verbs with a comma.

FIGURE 7.11
ASP.NET authorization rules are configured using the Edit Rule dialog.

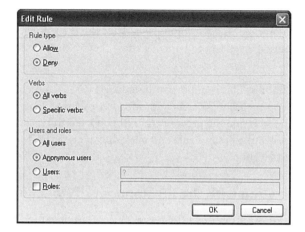

TIP | There are several HTTP verbs, but the only ones that ASP.NET recognizes for authorization rules are GET, HEAD, POST, and DEBUG.

7. Select the appropriate radio button in the Users and Roles section.
8. If the rule should apply to a particular role or roles, check the Roles check box and enter the role(s) in the text box. Separate multiple roles with a comma.
9. Click OK to apply the rule.

After a rule is configured, it appears in the list of local rules as shown in Figure 7.12.

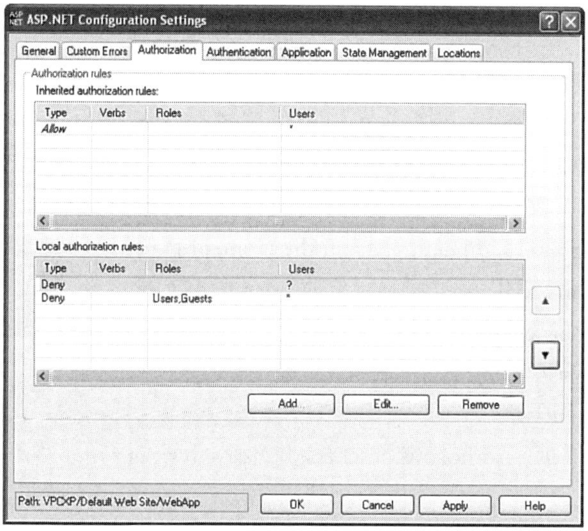

FIGURE 7.12
The Authorization tab shows a list of all configured authorization rules.

If a user is disallowed access to a Forms authentication site because of an authorization rule, that user is unable to proceed past the login page. After the credentials are entered, the login page refreshes. No message appears to let users know they've been denied because of an authorization rule.

The order of authorization rules is important because ASP.NET always applies them in the order in which they appear. Therefore, an authorization rule that appears below another authorization rule may override the previous rule. If you need to rearrange the order of authorization rules, select the desired rule and click the up arrow or down arrow button to move it to the desired location.

Configuring Authorization with the IIS Manager (IIS 7 Only)

In IIS 7, ASP.NET authorization is configured with the Authorization Rules icon, as shown in Figure 7.13.

FIGURE 7.13

IIS 7 provides an interface for configuring authorization rules with the Authorization Rules icon.

If you don't have an Authorization Rules icon in the IIS Manager, it's likely that you haven't enabled URL Authorization in IIS. To do that, follow these steps:

1. Open Programs and Features from the Control Panel.
2. Click the link to Turn Windows Features On or Off.
3. Expand Internet Information Services.
4. Expand World Wide Web Services.
5. Expand Security.
6. Check the URL Authorization check box as shown in Figure 7.14.

FIGURE 7.14
The URL Authorization check box installs the component in IIS 7 necessary for configuration of authorization rules.

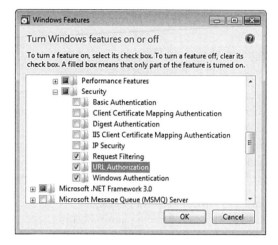

7. Click OK to add the feature.

To add a new authorization rule, double-click on the Authorization Rules icon, and then right-click and select Add Allow Rule or Add Deny Rule as shown in Figure 7.15.

FIGURE 7.15
Right-click to add either an Allow rule or a Deny rule in IIS 7.

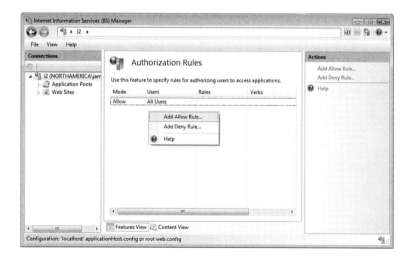

The interface for adding an Allow rule or a Deny rule is exactly the same, and the options available mirror those that are available for adding authorization rules in IIS 5 and 6. However, unlike the interface in IIS 5 and 6, you cannot rearrange the order of authorization rules in IIS 7. Instead, all Deny rules always appear before any Allow rules so that they are applied in the right order. Individual Allow and Deny rules are listed in the order in which they were created.

Why Not Windows Authentication?

You might often hear people say that using Windows authentication isn't appropriate over the Internet. There is a technical reason why that's so.

Windows authentication is actually a term that refers to one of two different authentication methods: NTLM or Kerberos. NTLM authentication relies on a special piece of information called a Windows token that is passed in the authorizing request. The Windows token contains a representation of your login and the groups to which you belong to. Kerberos authentication also transfers a special piece of information to identify you, but it is designed to work across servers that have a special trust relationship with each other.

In an Internet environment, authentication is often delegated to someone other than the client. For example, when you access a website on a remote Internet server, the process often involves you handing off your authentication information to an intermediary such as a proxy server. That intermediary then takes on the job of actually authenticating you to the web server.

NTLM authentication is explicitly designed to fail in this scenario. Therefore, in some cases such as this, Kerberos authentication can be used. However, Kerberos authentication requires that a trust relationship be configured between the computers taking part in the authentication process. That's something that you aren't going to be able to accomplish with a third-party proxy server or something similar.

For that reason, most websites on the Internet do not use Windows authentication. Instead, they use Basic authentication or something similar to Forms authentication in ASP.NET.

PART II

Creating ASP.NET Applications and Web Forms

CHAPTER 8

Creating Websites

IN THIS CHAPTER

The Structure of an ASP.NET Website

A few years ago, a common question often asked of people in the business community was "Do you have a web page?" Back then, having a presence on the Web often meant having a single page or a small group of unrelated pages filled with trivial information.

Today websites are made up of much more than a single page. They frequently contain pages that interact with databases, forms that users can use to post messages or send messages to the website's owner, and other interactive features.

> **TIP** An ASP.NET website is often referred to as a web application.

Special Folders in an ASP.NET Application

In addition to the images, pages, and other files that make up a website, there are also numerous special folders that you might find inside an ASP.NET web application.

The bin Folder

The bin folder is a special folder that contains compiled DLLs on which the web application relies. Depending on how your ASP.NET application is configured, you may or may not have a bin folder.

The App_Code Folder

The App_Code folder is a special folder that contains code files that define classes used in your Web forms. You can create your own classes for your own purposes by defining them inside a code file. That code file can then be added to the App_Code folder so that ASP.NET can automatically make your class available to all your Web forms.

➔ For more information on classes in an ASP.NET website, **see** Chapter 2, "ASP.NET Code Models."

> **NOTE** For a complete explanation of creating classes for use by your Web forms, read *Sams Teach Yourself ASP.NET 2.0 in 24 Hours, Complete Starter Kit* from Sams Publishing.

> **TIP** A *code file* is a file that contains only server-side code and is not related to a Web form. Code files that are written in C# have a .cs file extension and code files that are written in Visual Basic have a .vb file extension.

The Data Folder

The data folder (named App_Data by default) contains file-based databases for use by your ASP.NET application. Most commonly, these databases are SQL Server 2005 Express Edition databases.

You can create your own databases and store them in the App_Data folder. ASP.NET also creates databases automatically in some cases and places them in the App_Data folder. For example, if you use the ASP.NET membership features, an ASPNETDB.MDF file is automatically created in the App_Data folder to store your membership data.

→ For more information on using ASP.NET membership features, **see** "Configuring Authentication," **p. 186**.

> **TIP**   The App_Data folder is automatically configured with the proper permissions for your ASP.NET application to access the databases stored within it.

The App_GlobalResources Folder

The App_GlobalResources folder is used to store resource files that are used by your ASP.NET applications. Resource files are XML files with a .resx file extension that contain strings that your application can load dynamically. They are usually used in cases where an application needs to display text dynamically in different languages.

When you create a new resource file in Visual Web Developer, you are prompted to save the resource file into the App_GlobalResources folder.

> **NOTE**   For more information on using resource files in .NET Framework applications, see the InformIT Network website at www.informit.com.

The App_LocalResources Folder

The App_LocalResources folder is also used to store resource files, but unlike the App_GlobalResources folder, the App_LocalResources folder can be located at any level in the website and contains resources that are not used globally by the application. Each local resource file is used by a specific ASP.NET page and shares the page's name. For example, a local resource file for a page called info.aspx might be called info.aspx.resx. If the local resource file contains resources for a specific locale, the file will contain the locale code as well. For example, a resource file for the info.aspx page that contains resource strings for France would be called info.aspx.fr.resx.

> **NOTE** There can be many App_LocalResources folders at any place within a web application. There can be only one App_GlobalResources folder, and it must be located in the application root.

The App_WebReferences Folder

The App_WebReferences folder contains various files that are used for creating references to ASP.NET web services.

→ For more information on using ASP.NET web services, **see** Chapter 25, "Creating and Testing an ASP.NET Web Service."

The App_Browsers Folder

ASP.NET attempts to render code that works correctly in the browser that initiates the request to your application. In most cases, the code that ASP.NET generates renders correctly on all browsers, but in some cases you need to let ASP.NET know explicitly what capabilities are present in a browser that is accessing your site.

> **TIP** Every browser sends what's called a *user-agent string* that identifies what kind of browser it is. ASP.NET uses the browser's user-agent string to identify different browsers.

ASP.NET 2.0 introduced a new type of file called a *browser definition file*. A browser definition file is an XML file with a `.browser` extension that contains information regarding the capabilities of one or more browsers. In some cases, the browser definition file contains information about which browsers support features such as cookies, JavaScript, and so on.

In other cases, there may be more intricate requirements for the rendering of a specific control. For example, suppose that users are browsing your website from a browser running on a cell phone and a particular ASP.NET control is not rendering correctly. In such cases, a developer can create a special class called a *control adapter* that manages how ASP.NET renders the control for that particular browser, and the mapping of the control adapter to the control is created inside a browser definition file.

> **NOTE** You can find excellent coverage of control adapters by reading *Professional ASP.NET 2.0 Server Control and Component Development* from Wrox Professional Guides.

The App_Themes Folder

The App_Themes folder is the storage area for ASP.NET themes that are available for your use in your web application. The App_Themes folder contains one subfolder for each available theme.

➜ For more information on using themes in ASP.NET, **see** Chapter 19, "Using ASP.NET Themes and Skins."

Creating one of these folders in your web application is easy with Visual Web Developer. Simply select your project in Solution Explorer (the top-level folder of your web application) and select Website, Add ASP.NET Folder from the menu, as shown in Figure 8.1 to reveal a menu of folder names. Alternatively, you can right-click on the project in Solution Explorer and select Add ASP.NET Folder from the menu.

FIGURE 8.1

Adding special ASP.NET folders is easy in Visual Web Developer. Make sure you first select the project in Solution Explorer.

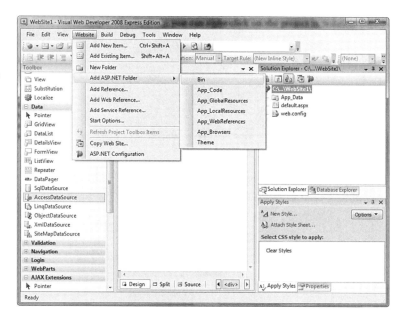

Creating a Web Application in Visual Web Developer

You can create two types of ASP.NET projects: the website project and the web application project. For the purposes of this book, we'll cover the website project model because that's the kind of project Visual Web Developer creates.

➜ For more information on the difference between the web application model and the website model, **see** "ASP.NET Compilation," **p. 32**.

First, you need to create a website in Visual Web Developer. You'll build on this website throughout the rest of this book.

1. Select File, New Web Site from the main menu to display the New Web Site dialog shown in Figure 8.2.

FIGURE 8.2

The New Web Site dialog in Visual Web Developer contains several templates for creating ASP.NET applications.

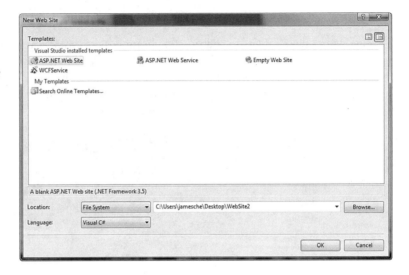

2. If you are using the full version of Visual Studio, click the Framework Version button and select .NET Framework 2.0, as shown in Figure 8.3.

Framework Version Drop-down

FIGURE 8.3

The Framework Version drop-down enables you to target a specific version of the .NET Framework.

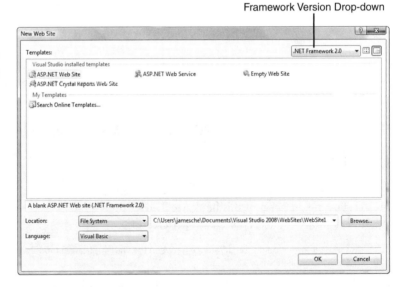

NOTE You can choose a later version of the .NET Framework if you choose, but because this application doesn't use any .NET Framework 3.0 or 3.5 features, selecting .NET Framework 2.0 uses the least amount of overhead.

3. Select ASP.NET Web Site from the list of templates.

4. Select File System, HTTP, or FTP from the location drop-down.

5. Select either Visual C# or Visual Basic from the Language drop-down.

> **NOTE** I'll provide code samples in both Visual Basic and C#, so choose the language that you feel most comfortable with.

6. Enter the path for the new website, or click Browse to select a path. If the path you enter does not exist, Visual Web Developer creates it for you.

7. Click OK to create the website.

If you click the Browse button to select a path, you are presented with Visual Web Developer's Choose Location dialog, as shown in Figure 8.4.

FIGURE 8.4

The Choose Location dialog in Visual Web Developer enables you to create a website easily in the location you choose.

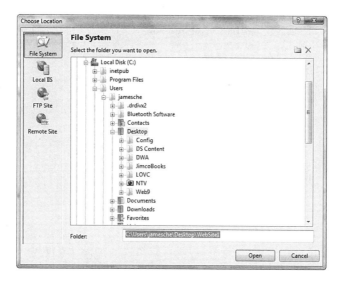

The Choose Location dialog enables you to choose between four different types of websites by clicking one of the buttons along the left edge.

File System

The File System button enables you to create a disk-based web application, as shown previously in Figure 8.4. If you specify a path that does not exist, Visual Web Developer prompts you to create a new folder.

> **TIP** The file system option is the easiest option to work with if you have no prefer-
> ence. It also makes it easy to move the web application to another computer or
> another location on the same computer if necessary.

Local IIS

The Local IIS button enables you to create a web application on the local web server. You
cannot use this option to create a web application on a remote web server.

You can create a new web application by clicking the Create New Web Application button,
as shown in Figure 8.5. You can also choose to create a new virtual directory by clicking the
Create New Virtual Directory button.

FIGURE 8.5
The Local IIS option
makes it easy to cre-
ate a new web appli-
cation on the local IIS
web server.

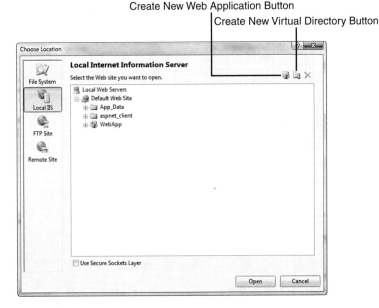

> **NOTE** The Local IIS option does not require the FrontPage Server Extensions on the
> web server.

If you're using IIS 7, you must turn on the IIS Metabase and IIS 6 Configuration
Compatibility feature as shown in Figure 8.6. This option is available when you select the
Programs and Features link in the Control Panel and then click the Turn Windows
Features On or Off link.

FIGURE 8.6

IIS Metabase and IIS 6 Configuration Compatibility must be enabled if you want to use the Local IIS option when using Windows Vista.

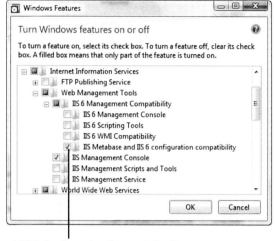

IIS Metabase and IIS 6 Configuration Compatibility Feature

FTP

To create a new web application at an FTP location, click the FTP Site button and fill in the necessary information, as shown in Figure 8.7.

FIGURE 8.7

You can create a new web application at an FTP location as well.

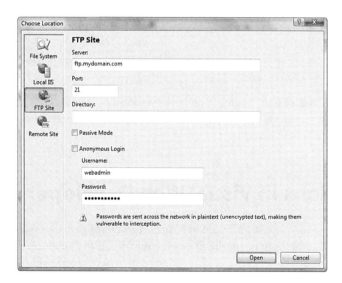

Notice that Visual Web Developer allows you to enable and disable passive FTP from within the FTP Site dialog.

TIP	If you have trouble creating the application with the default settings, check the Passive Mode check box and try again.

Remote Site

To create a web application on a remote website, use the Remote Site button shown in Figure 8.8.

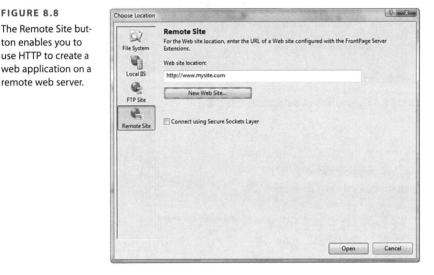

This method uses HTTP to create the web application. If you want to use this method, the remote web server must be configured with ASP.NET 2.0 or later and it must be running the FrontPage Server Extensions.

Start Options in Visual Web Developer

When you're ready to test a website in Visual Web Developer, you start the application by selecting one of the options on the Debug menu. When the application starts, the Start Options in Visual Web Developer determine what action Visual Web Developer takes.

The Start Options in Visual Web Developer are located in the Property Pages for your project. They are accessible if you select the project in Solution Explorer and then select View, Property Pages from the main menu.

As shown in Figure 8.9, your project has three categories in the Property Pages. This chapter covers only the Start Options category. The other options are covered in subsequent chapters.

FIGURE 8.9
The Start Options in Visual Web Developer control what happens when you run your application.

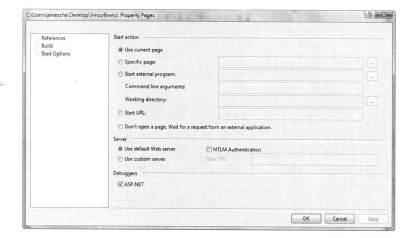

Start Actions

There are five choices for the start action. The selected option is executed whenever you preview the site in a browser or use one of the options on the Debug menu to start the application.

- **Use Current Page**—Specifies that the page that is currently selected or open in Visual Web Developer will be opened in your browser when the site is started. If a folder is selected, Visual Web Developer launches a browser and issues a request for that folder. If a default document is located in the folder, that page is displayed. Otherwise, a folder listing is displayed, in most cases.

- **Specific Page**—When selected, this option causes a specific page to be launched when the site is started. You can click the browse button (...) to the right of the text box to select a page, as shown in Figure 8.10.

TIP   You can also specify a specific startup page by right-clicking on the page in Solution Explorer and selecting Select As Startup Page from the menu.

FIGURE 8.10

When browsing for a specific start page, you are presented with a list of all pages in the website.

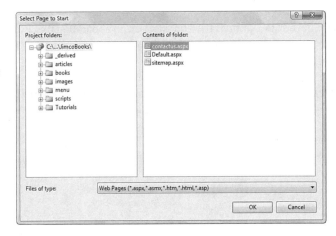

- **Start External Program**—This option causes another application to be launched when the web application is started. You can specify command-line arguments as well as a working directory. This option is especially useful in cases where another application issues requests to your web application instead of users browsing it directly from a browser.

- **Start URL**—Enables you to specify a particular URL that is always requested when you start your web application.

- **Don't Open a Page**—If this option is selected, Visual Web Developer makes sure your application is compiled and ready to execute when it is started, but it doesn't actually open a page from the application. This is useful if you want to manually launch another application that will be making requests against your web application.

Server Options

The Server section of the Start Options dialog enables you to configure the web server that is used to host your web application. The Use Default Web Server option causes one of three things to happen based on the location of the website open in Visual Web Developer:

- If a disk-based website is open in Visual Web Developer, the website is opened in the ASP.NET Development Server.

- If a server-based website is open via HTTP, this option uses the web application's HTTP path to browse the website.

- If a server-based website is open via FTP, this option is disabled.

If you are using the ASP.NET Development Server, you also have the option of enabling NTLM authentication by using the NTLM Authentication check box. Using NTLM authentication helps to prevent someone else from running code on the ASP.NET Development Server using your credentials. If the website open in Visual Web Developer is a server-based website, the NTLM Authentication check box is not visible.

> **NOTE**
>
> NTLM stands for *New Technology LAN Manager*. It's an authentication mechanism that Microsoft introduced many years ago in Windows NT.
>
> Unless you know that you have a specific need to enable NTLM authentication, you can leave it disabled.

You also have the option of using a custom URL in Visual Web Developer's start options. Selecting this option enables you to use a different URL for browsing your application than you use for opening the application in Visual Web Developer.

Finally, there is a check box for the ASP.NET debugger. When this check box is checked, you can debug server-side ASP.NET code when you launch your application.

→ For more information on debugging ASP.NET applications, **see** Chapter 27, "Debugging ASP.NET Applications."

> **TIP**
>
> If you are using another web design tool, such as Expression Web, along with Visual Web Developer, it's best to ensure that both are using the same method of previewing your page. This ensures that what you see is consistent across both applications.

CHAPTER 9

Creating ASP.NET Web Forms

IN THIS CHAPTER

Creating Web Forms in Visual Web Developer

When you create a new website in Visual Web Developer, a new Web form is created for you automatically. Although this first page is enough to get you started, eventually you will need to create new pages.

To create a new web page in Visual Web Developer, select File, New File from the main menu to display the Add New Item dialog as shown in Figure 9.1.

FIGURE 9.1

The Add New Item dialog in Visual Web Developer contains a long list of items you can add to your web application.

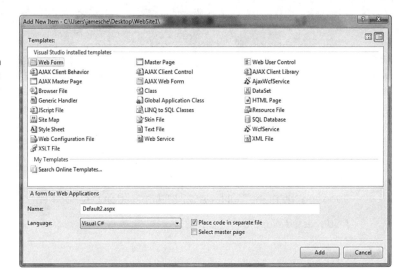

Creating ASP.NET Web Forms

When you create a new Web form, you can select the language of your choice in the Language drop-down you saw in Figure 9.1. ASP.NET enables you to mix pages that use different languages in your website, so you can have some pages written in C# and others in Visual Basic. If you're the only developer working on your web application, you're likely to pick your preferred language and stick with it. However, if you have two or more developers creating pages for you, it's nice to allow those developers to use the languages they prefer.

You also have the option to place the server-side code in a separate file (using the code-behind code model) or include it inline. If you'd prefer to use the code-behind model, check the Place Code in Separate File check box, also shown previously in Figure 9.1. If you leave the check box unchecked, Visual Web Developer does not create a code-behind file and the page is created for use with inline code.

→ For more information on code-behind and inline code models, **see** "Server-Side Code Models," **p. 24**.

If you're using ASP.NET master pages and you want to attach the new page to a master page, check the Select Master Page check box shown previously in Figure 9.1. If you check that check box, Visual Web Developer enables you to browse to the desired master page after the new Web form has been created.

→ For more information on ASP.NET master pages, **see** Chapter 10, "Creating and Using Master Pages."

Other File Types Available in Visual Web Developer

The following are some of the commonly used types of files available in Visual Web Developer:

- **Web Form**—Creates an ASP.NET Web form.
- **HTML Page**—Creates a static HTML file. Pages of this type cannot contain any ASP.NET controls or features.
- **Style Sheet**—Creates a new CSS file.
- **Site Map**—Creates a new ASP.NET sitemap file called `web.sitemap`.
- **JScript File**—Creates a new JScript file with a `.js` file extension. This file can be used for any client-side scripts used in your pages.
- **Master Page**—Creates a new ASP.NET master page with a `.master` file extension.
- **Global Application Class**—Creates a new `global.asax` file that can be used for application-level code.

→ For more information on using the `global.asax` file, **see** "Application and Session Events," **p. 42**.

- **Mobile Web Form**—Creates a new mobile Web form for use when developing applications for mobile devices such as cell phones and PDAs.
- **Mobile Web User** Control—Creates a new mobile user control for use with mobile devices.

> **N O T E** Developing applications for mobile devices is beyond the scope of this book. For details on how to create ASP.NET applications for mobile devices, read *ASP.NET Unleashed, Second Edition* from Sams Publishing.

- **Skin File**—Creates a new skin file for use with ASP.NET skins.

→ For more information on ASP.NET skins and skin files, **see** "Default Skins and Named Skins," **p. 279**.

- **Web User Control**—Creates a new user control with an `.ascx` file extension.
- **Class**—Creates a new class file for defining your own class.

- **Web Configuration File**—Creates a new web configuration file called `web.config`.
- **VBScript File**—Creates a new VBScript file with a `.vbs` file extension.

CAUTION   Client scripts written in VBScript are supported only in Internet Explorer.

- **Browser File**—Creates a browser definition file with a `.browser` file extension.

Creating Web Pages in Expression Web

As strong of a development tool as Visual Web Developer is, you may find yourself wanting to use Expression Web to design some of your web pages. Expression Web was created explicitly for web design, and many web designers find it more pleasurable to use as web design tool.

NOTE   Previous versions of Visual Web Developer did not have the robust web design tools and CSS tools that Visual Web Developer 2008 has, so the need to use a separate tool for designing web interfaces has been largely mitigated.

Expression Web's dialog for creating new files contains many of the file types used in ASP.NET applications. To create a new web page in Expression Web, select File, New, Page from the main menu. The New dialog (shown in Figure 9.2) includes ASP.NET file types, both in the General and ASP.NET categories.

FIGURE 9.2
Many ASP.NET file types can be created with Expression Web.

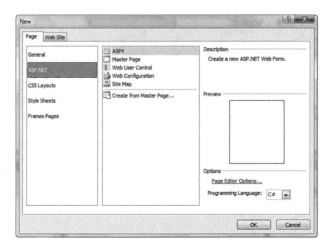

| TIP | You can also create a new ASP.NET Web form directly from the Expression Web menus. We'll cover that later in this section. |

The following ASP.NET files types can be created from the New dialog in Expression Web:

- **ASPX**—This option creates a new ASP.NET Web form with an `.aspx` file extension. You can choose between C#, VJ#, and Visual Basic as your language.

- **Master Page**—Creates a new ASP.NET master page with a `.master` file extension.

- **Web User Control**—Creates a new ASP.NET user control with an `.ascx` file extension.

  → For more information on ASP.NET user controls, **see** "What Are User Controls?," **p. 164**.

- **Web Configuration**—Creates a new web configuration file called `web.config`.

  → For more information on ASP.NET web configuration files, **see** "ASP.NET Configuration Files," **p. 66**.

- **Site Map**—Creates a new ASP.NET sitemap file called `web.sitemap`.

You also have the option of creating a new ASP.NET Web form based on an existing ASP.NET master page. To do so, choose the Create from Master Page item in the New dialog shown previously in Figure 9.2.

When you create an ASP.NET web page in Expression Web, you have the option of choosing a language. Your choices are C#, Visual Basic, and VJ#. Your choice of language determines which language Expression Web specifies in the `@ Page` directive of the Web form.

Because Expression Web does not support ASP.NET server-side code, there is no consequence to choosing one language over another. However, Visual Web Developer does not support ASP.NET development using VJ#, so it's best to choose either Visual Basic or C# as your programming language when creating web pages in Expression Web so that you can use Visual Web Developer, if you choose, to write server-side code easily for your page.

You can also create ASP.NET Web forms by selecting File, New, ASPX from the main menu in Expression Web. Doing so creates an ASP.NET Web form that includes an `@ Page` directive specifying C# as the language. There is no way to change this menu item so that it creates a page using any other language, so if you want to use Visual Basic as your server-side language, you need to be sure to use the New dialog, as previously discussed, to create your Web forms.

Choosing the Right Tool for ASP.NET Application Development

One of the challenges of using both Expression Web and Visual Web Developer for ASP.NET application development is that the tools share a fair amount of functionality. As you've seen, both are capable of creating many of the files that you'll use in your ASP.NET application.

The greatest difference between the two tools is in the support of server-side code. As a design tool, Expression Web is a poor choice for writing ASP.NET code. Although you can use it for such code if you wish, you won't get IntelliSense support, color-coding, or any of the other features that make writing server-side code easier.

Using the Code-Behind Model

Although Expression Web doesn't have a template for creating code-behind files, you can use Expression Web to edit code-behind files if you choose. However, you won't get IntelliSense or color-coding because Expression Web doesn't recognize code-behind syntax. Therefore, you'll probably want to create your code-behind files in Visual Web Developer.

When you create a Web form in Visual Web Developer, you are offered the choice of placing the server-side code in a separate file. When you choose this option, Visual Web Developer creates two files: the `.aspx` file and another file that contains server-side code as shown in Figure 9.3.

FIGURE 9.3

If you choose to place the server-side code in a separate file, Visual Web Developer creates two files when you create a Web form.

> **TIP** I'm going to walk you through how you can create a code-behind file in Expression Web only because there's a chance that you might want to implement the code-behind model after a Web form has already been created. However, I strongly urge you to use Visual Web Developer for any code-behind Web forms because it's designed for code-behind.

As I already mentioned, Expression Web does not enable you to create code-behind files. Therefore, if you create your ASP.NET Web forms in Expression Web and you want to use the code-behind model, you need to follow these steps:

1. Create the ASP.NET Web form in Expression Web.

2. Create a new Text File.

3. Select File, Save As.

4. Select All Files in the Save As Type drop-down.

5. Name the file using the same name that you used for the .aspx page but add a .cs file extension if you're using C# or a .vb file extension if you're using VB, as shown in Figure 9.4.

FIGURE 9.4

You can create code-behind files manually in Expression Web if you use the code-behind naming syntax to save a text file, but it's hardly worth the effort because it involves many steps to do something that's automatic in Visual Web Developer.

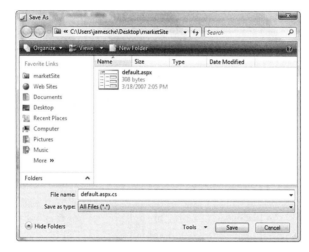

6. Add the ASP.NET code-behind code to the file.

7. Edit the @ Page directive for the Web form so that it uses the code-behind file you created.

→ For more information on the @ Page directive in ASP.NET Web forms, **see** "ASP.NET Directives," **p. 22**.

As you can see, implementing the code-behind model in Expression Web can be more trouble than it's worth. It's much easier to use Visual Web Developer instead to create your Web forms. You can then design the Web form in Expression Web. Keep in mind, however, that because Expression Web does not recognize the code-behind syntax, it does not display your code-behind files nested under the associated Web forms as you see them displayed in Visual Web Developer.

Using the Inline Code Model

It is quite easy to add inline ASP.NET code to a Web form created with Expression Web. When you create a Web form in Expression Web, the following @ Page directive is added to the page:

```
<%@ Page Language="C#" %>
```

or

```
<%@ Page Language="VB" %>
```

To add server-side code to the page in the inline code model, you simply have to add a new `<script>` block directly under the @ Page directive with a runat attribute set to server like so:

```
<%@ Page Language="C#" %>
<script runat="server">
    // server-side code goes here
</script>
```

Expression Web marks this code as invalid if you are using the default settings because XHTML requires that `<script>` tags be placed within a parent tag, but you can ignore that warning. ASP.NET uses the code within the `<script>` block to generate the page that is sent down to the browser, and after it has used the code to do that, it removes the `<script>` block from the page.

Whether you choose inline code or code-behind code, you should write the code in Visual Web Developer. As you'll see as you work through the rest of this book, Visual Web Developer adds significant capabilities that support writing ASP.NET code, all of which are absent in Expression Web.

A Suggested Workflow

I've used Visual Web Developer and Expression Web together for several ASP.NET applications. As I developed these sites, it became clear to me that each product has its own strengths and weaknesses. The new features that Expression Web brings to Visual Web Developer 2008 close the gap a bit, but there are still some clear delineations between the two products. The following sections walk you through the workflow that I find most suitable based on the strength of individual features of each product

Use Either Tool to Create the Website

The tool that you choose to create the website is unimportant because neither tool has any advantage over the other. However, if you use Expression Web to create your website, keep in mind the templates that are used in Expression Web are not targeted at ASP.NET. As such, they generate many files that are not ASP.NET files.

> **NOTE** When I refer to creating the website, I'm not referring to the design process of a web application. Instead, I'm referring to the specific act of using the New Web Site menu item to create the folders and baseline files for a site.

Use Visual Web Developer to Create Pages

Unless I don't plan on having any server-side code for a page, I create all my pages with Visual Web Developer. If I'm going to use the code-behind model, I always create my pages in Visual Web Developer. If I'm using the inline code model, I occasionally create a page in Expression Web, but I still use Visual Web Developer most often because it creates the necessary `<script>` block for me.

Do Design Work in Either Tool

The previous version of Visual Web Developer lacked the excellent CSS tools and other design features that Visual Web Developer 2008 contains. These enhancements to Visual Web Developer 2008 are made possible by the inclusion of the Expression Web designer in Visual Web Developer 2008. The differences between Expression Web and Visual Web Developer therefore have been blurred to some degree. However, there are still some features (especially those found when working with images) that are more full-featured in Expression Web.

Even so, for most users, neither tool carries a distinct advantage in the design category.

Use Either Tool to Configure ASP.NET Controls

Setting the properties and configuring ASP.NET server controls can be accomplished easily with either tool. As shown in Figures 9.5 and 9.6, ASP.NET server controls provide equal design-time functionality in both tools. The developers of Expression Web obviously put a lot of work into making sure that ASP.NET server controls provide the same designer properties in Expression Web as they do in Visual Web Developer.

Use Either Tool to Preview Your Pages

Both Expression Web and Visual Web Developer use the ASP.NET Development Server for testing disk-based websites, and both are capable of using the FrontPage Server Extensions to open server-based websites. Therefore, if you are previewing pages to check design features, either tool is equally capable.

FIGURE 9.5

An ASP.NET server control being edited in Expression Web looks just as it does in Visual Web Developer.

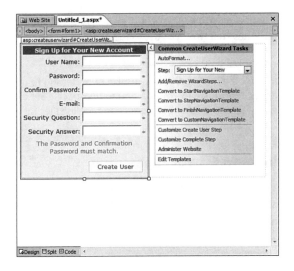

FIGURE 9.6

This control is being edited in Visual Web Developer, but it looks just as it does while being edited in Expression Web.

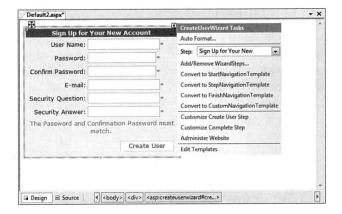

> **TIP** Expression Web relies on the FrontPage Server Extensions for local IIS websites, but Visual Web Developer does not use the FrontPage Server Extensions for local IIS websites.

Test ASP.NET Code in Visual Web Developer

If you are testing pages that use ASP.NET server-side code, using Visual Web Developer is the best option. Unlike Expression Web, Visual Web Developer enables you to debug ASP.NET pages, meaning you can step through your code, set breakpoints where you'd like, and so on.

→ For more information on debugging ASP.NET applications, **see** Chapter 27, "Debugging ASP.NET Applications."

Publish Your Website with Expression Web

In most cases, Expression Web is the best tool to use for copying your web application from one place to another. The main reason for this is that Expression Web has the capability to determine which files have changed and copy only those files. Expression Web can also optimize your HTML when you copy the files.

Visual Web Developer does have the capability to synchronize files between two computers, but it does not have the capability to copy only changed files from a source computer to a destination computer.

There is one exception to this recommendation. If you want to precompile your web application, Visual Web Developer is the best choice because it enables you to configure precompilation in the user interface.

NOTE | I don't cover publishing a website with Expression Web in this book. If you want full details on publishing in Expression Web, read *Special Edition Using Microsoft Expression Web* from Que Publishing.

➔ For more information on deploying websites with Visual Web Developer, **see** Chapter 30, "Publishing an ASP.NET Application."

➔ For more information on precompiling ASP.NET websites, **see** "ASP.NET Compilation," **p. 32**.

As this suggested workflow has shown, if you create a Web form in Expression Web and you want to move it to a code-behind model, it's a time-consuming endeavor. That's just one example of how changing tools midstream can be troublesome. Choosing the right tool from the beginning is going to save you plenty of time and spare you lots of headaches.

PART III

Master Pages and User Controls

CHAPTER 10

Creating and Using Master Pages

IN THIS CHAPTER

An Introduction to Master Pages

When Microsoft decided to stop developing FrontPage, I got many emails from web designers asking me how to best go about converting a website from FrontPage to Expression Web. My answer was always the same: Don't worry about converting your site. Instead, use this as an opportunity to redesign your site and give it a fresh appearance. That recommendation was always met with resistance because redesigning a website is a daunting task. However, if you design your site to be easily updated and maintained, it's not nearly as hard as you might think.

ASP.NET master pages can make it easy to create and maintain a web application with a consistent look and feel. A master page is a special kind of ASP.NET page that is used somewhat like a template for other ASP.NET pages. When another ASP.NET page uses an ASP.NET master page, it takes on all the qualities of the master page, including the appearance and any code associated with the master page. However, you can define areas in the master page that a page using that master page can override with its own content by using ContentPlaceHolder controls.

Each time you create a new ASP.NET Web form, you have the option of selecting a master page to use with it. If you select a master page, the new Web form immediately takes on the appearance of the master page and is referred to as a *content page* for the master page. If an area of that master page contains a ContentPlaceHolder control, you have the option of either using the content that the master page provides for the ContentPlaceHolder control or of creating content for the ContentPlaceHolder control that is unique to the content page.

Most ASP.NET developers use master pages to define a common user interface for their web applications. Content that remains the same on all pages is contained within the master page and outside any ContentPlaceHolder controls. However, any area of the page that should contain page-specific data includes a ContentPlaceHolder control. Figure 10.1 illustrates this concept.

The master page shown in Figure 10.1 contains navigational controls, a logo, and copyright text that will be included on all pages that use the master page. It also contains a ContentPlaceHolder control named `mainContent`. When a content page uses this master page, only the `mainContent` section of the page is editable. The rest of the page is locked and content is provided by the master page. You'll have an opportunity to see this concept in action later in this chapter.

FIGURE 10.1

A typical ASP.NET master page showing a single ContentPlaceHolder control.

Structure of Master Pages and Content Pages

As previously mentioned, a master page consists of regular page content along with one or more ContentPlaceHolder controls. Unlike a regular ASP.NET Web form, a master page uses a @ Master directive at the top of the page. The following code shows the @ Master directive from the master page shown previously in Figure 10.1.

```
<%@ Master Language="C#" AutoEventWireup="true"
➥CodeFile="MasterPage.master.cs" Inherits="MasterPage" %>
```

→ For more information on ASP.NET directives, **see** "ASP.NET Directives," **p. 22**.

Other than the different directive used to define the page, master pages are very much like any other ASP.NET Web form. Content pages, on the other hand, are quite different from other ASP.NET pages. Because a content page gets a large part of its content from the master page, it does not contain the traditional HTML tags that you're used to seeing. The code in Listing 10.1 contains all the code visible in Source view after a master page is used to create a Web form as a content page.

Listing 10.1   Content Page Code

```
<%@ Page Language="C#" MasterPageFile="~/MasterPage.master"
➥AutoEventWireup="true" CodeFile="products.aspx.cs" Inherits="products"
➥Title="Our Products" %>
<asp:Content ID="Content1" ContentPlaceHolderID="head" Runat="Server">
</asp:Content>
<asp:Content ID="Content2" ContentPlaceHolderID="mainContent" Runat="Server">
</asp:Content>
```

The first thing that you'll notice is the `MasterPageFile` attribute in the @ Page directive. This attribute configures the connection between the content page and the master page. The only other code in the page consists of two Content controls (indicated by the `<asp:Content>` tags) called `Content1` and `Content2`.

Content controls are ASP.NET controls that correspond to specific ContentPlaceHolder controls on the master page. Each Content control has a `ContentPlaceHolderID` attribute that specifies the ContentPlaceHolder control on the master page that corresponds to the Content control. For example, anything that is entered into the `Content2` Content control in Listing 10.1 will appear inside the area indicated by the `mainContent` ContentPlaceHolder control shown previously in Figure 10.1.

> **TIP** Remember that ContentPlaceHolder controls belong on master pages and Content controls belong on content pages.

A master page can also provide content itself for a particular ContentPlaceHolder control. For example, you might have a ContentPlaceHolder control that contains a telephone number for your office, but you have some pages that refer to a different office with a different phone number. If you enter the telephone number into a ContentPlaceHolder control, any page that uses the master page will automatically show the telephone number you entered, as shown in Figure 10.2.

FIGURE 10.2

The phoneContent ContentPlaceHolder control contains a phone number that was entered into the control on the master page.

On the pages where you need to specify a different phone number, simply click the Smart Tag button as shown in Figure 10.3 and select Create Custom Content. When you do, the content from the master page is replaced with empty content so that you can provide your own.

FIGURE 10.3

A Content control can provide its own unique content by using the Smart Tag for the Content control.

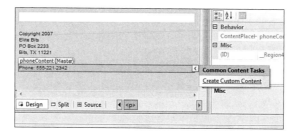

If you'd like to revert back to the content from the master page, click the Smart Tag button again and select Default to Master's Content. When you do, any content that you've added to the Content control is removed and replaced with the content from the master page.

CAUTION

> If you switch to the master page's content, any information that exists within the Content control is deleted. You can undo that operation, but only if you haven't already made other edits. Keep in mind that changing the Content control back to using custom content does not restore the previous content.

Creating a Master Page

The application that you'll be creating throughout the rest of this book will use a master page so that you can easily change the appearance of the website in the future. In this section you will create the master page and begin to build the user interface for the application.

To create the master page, follow these steps:

1. Open the web application that you created in Chapter 8.

TIP

> If you haven't yet created a new website, create a new one-page or empty website now. If you don't know how, refer to Chapter 8.

2. Select File, New File and select Master Page from the list of templates, as shown in Figure 10.4.

3. Choose a language from the Language drop-down and check the Place Code in Separate File check box as shown in Figure 10.4.

FIGURE 10.4

Visual Web Developer provides a Master Page template so that you can easily create new master pages.

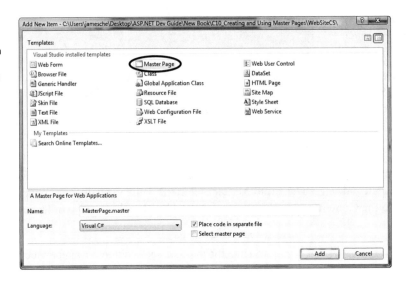

You do not have to choose the same language that you chose when you created your web application. However, unless you have multiple developers working on your site, there's no need to mix languages. Choose the language you're most comfortable with.

4. Name the new master page **MasterPage.master** and click Add to add it to your website.

If you're not already in Design view, click the Design tab at the bottom of the design surface in Visual Web Developer to switch into Design view. Your new master page is blank except for one empty ContentPlaceHolder control, as shown in Figure 10.5.

FIGURE 10.5

When you create a new master page, Visual Web Developer adds a single ContentPlaceHolder control automatically.

When I'm creating master pages, I prefer to design the page elements that all pages will use, and then add the ContentPlaceHolder controls after the page layout is complete. Let's add some content to the master page you just created.

Adding Content to the Master Page

To complete the layout of the master page, we'll add a logo, a couple of navigation controls, a ContentPlaceHolder control that will contain the main page content, and copyright information for a fictitious company called Elite Bits.

> **NOTE** The Elite Bits logo is located in the Examples\Ch10\Files folder on the website for this book at www.quepublishing.com.

1. Create a new folder labeled `images` in your website.
2. Copy the `elitebitslogo.jpg` file into the `images` folder.

> **TIP** You can drag and drop the JPEG file into the `images` folder in Solution Explorer or you can use Windows Explorer to copy the file. If you use Windows Explorer, right-click on the project name in Solution Explorer and select Refresh Folder to refresh the view after you copy the file so that the image file becomes visible in the list.

3. Delete the `ContentPlaceHolder1` control from the new master page.
4. Drag the `elitebitslogo.jpg` file from the `images` folder in Solution Explorer onto the master page.
5. Type **Elite Bits Logo** in the Accessibility Properties dialog as shown in Figure 10.6.

FIGURE 10.6
The Accessibility Properties dialog prompts you to enter information that keeps your site accessible.

> **NOTE** If you have configured the options in Visual Web Developer so that the Accessibility Properties dialog is not displayed, you can skip step 5.

6. Press Enter to add a new line after the logo image.
7. Double-click the SiteMapPath control in the Navigation section of the toolbox to add a new SiteMapPath control.
8. Place the insertion point to the right of the SiteMapPath control you just added and press Enter to add a new line after the SiteMapPath control.

9. Double-click on the Menu control in the Navigation section of the toolbox to add a new Menu control.

10. Press the right-arrow key to deselect the Menu control you just added and press Enter to add a new line after the Menu control.

11. Double-click on the ContentPlaceHolder control in the Standard section of the toolbox to add a new ContentPlaceHolder control.

12. Press the right-arrow key to deselect the ContentPlaceHolder control you just added and press Enter to add a new line after the ContentPlaceHolder control.

13. Press Shift+Enter to insert a new line and a new <p> element and type some text for your copyright and company information.

Your master page should now look similar to the one shown in Figure 10.7.

FIGURE 10.7
Your new master page should look similar to the one shown here.

Your master page now has a ContentPlaceHolder control and some default content. You could use it for your website right now, but we'll first make a few changes to make it more attractive in appearance and also to make it easier to maintain in case you want to make changes later on.

Formatting the Master Page

Let's apply some formatting to the content you've just added to give the master page a more pleasing appearance. You'll use some of the automatic formatting capabilities of the ASP.NET controls along with some cascading style sheet (CSS) code for other content.

To automatically format the ASP.NET controls on the master page, click the Smart Tag button next to the SiteMapPath control and select Auto Format as shown in Figure 10.8.

Select a formatting scheme in the AutoFormat dialog that suits your preference. For this master page, I chose the Classic formatting as shown in Figure 10.9.

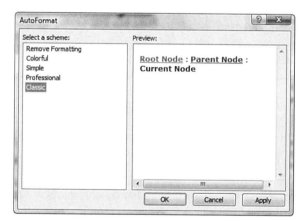

Follow the same steps outlined for the ASP.NET controls to apply the Classic auto-formatting for the Menu control. After applying the formatting to the Menu control, your master page should look like the one shown in Figure 10.10.

FIGURE 10.10

The auto-formatted ASP.NET controls make the page look much more professional.

Now you need to create a new CSS style and apply it to the copyright text on the page. You're going to use the Manage Styles window (new to Visual Web Developer 2008) for this task.

NOTE

The Manage Styles task pane is one of several powerful features that Visual Web Developer 2008 offers as a result of the Expression Web designer being incorporated into Visual Studio 2008.

For more information on Microsoft Expression Web, read my book, *Special Edition Using Microsoft Expression Web*, from Que Publishing.

→ For more information on using CSS with Visual Web Developer, **see** Chapter 17, "Creating and Managing CSS Styles."

If the Manage Styles window is not already visible, select Format, CSS Styles, Manage Styles to display it. Select the New Style link in the Manage Styles window as shown in Figure 10.11.

When you click the New Style link, you're presented with the New Style dialog, another new feature in Visual Web Developer's CSS arsenal. You'll use a CSS ID for the copyright block on the master page. To do that, follow these steps:

1. Type **#Copyright** in the Selector text box of the New Style dialog.

2. Select New Style Sheet from the Define In drop-down. This creates the new style in a new .css file.

3. Select Font in the list of categories.

FIGURE 10.11

The Manage Styles window is a new addition to Visual Web Developer 2008, and it adds unprecedented CSS capabilities.

New Style Link

4. Select Arial, Helvetica, sans-serif from the Font-family drop-down.

5. Select x-small from the Font-size drop-down.

> **TIP** Notice that Visual Web Developer displays the CSS code for your new style along with a preview at the bottom of the New Style dialog.

6. Select Border in the list of categories.

> **TIP** Any category that is included in your new style will show up bolded in the category list.

7. Under Border-style, make sure that the Same For All check box is checked and select Solid from the Top drop-down.

8. Under Border-width, make sure that the Same For All check box is checked and select Thin from the Top drop-down.

The New Style dialog should look like the one shown in Figure 10.12. Click OK to create the new style and click Yes when Visual Web Developer asks you whether you want to link the new style sheet to your page.

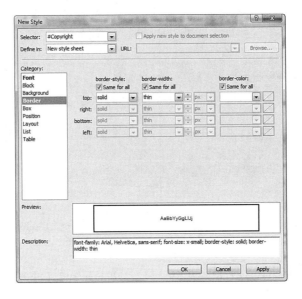

FIGURE 10.12

The New Style dialog with the new CSS ID configured.

Figure 10.13 shows the new CSS ID as it appears in the Manage Styles window. The small dot that appears next to the style is red in color, indicating that the style is a CSS ID.

FIGURE 10.13

The new CSS ID appears in the Manage Styles task pane with a red dot next to it.

To apply the new CSS ID to the copyright text, you'll use the Apply Styles window. The Apply Styles window looks similar to the Manage Styles window, but it's more suited to applying styles to page elements.

To apply the #Copyright CSS ID to the copyright text, follow these steps:

1. Click anywhere inside the copyright text to select the <p> element.

2. If the Apply Styles window is not visible, select Format, CSS Styles, Apply Styles to access it.

3. Click on the #Copyright CSS ID in the Apply Styles window as shown in Figure 10.14 to apply the style.

FIGURE 10.14
Applying a CSS style to a page element is as simple as clicking on the style in the Apply Styles window.

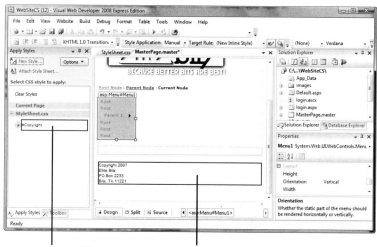

Style in Apply Styles Window   Style Applied to Paragraph

Now let's complete the final step in configuring the master page, configuring the SiteMapPath and Menu controls that we added earlier.

Configuring Navigation Controls

ASP.NET navigation controls have a lot of functionality built in to them that you can tap into without writing any code at all. For example, the SiteMapPath control automatically reads your site's navigation structure from a special file called a *sitemap* file. Other controls use the sitemap file as well.

The following sections show you how to create a sitemap file for your application and configure the controls to use it for navigation structure.

Creating a Sitemap File

The sitemap file is an XML file that defines the structure of your website. When ASP.NET first loads your application, it looks for a file called web.sitemap in your application's root folder and uses it to feed your navigation controls. This is, of course, the default behavior, which you can certainly change, but this book doesn't go into those details.

> **NOTE** Scott Guthrie (considered by many to be the father of ASP.NET) has a great blog post that provides plenty of links demonstrating how to work with a sitemap file. You can access that post at weblogs.asp.net/scottgu/archive/ 2005/11/20/431019.aspx.

Follow these steps to create a sitemap file that will feed the navigation controls:

1. Make sure that your web application is open in Visual Web Developer and select File, New File.

2. From the list of installed templates, choose Site Map and click Add to add a new Web.sitemap file to your application.

3. Replace the existing XML code in the sitemap file with the code shown in Listing 10.2.

Listing 10.2   Web.sitemap Code

```
<?xml version="1.0" encoding="utf 8" ?>
<siteMap xmlns="http://schemas.microsoft.com/AspNet/SiteMap-File-1.0" >
    <siteMapNode url="default.aspx" title="Home"  description="Home Page">
        <siteMapNode url="bits.aspx" title="Bits"
        ➥description="Listing of Bits">
            <siteMapNode url="softbits.aspx" title="Soft Bits"
            ➥description="Software Bits" />
            <siteMapNode url="hardbits.aspx" title="Hard Bits"
            ➥description="Hardware Bits" />
        </siteMapNode>
        <siteMapNode url="contact.aspx" title="Contact"
        ➥description="Contact Us" />
        <siteMapNode url="login.aspx" title="Member Section"
        ➥description="For registered members only.">
        <siteMapNode url="members/productlist.aspx" title="Products"
        ➥description="List of Products" />
        </siteMapNode>
    </siteMapNode>
</siteMap>
```

Save the sitemap file. You'll preview a page shortly, but first you need to configure the Menu control to use the new sitemap file.

Configuring the Menu to Use the Sitemap File

Unlike the SiteMapPath control, the Menu control does not automatically use a sitemap file. You have to configure the Menu control to use the sitemap file. To do that, follow these steps:

1. Click the Smart Tag button next to the Menu.
2. Select New Data Source from the Data Source drop-down.
3. Select Site Map in the Data Source Configuration Wizard dialog as shown in Figure 10.15 and click OK.

FIGURE 10.15

The Data Source Configuration Wizard is an easy way to configure a data source for the Menu control.

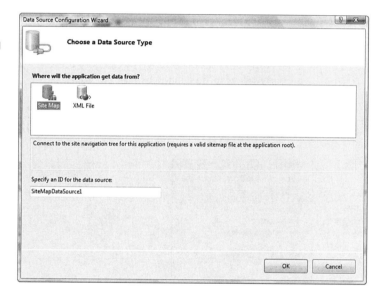

After the data source has been configured, you will see a SiteMapDataSource control on the master page as shown in Figure 10.16.

FIGURE 10.16

The master page now contains a SiteMapDataSource control that connects the Menu control to the sitemap file.

> **NOTE**   The SiteMapDataSource control is not visible when the page is browsed.

As shown in Figure 10.16, the Menu control displays one item labeled Home. What you want it to display is all the items from the sitemap file. By default, a Menu control displays only one level of menu items. To change the Menu so that it displays all the items from the sitemap file, follow these steps:

1. Select the Menu control.
2. If the Properties window is not visible, press F4 to display it.
3. Locate the `StaticDisplayLevels` property.

> **TIP**   If the Properties window is sorted by category, the `StaticDisplayLevels` property will be located in the Behavior category.

4. Set the StaticDisplayLevels property to **2** as shown in Figure 10.17.

FIGURE 10.17

The `Static-DisplayLevels` property controls how many levels are displayed in the Menu control.

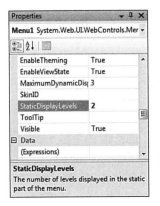

After you make that change, the Menu control should immediately change to show all the top-level menu items.

While you are looking at the properties of the Menu control, let's make one more modification to make the Menu control fit with the layout of the master page. Select the Menu if it's not already selected and locate the Orientation property. Change the Orientation property to Horizontal to display the menu in a horizontal fashion.

> **TIP**   The Orientation property is located in the Layout category in the Properties window.

Connecting a Page to the Master Page

To test the master page and the navigation controls you've configured, you need to connect a page to the master page. You can connect a page to a master page when you create the page or you can connect it afterward.

Connecting a New Page

To connect a new page to a master page, simply check the Select Master Page check box as shown in Figure 10.18. When this check box is checked, Visual Web Developer prompts you to select the master page when the new page is created.

FIGURE 10.18

The easiest way to connect a page to a master page is to do it when the page is created.

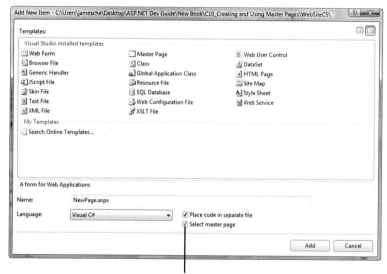

Select Master Page Check Box

Connecting an Existing Page

To connect a master page to an existing page, first set the `MasterPageFile` property of the page to the location of the master page. To do that, you simply click on the page away from any ASP.NET controls and then click the ellipsis button next to the `MasterPageFile` property in the Properties window as shown in Figure 10.19.

If you close the page after setting the MasterPageFile property and reopen it in Visual Web Developer, you'll see a master page error because a content page cannot contain HTML markup outside of Content controls. Therefore, you'll need to delete all content in the page except for the @ Page directive.

FIGURE 10.19

The
MasterPageFile
property configures
the connection
between a page and
a master page.

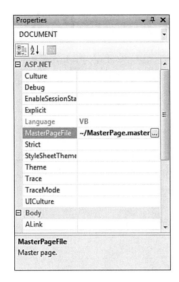

If the page contains content that you want to keep, paste that content into a Content control after the page has been successfully attached to the master page. To do that, click the Smart Tag button on an existing Content control and select Create Custom Content as shown in Figure 10.20. Doing so unlocks the Content control so that you can place content within it.

FIGURE 10.20

To create custom
content for a Content
control, use the
Smart Tag button.

Follow these steps to attach the master page to the `default.aspx` file that was created when you created the web application:

1. Open the `default.aspx` page.
2. Switch to Design view if necessary.
3. Click inside an empty portion of the page.
4. Locate the `MasterPageFile` property and click the ellipsis button.
5. Select `MasterPage.master` and click OK.
6. Save the page and close it.
7. Reopen the page. You'll see a master page error.
8. Switch to Code view and delete all code except for the `@ Page` directive.
9. Switch back to Design view.

The default page should now be attached to the master page and you should see the content from the master page. Save the page and preview it in a browser to test the page and the navigation control.

> **N O T E**   Because you haven't created the other pages for the site, clicking on links on the menu makes requests for nonexistent pages.

> **T I P**   In addition the methods already described, you can also connect pages to master pages by using the `web.config` file or by using server-side code. We won't go into the details of that here, but information is available on the MSDN website at msdn.microsoft.com.

Checkpoint

Here's what you completed in this chapter:

- The website
- The master page with navigation controls
- An external style sheet for CSS styles
- The sitemap file to feed navigation structure to navigation controls
- The home page attached to the master page

In the next chapter, you'll learn how to use ASP.NET user controls so that you can reuse portions of a page easily.

CHAPTER 11

Creating and Using User Controls

IN THIS CHAPTER

What Are User Controls?

As you develop Web forms for a web application, it's likely that you'll identify some parts of a page that can be reused in several other pages. In Chapter 14 of this book, you will be creating a login interface for some membership pages. Although most web applications have a login page that contains a login interface, that same login interface can also be used in other pages so that users can log in from several places in the site. When you create the login interface as an ASP.NET user control, you can easily reuse it in any page.

ASP.NET user controls are created just like Web forms, but there are several differences between the two. Table 11.1 lists the differences between a Web form and a user control.

Table 11.1   Differences Between Web Forms and User Controls

Web Form	User Control
.aspx file extension	.ascx file extension
Defined with an @ Page directive	Defined with an @ Control directive
Contains an <html>/<body>/<form> element	Does not contain an <html>/<body>/<form> element

> **NOTE** Another difference between a Web form and a user control is that a Web form derives from the Page class and a user control derives from the UserControl class. However, the topic of programmatic inheritance is beyond the scope of this book so we won't go into detail on this difference.

Creating a User Control

To create an ASP.NET user control, follow these steps:

1. Select File, New File.
2. From the list of templates, choose Web User Control.
3. Select a language for the user control's server-side code.

> **TIP** The user control's language does not have to match the page on which it is being used.

4. If you'd like for the server-side code to be in a code-behind file, check the Place Code in Separate File check box.

→ For more information on code-behind files in ASP.NET, **see** "Code-Behind Server-Side Code," **p. 26.**

5. Click Add to add the new user control to your web application.

After the user control has been created, you can add ASP.NET controls to it just as you would a Web form. Follow these steps to add the basic controls that you'll build upon in Chapter 14.

1. If you aren't in Design view, click the Design button.

2. If the toolbox isn't visible, press Ctrl+Alt+X to display it.

3. Double-click on the LoginView control in the Login section of the toolbox to add it to the user control.

4. Click inside the LoginView control.

5. Double-click on the Login control in the Login section of the toolbox to add it to the user control inside the LoginView control.

> **NOTE** You're not expected to know how to use the LoginView or Login controls at this point. You'll configure them later in Chapter 14.

Your user control should now look like the one shown in Figure 11.1. Select File, Save WebUserControl.ascx As and save the user control as login.ascx.

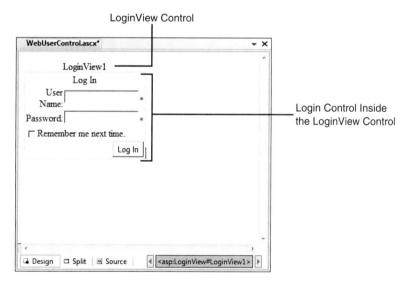

FIGURE 11.1
The user control contains a LoginView control and a Login control.

> **TIP** After you save the user control as login.ascx, you can right-click on WebUserControl.ascx in Solution Explorer and delete it if you want to.

Adding User Controls to a Page

To add a user control to a page, simply drag and drop the user control from Solution Explorer onto the page. When you do so, Visual Web Developer adds an @ Register directive to the Web form that looks like the following:

```
<%@ Register src="~/login.ascx" tagname="login" tagprefix="uc1" %>
```

> **TIP**
>
> The tilde in the src attribute is an ASP.NET convention that points to the root directory of your web application. You can use a tilde anywhere in your ASP.NET files to indicate the root of the application.

The @ Register directive tells Visual Web Developer the name of the user control file, the tag name that is used for the user control, and the tag prefix. The tag name and tag prefix are used in the HTML source for the Web form. The format is as follows:

```
<tagprefix:tagname ID="controlID" runat="server" />
```

Therefore, the user control registered by the example @ Register directive shown previously would appear as follows in Source view:

```
<uc1:login ID="login1" runat="server" />
```

Of course, it's not necessary for you to know all this because Visual Web Developer automatically takes care of it when you drag and drop the user control onto your page.

Creating a User Control

Follow these steps to create a new ASP.NET Web form and add the user control to it:

1. Select File, New File.
2. From the list of templates, select Web Form.
3. Change the name to login.aspx.
4. Place a check in the Select Master Page check box.
5. Click Add to add the new Web form.
6. In the Select a Master Page dialog, select the MasterPage.master master page and click OK.
7. Switch to Design view if necessary.
8. Drag the login.ascx user control from Solution Explorer into the mainContent Content control as shown in Figure 11.2.

login.ascx User Control in Solution Explorer

FIGURE 11.2

The `login.ascx` user control has been dropped into the `mainContent` Content control.

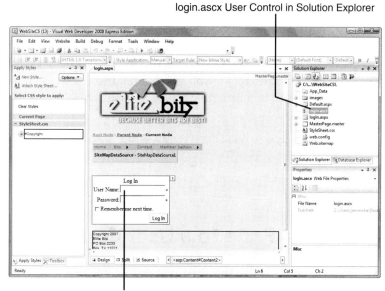

login.ascx User Control in the Web Form

Editing a User Control

After you've added the user control to the page, you can edit it by either opening the `login.ascx` file from Solution Explorer or by clicking the Smart Tag button on the user control within the Web form and selecting Edit User Control, as shown in Figure 11.3.

FIGURE 11.3

You can edit a user control by selecting the Edit User Control link in the Smart Tag options for the user control.

If you edit a user control by opening it in Solution Explorer, you can refresh the user control in the Web form to see the changes by selecting the Refresh Contents link, as shown previously in Figure 11.3.

One thing you may notice about user controls is that you cannot apply CSS styles or other formatting to them when they are on a Web form. If you want to format a user control's appearance, you need to format it by editing the user control file or use a theme to alter its appearance.

→ For more information on using CSS in Visual Web Developer, **see** Chapter 17, "Creating and Managing CSS Styles."

→ For more information on ASP.NET themes, **see** "Introduction to ASP.NET Themes," **p. 270**.

Converting a Page to a User Control

Because user controls are so beneficial as reusable components, you may very well find yourself wanting to convert an ASP.NET page into a user control. For example, suppose you have created a login page for your web application and then you later add a web forum. You'd like to add the login interface to the forum home page and also to several other pages within the forum. You could re-create the login interface on all those pages, but it would be a lot easier to convert the login page into a user control so that you could just drag and drop it onto the pages where you want a login interface.

> **N O T E**
>
> If your login interface contains server-side code that authenticates users, a user control becomes even more attractive because it prevents you from having to write the same code more than once.

Converting a page into a user control is actually quite easy. Only four steps are involved:

1. Change the @ Page directive to an @ Control directive.
2. Remove the Title attribute from the @ Control directive.

> **T I P**
>
> There might be other attributes that you'll have to remove. Visual Web Developer underlines any invalid attributes with a red line.

3. Remove the <html>, <body>, and <form> elements from the page.

N O T E Any content within the page can remain, but it must not be inside any of the elements indicated in step 3.

4. Save the page with an **.ascx** file extension.

If you have a code-behind file associated with the page you're converting, you need to make other changes. You need to change the name of the code-behind file to pagename.ascx.vb or pagename.ascx.cs, depending on your language, and you need to change the class for the control to derive from UserControl instead of Page.

The following code shows the code-behind class declaration for a page:

If you are using C#:

```
public partial class login : System.Web.UI.Page
```

If you are using Visual Basic:

```
Partial Class login
    Inherits System.Web.UI.Page
```

To convert this class to a user control class, you would change the code to the following:

If you are using C#:

```
public partial class login : System.Web.UI.UserControl
```

If you are using Visual Basic:

```
Partial Class login
    Inherits System.Web.UI.UserControl
```

Checkpoint

Here's what you completed in this chapter:

- A login user control for any page to provide a login interface
- A login page containing the login user control

In the next chapter, you'll create a database to store members for your website. As you complete the next section, you'll finish building your login user control and you'll create the other pages for your membership system.

PART **IV**

ASP.NET Membership

CHAPTER 12

Configuring a Membership Database

An Introduction to ASP.NET Membership

One of the most common questions I see from web designers is, "How do I password protect my site or part of my site?" The most common method of password-protecting content is to set permissions on files and folders so that only someone who has been given permission can access them. That technique works great, but it has some shortcomings. When using this technique:

- Managing users and groups is sometimes not possible because it often must be done on the web server itself.
- You don't have the capability of allowing users to create their own account.
- Users cannot retrieve or reset a lost password.
- Designers cannot implement a web-based login system.

ASP.NET membership was designed to address these and other shortcomings. The membership features of ASP.NET make it easy to implement a password-protected website (or part of a site) that is completely web-based.

The Membership Provider

ASP.NET has many built-in capabilities that developers can take advantage of without writing any code. Part of what makes that possible is a collection of pre-built components called *providers* that supply a specific type of functionality.

ASP.NET membership uses a built-in membership provider to make its features available to you. The membership provider dictates specifics about how the membership system is implemented. For example, some of the capabilities provided by the default membership provider are

- A connection to a SQL Server 2005 Express Edition database.
- Password strength and length requirements.
- Login capability for the website or the protected part of a site.
- Capability to create users and for users to create their own accounts.
- Ability for users to retrieve a lost password or reset it.
- Access to controlled content based on users and/or groups.

Some of the capabilities of the default membership provider can be modified. For example, you can modify the database connection string so the membership provider uses a SQL Server 2005 or SQL Server 2000 database without changing providers. However, some changes require that you either modify the default provider or use a different provider.

Suppose you want to use a MySQL database for your membership system. To do that, you need to use a custom provider to provide that functionality. However, that custom provider has to provide only the portion of the membership system that communicates with the database. Other login functionality can be provided by existing ASP.NET membership features.

| TIP | The creation of custom membership providers is far beyond the scope of this book. However, in most cases, if you desire specific functionality, you can find a third-party provider that you can use at no charge. |

For the purposes of this book, you don't really need to understand the provider model or how it all works, but it's helpful in seeing the big picture to know that the functionality of your membership system is supplied by the membership provider.

Using the Default Membership Database

By default, the membership provider uses SQL Server 2005 Express Edition. ASP.NET automatically creates the SQL Server 2005 Express Edition database in the App_Data folder of your website, as shown in Figure 12.1.

FIGURE 12.1
The default membership database is created in the App_Data folder of your website, as shown here.

ASP.NET creates the default membership database the first time that you interact with one of the ASP.NET Login controls in the browser or if you administer the website to add users, roles, and so on.

→ For more information on administering users and roles, **see** "Users and Roles," **p. 186**.

We use the default membership database as we complete the web application in this book.

Using SQL Server 2000 or SQL Server 2005 for Membership

A SQL Server 2005 Express Edition database is fine for many users, but if you expect more than a few dozen people to use your website at any one time, you might want to use a more robust database engine. In those cases, it's quite simple to configure the membership provider to use SQL Server 2000 or SQL Server 2005.

NOTE
Your hosting company may also provide a restriction on using SQL Server 2005 Express Edition. If you're not sure about the kinds of databases you can use with ASP.NET membership, check with your hosting company.

TIP
You're not limited to using Microsoft's database technologies. In fact, many web designers prefer MySQL because it's often more affordable to host. You can download an ASP.NET 2.0 membership provider and instructions for using MySQL at www.codeproject.com/aspnet/MySQLMembershipProvider.asp. This provider will work perfectly fine on a .NET Framework 3.5 application.

If you choose to use the MySQL provider from The Code Project, you can skip this section because it doesn't apply to MySQL.

Configuring the Database

ASP.NET comes with a utility called aspnet_regsql.exe for configuring a SQL Server database for use with ASP.NET membership. The aspnet_regsql.exe utility can be used as a command-line tool, but it also offers a wizard interface that makes it fast and easy to configure your database for ASP.NET membership.

NOTE
If you need to add ASP.NET membership services to a SQL Server instance provided by your hosting company, the company needs to use the aspnet_regsql tool. You can't configure it yourself.

To configure SQL Server 2000 or SQL Server 2005 for ASP.NET membership, follow these steps:

1. Create a new, blank database.

NOTE
For more information on how to create a new blank database in your version of SQL Server, see SQL Server Books Online, which comes with SQL Server.

2. Click the Windows Start button and select All Programs. Click the Accessories program group and select Command Prompt to launch a command prompt.

3. At the command prompt, type the following command and press Enter:

   `cd %windir%\microsoft.net\framework\v2.0*`

4. At the command prompt, type **aspnet_regsql** and press Enter to launch the ASP.NET SQL Server Setup Wizard, as shown in Figure 12.2.

FIGURE 12.2

The ASP.NET SQL Server Setup Wizard is a fast and convenient way to add ASP.NET membership capabilities to an existing database.

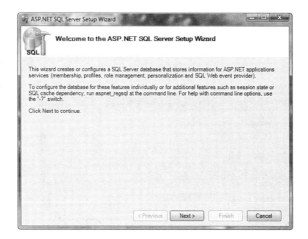

5. Click Next to proceed to the next step.

6. Select the Configure SQL Server for Application Services radio button, as shown in Figure 12.3, and click Next.

FIGURE 12.3

The ASP.NET SQL Server Setup Wizard can configure or remove ASP.NET services from a database. In this case, the ASP.NET application services are to be configured.

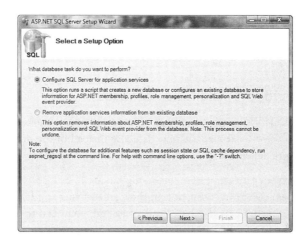

7. Enter the name of your SQL Server in the Server text box.

> **TIP**
>
> If you're running a default installation of SQL Server 2005 Express Edition, you must specify the server name using a fully qualified syntax (that is, server\SQL-EXPRESS.) If SQL Server is running on the local computer, you can use local-host\SQLEXPRESS for the server name.

8. Select the Windows Authentication radio button.

9. Select the blank database that you created in step 1 from the database drop-down. The completed step is shown in Figure 12.4.

FIGURE 12.4

To add ASP.NET membership services to a database, you'll need to specify the SQL Server instance and database name.

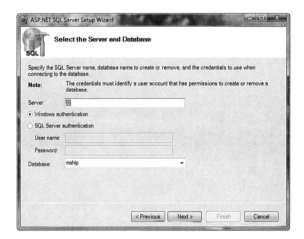

10. Click Next to confirm your settings, and then click Next again to configure the database. After the database has been configured, click Finish.

Configuring the Provider for the New Database

After you've added ASP.NET membership services to the new database, you need to configure the membership provider to use the new database instead of the default SQL Server 2005 Express Edition database.

The membership provider locates the membership database, using a connection string located in the <connectionStrings> section of the machine.config file. To redirect the membership provider to the new database you've created, you need to override the connection string located in the machine.config file with a new connection string that points to your new database.

→ For more information on ASP.NET configuration files, **see** "ASP.NET Configuration Files," **p. 66**.

You could change the connection string in the `machine.config` file and point it to your new database, but if you do that, you are altering the configuration of all applications on the computer that use that connection string. A better option would be to specify a new connection string for your specific application.

If you're using IIS 5 or IIS 6 (including IIS 5.1 on Windows XP,) the following section describes how to configure the connection string for your new database. If you are using IIS 7 on Windows Vista or Longhorn Server, you can skip ahead to the "Configuring the Connection String in IIS 7" section. If you are using a disk-based website, skip ahead to the "Configuring the Connection String in a Disk-based Application."

Configuring the Connection String in IIS 5 or IIS 6

If you're using IIS 5 or IIS 6, the easiest way to configure your connection string is the use the ASP.NET tab in the Internet Information Services manager.

1. Open Control Panel and double-click on Administrative Tools.
2. Double-click Internet Information Services to open the Internet Information Services manager.
3. Expand the nodes until you can see your ASP.NET application.
4. Right-click on your ASP.NET application and select Properties as shown in Figure 12.5.

FIGURE 12.5
You can modify the properties of your specific web application with the Internet Information Services manager.

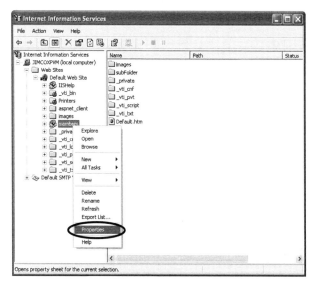

5. Select the ASP.NET tab in the properties of your ASP.NET application.
6. Click the Edit Configuration button as shown in Figure 12.6.

FIGURE 12.6
The Edit
Configuration button
allows you to edit
the ASP.NET configu-
ration of your appli-
cation.

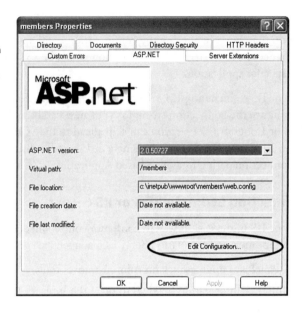

7. Select the LocalSqlServer connection string on the General tab and click the Edit button as shown in Figure 12.7.

FIGURE 12.7
You can modify the
existing connection
string by clicking the
Edit button as shown
here.

8. Enter your new connection string and click OK.

After you modify the connection string, the LocalSqlServer entry in the ASP.NET Configuration Settings appears bolded as shown in Figure 12.8. When an entry appears bolded, it means that the entry is overriding a setting that is defined higher in the configuration hierarchy. In this specific case, your new connection string overrides the connection string that is defined in the `machine.config` file.

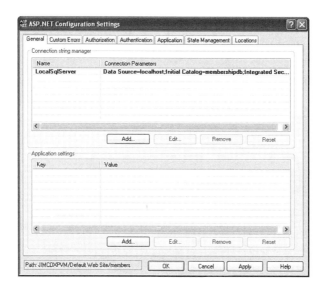

| TIP | You can reset the connection string to the inherited connection string by selecting it and clicking the Reset button. |

Configuring the Connection String in IIS 7

To configure the connection string in IIS 7, follow these steps:

1. Open Administrative Tools in the Control Panel.
2. Double-click on Internet Information Services (IIS) Manager.
3. Expand the nodes until your web application is visible.
4. Click on your web application to select it.
5. Double-click on the Connection Strings icon in the ASP.NET area as shown in Figure 12.9.

FIGURE 12.9

The Connection Strings icon in the ASP.NET area of IIS 7 enables you to configure connection strings.

6. Double-click the LocalSqlServer connection string to edit it.

7. Enter your new connection string as shown in Figure 12.10.

FIGURE 12.10

Enter a new connection string that points to your SQL Server 2000 or SQL Server 2005 instance.

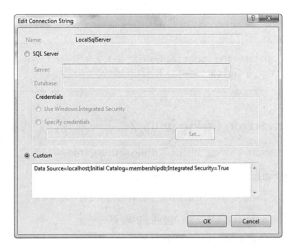

8. Click OK to finish editing the connection string.

The entry type for an edited connection string is Local as shown in Figure 12.11, meaning that the connection string is no longer inherited from the `machine.config` file.

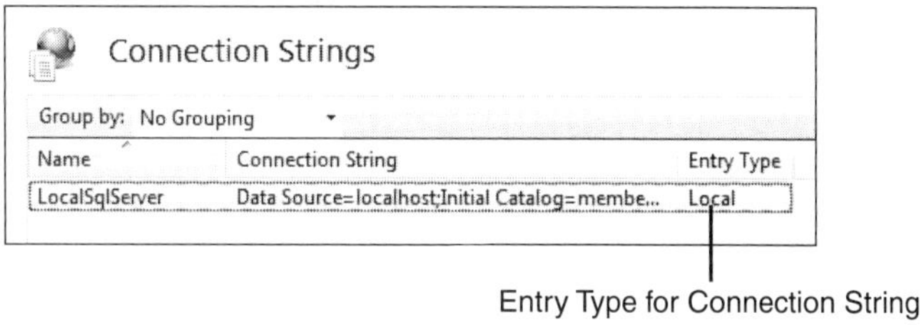

FIGURE 12.11
After the connection string has been edited, the entry type changes to Local.

Connection Strings

Group by: No Grouping ▾

Name	Connection String	Entry Type
LocalSqlServer	Data Source=localhost;Initial Catalog=membe...	Local

Entry Type for Connection String

CAUTION If you select the LocalSqlServer connection string and click Remove, it removes the connection string entirely, thereby breaking your membership features for the application. The only way to revert to the default connection string is to edit the configuration file manually, as described in the next section.

Configuring the Connection String in a Disk-based Application

As the preceding sections have shown, IIS provides a friendly user interface for editing the connection string for your application. Under the covers, IIS is simply making modifications to a local web.config file in your website. If your application is a disk-based website, you need to make those same modifications to the web.config file manually.

As I mentioned previously, the machine.config file contains a definition for the LocalSqlServer connection string. That entry looks like this:

```
<connectionStrings>
<add name="LocalSqlServer" connectionString="data
➥source=.\SQLEXPRESS;Integrated
➥Security=SSPI;AttachDBFilename=¦DataDirectory¦aspnetdb.mdf;
User Instance=true" providerName="System.Data.SqlClient"/>
</connectionStrings>
```

The <connectionStrings> section can appear in any configuration file, so to alter the LocalSqlServer connection string, you need to add a new <connectionStrings> section to the web.config file in the root of your web application. To do that, follow these steps:

1. If you don't have a web.config file in the root of your web application, select File, New File and add a new Web Configuration File.

2. Open the web.config file in Visual Web Developer 2008.

3. Add the following direction under the opening <configuration> element:
```
<connectionStrings>
        <remove name="LocalSqlServer" />
        <add connectionString="Data Source=localhost;Initial
➥Catalog=membershipdb;Integrated Security=True" name="LocalSqlServer"
➥providerName="System.Data.SqlClient" />
</connectionStrings>
```

> **NOTE** You'll need to use your own connection string that points to your database. The connection string in step 3 is only an example.

4. Save the `web.config` file.

The first line in the `<connectionStrings>` section removes the current `LocalSqlServer` connection string. If you don't first remove the existing connection string, you get an error when you add the new connection string.

> **TIP** To revert to the default connection string that is configured in the `machine.config` file, simply remove the `<connectionStrings>` section from your `web.config` file.

Checkpoint

Here's what you completed in this chapter:

- A review of the basics of ASP.NET membership features

In the next couple of chapters, you'll create users and roles for the members-only portion of the web application and you'll have an opportunity to apply some of the knowledge you have acquired.

CHAPTER 13

Adding and Managing Users and Roles

IN THIS CHAPTER

Users and Roles

When you are developing a membership system for a web application, you'll often restrict access to particular pages (or the entire website), to particular users, or to one or more groups (or roles) of users.

A user is a visitor to your website with a known identity who is identified by a username. In the context of an ASP.NET membership website, a username can be provided by a network administrator (for example, a Windows login username), or it can be a username defined in the ASP.NET membership database and applicable only to the ASP.NET website.

A *role* is a group of one or more users with an explicit identity. A role can be a Windows group, or it can be a role defined only in the ASP.NET membership database.

To control access to your website using ASP.NET membership, the ASP.NET application must identify the user by username in a process known as *authentication*.

Configuring Authentication

When using ASP.NET membership features, the most common type of authentication is ASP.NET forms authentication. Forms authentication is well-suited to authenticating users accessing your website over the Internet.

→ For more information on ASP.NET forms authentication, **see** "Understanding Forms Authentication," **p. 102**.

Here are some of the reasons why using forms authentication is recommended for an Internet site:

- User information is stored in a database and users can create their own accounts easily if necessary.
- Users can change or retrieve lost passwords easily.
- You can create a login web page that shares the look and feel with the rest of your website.
- ASP.NET provides full functionality for authentication and authorizing users without writing any additional code.

> **NOTE** It's possible to use Windows authentication with ASP.NET membership, but doing so is most common in intranet environments.
>
> For more information on using Windows authentication with ASP.NET membership features, check out Scott Guthrie's blog post at weblogs.asp.net/scottgu/archive/2006/07/12/Recipe_3A00_-Enabling-Windows-Authentication-within-an-Intranet-ASP.NET-Web-application.aspx.

The following steps show you how to configure forms authentication for your website. Open the website you created in Chapter 8. To configure the authentication for the website, follow these steps:

1. Click the ASP.NET Configuration button at the top of the Solution Explorer, as shown in Figure 13.1.

FIGURE 13.1

The ASP.NET Configuration button provides an easy means of launching the ASP.NET configuration website.

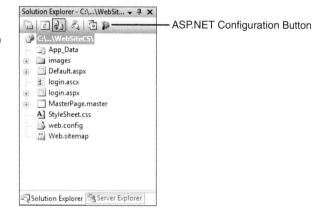

2. In the ASP.NET Web Site Administration Tool, click the Security tab.
3. Click the Select Authentication Type link, as shown in Figure 13.2.

FIGURE 13.2

The Select Authentication Type link allows you to choose between authentication types for your website.

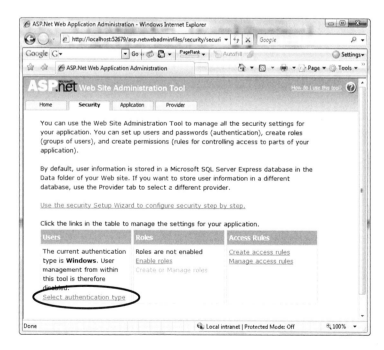

4. Choose the From the Internet option as shown in Figure 13.3, and then click Done.

FIGURE 13.3

When you select the From the Internet option, your web application is configured for ASP.NET forms authentication.

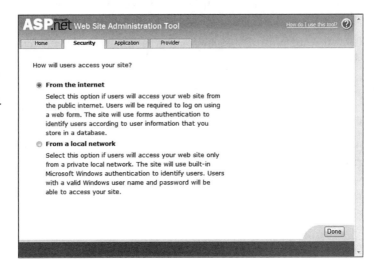

When you choose the From the Internet option, the Web Site Administration Tool configures your application to use ASP.NET forms authentication. By default, all users are allowed to access any portion of the website. Therefore, even though the website is now configured to use forms authentication, no one is required to log in to view the site. Later in this chapter, you'll configure a portion of the website as a members-only section that will require users to log in.

Adding New Users

When using ASP.NET membership with forms authentication, you can add new users to the site with the Web Site Administration Tool. When you add users to the site, information is added to the membership database so that the user can log in to the website with the username and password that you assign.

TIP   As you'll see in the next chapter, you can also create a web page where users can sign themselves up with an account for your website.

Now you can try adding a new user to the website. For now, you'll just add the user account. Later in this chapter, you'll create some roles and configure a specific portion of the website that only registered users can access.

1. Open the web application you've been working on throughout this book.

N O T E | If you haven't completed the website up to this point, you can download the website from www.quepublishing.com.

2. Open the Web Site Administration Tool and click the Security tab.

3. Click the Create User link as shown in Figure 13.4.

FIGURE 13.4
Click the Create User link to create a new user for your website.

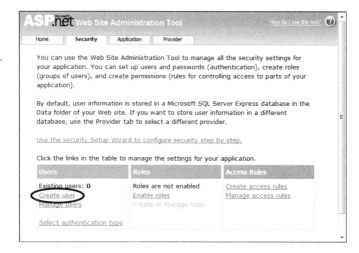

4. Enter the information for your new user into the form (use your own first name for the user name) and click Create User as shown in Figure 13.5.

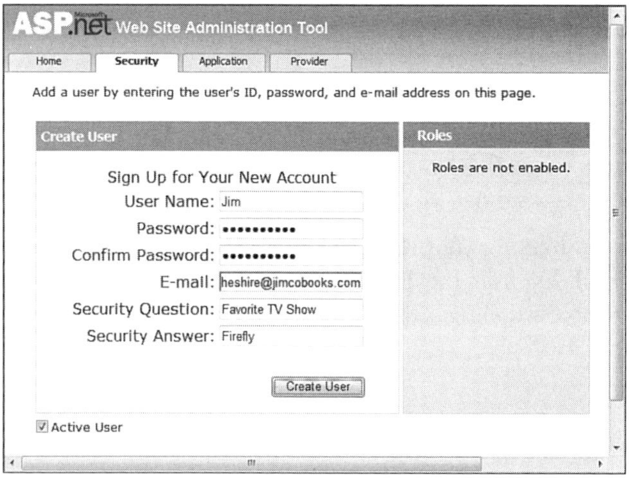

FIGURE 13.5
Fill in the form and click Create User to create a new user.

| T I P | If you get an error when working with the Web Site Administration Tool, try closing your browser and relaunching the Web Site Administration Tool from Solution Explorer. |

| T I P | One thing you may have noticed is that the membership provider has pretty tough password requirements. You can change the requirements if you wish. There's a good blog post on that at weblogs.asp.net/owscott/archive/2005/05/11/406550.aspx. |

Enabling and Adding Roles

Most sites that authenticate users before allowing access don't give everyone the same level of access. For example, basic users might be able to read information, whereas some other users might be able to modify data. You might also want to have some pages that only some users are allowed to access.

For example, if you have a page that allows for reviewing and editing user account information, you would want to tightly control who can access that page. You could manually assign access rights to your site each time you create a new user, but that can quickly become cumbersome because you'd have to manually set access rights to every resource.

Creating roles for your users is a much more effective way to manage access to your website. A *role* is a named group of users. After you create a user, you can assign him or her to one or more roles. You can then grant or deny access to a file or folder of your website based on the role.

| N O T E | When a new user is added to your website, he or she is not added to any particular role by default. To make a user a member of a role, the user must be explicitly added to the role. |

You'll create two roles for your website; Users and Editors. Users will be able to access the website and read data from the database. Editors will also be able to read data, but they'll also be able to access the pages that allow for editing the data.

Enabling Roles

Before you can add new roles to your website, you need to enable roles. To do that, follow these steps:

1. Open the website in Visual Web Developer if you haven't already opened it.
2. Open the Web Site Administration Tool and click the Security tab.
3. Click the Enable Roles link as shown in Figure 13.6.

FIGURE 13.6

The Enable Roles link adds information to your web configuration file so that you can take advantage of this powerful feature.

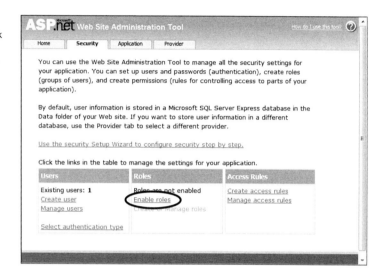

When you click the Enable Roles link, the Create or Manage Roles link activates so that you can create some new roles for your website.

Creating Roles

Next, you'll create the User and Editor roles as described previously.

1. Click the Create and Manage Roles link that activated when you enabled roles.
2. Type **Users** for the role name and click Add Role, as shown in Figure 13.7.

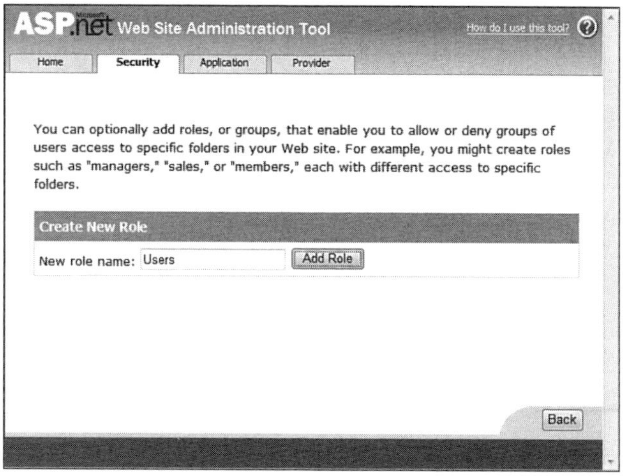

FIGURE 13.7

Enter the role name and click Add Role to create the role.

3. Type **Editors** for the second role name and click Add Role.

You should now see both new roles listed, as shown in Figure 13.8.

FIGURE 13.8
Each role is listed in a table, along with links to manage or delete each role.

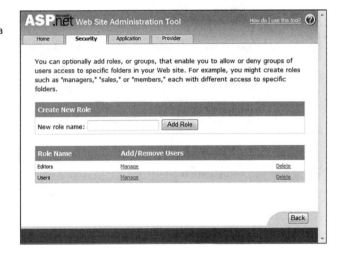

Adding a User to a Role

Now that you've created each role, it's time to add the user you created earlier to the Editors role.

1. Click the Manage link next to the Editors role as shown previously in Figure 13.8.
2. Enter the name of your user and click the Find User button.
3. Place a check in the User Is In Role check box as shown in Figure 13.9.

FIGURE 13.9
To add a user to the group, check the User Is In Role check box.

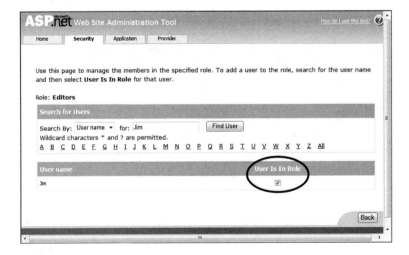

Now that you've created your roles and added a user to the Editors role, you can create an access rule for the site.

Configuring Access Rules

As mentioned previously, users in the Editors role can edit data in the website. The web page that will allow for editing of data will be in a folder called `editor`. Now you can create the access rule that prevents everyone other than members of the Editors role from accessing that folder.

1. Create a new folder in the root of your website called **editor**.
2. Click the Create Access Rules link as shown previously in Figure 13.6.
3. Select the `editor` folder from the folder list as shown in Figure 13.10.

FIGURE 13.10
Select the folder to which you want the access rule to apply.

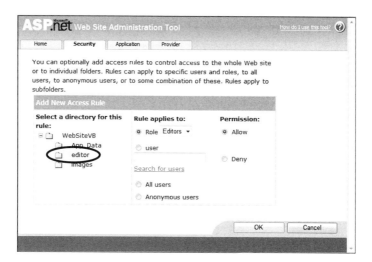

4. Select the Role radio button and select the Editors role from the drop-down, as shown previously in Figure 13.10.
5. Select the Allow radio button and click OK to add the access rule.
6. Click the Create Access Rules link again.
7. Select the `editor` folder if it's not already selected.
8. Select the All Users radio button.
9. Select the Deny radio button.
10. Click OK to add the new access rule.

Click the Manage Access Rules link to review your access rules. Your access rules should look like the ones shown in Figure 13.11.

FIGURE 13.11
Your completed access rules should look like the ones shown here.

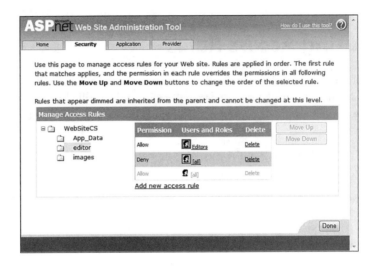

You might be a little confused at this point. After you created the access rule allowing the Editors role to access the editor folder, you then created another access rule that denied everyone access to it. You may be thinking that this is going to deny users in the Editors role from accessing the folder, but it won't. Access rules are applied from the top down and the first rule that applies wins. Therefore, if a user who is a member of the Editors group tries to access the editor folder, he or she will meet the criterion for the first access rule, so that rule will apply and access will be granted. Anyone else who tries to access the editor folder will be denied access.

> **TIP** You can modify the order of access rules in the Manage Access Rules page by clicking the Move Up and Move Down buttons.

What Happens Under the Hood?

The Web Site Administration Tool makes configuring ASP.NET security easy, but if you don't know what it's actually doing, it quickly becomes a black box.

The Web Site Administration Tool is a user interface that allows for easy manipulation of the ASP.NET membership database and also the configuration file (web.config) in your application. When you add users and roles, they are added to the membership database. When you add a user to a role, it also modifies the membership database.

The other changes you made to the security of the website in this chapter caused the Web Site Administration Tool to modify the `web.config` file for your website. Let's look at the configuration changes you made in the Web Site Administration Tool and the corresponding entries that were made in the configuration files for the application.

Configuring Authentication

When you chose the From the Internet option for the authentication of your website, the Web Site Administration Tool enabled ASP.NET Forms authentication for your site by adding the following entry to the `web.config` file in the root of your web application:

```
<authentication mode="Forms" />
```

This enables Forms authentication with all the default settings.

Enabling Roles

When you enabled roles, the Web Site Administration Tool added the following entry to the `web.config` file in the root of your web application:

```
<roleManager enabled="true" />
```

This enables ASP.NET roles with the default configuration.

> **N O T E**   You can read about the `<roleManager>` element on the MSDN website at msdn2.microsoft.com/en-us/library/ms164660(vs.90).aspx.

Creating Access Rules

When you created access rules for the editor folder of the web application, the Web Site Administration Tool added a new `web.config` file in the editor folder and added the access rules to it by adding the following code inside of a `<system.web>` section:

```
<authorization>
    <allow roles="Editors" />
    <deny users="*" />
</authorization>
```

This is one area where I think the Web Site Administration Tool falls short. Because it adds new configuration files to the website when you create access rules, the Web Site Administration Tool can create an administrative nightmare. If you have many access rules for many different folders, it can become difficult to manage.

ASP.NET provides a more sensible approach to configuring different settings for different parts of a website, using a `<location>` element in the `web.config` file. To use a `<location>`

element to apply the access rule for the editor folder, you can add the following code to the web.config file in the root of the web application (the code should be added between the closing </system.web> element and the closing </configuration> element):

```
<location path="editor">
    <system.web>
      <authorization>
        <allow roles="Editors" />
        <deny users="*" />
      </authorization>
    </system.web>
</location>
```

If you use this method instead of a separate web.config file, it becomes easier to manage access rules because they are all contained in one file. However, for the purposes of the web application we're creating in this book, we'll leave the separate web.config file in the editors folder because we won't have enough access rules to make things difficult.

Checkpoint

Here's what you completed in this chapter:

- Created the membership database
- Created a user for the website
- Created two new roles and assigned the user to the Editors role
- Created access rules for the editor folder of the website

In the next chapter, you'll complete the login page and you'll create other pages for users to create an account for themselves and otherwise manage their accounts.

CHAPTER 14

Adding and Configuring Login and User Management Pages

IN THIS CHAPTER

Configuring the Login Control

The core ASP.NET control for use in a membership system is the Login control. The Login control is highly customizable; all you need to do is set properties of the control.

Chapter 11 walked you through the creation of a user control called login.ascx that contained a Login control. However, not much was done to configure the Login control's appearance or behavior. Let's do that now.

Configuring the Appearance of the Login Control

Chapter 10 covered using the AutoFormat of ASP.NET controls to add some navigation controls to a master page. You can use the same method to automatically change the format of the Login control so that it fits better with the overall appearance of the website.

1. Open the web application in Visual Web Developer.
2. Open the login.ascx user control.
3. Select the Login control.

> **TIP** The Login control is inside a LoginView control. Make sure you select the Login control and not the LoginView control.

4. Click the Smart Tag button for the Login control and select the AutoFormat link.
5. Select the Professional option in the AutoFormat dialog, and click OK to apply the formatting.

After applying the formatting to the Login control, drag the right edge of the control and increase the width of the control to 250px, as shown in Figure 14.1

FIGURE 14.1
The Login control has now been automatically formatted and resized to make it more professional looking.

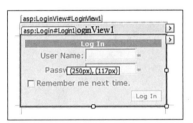

> **TIP** You can explicitly change the Width property of the Login control as an alternative to dragging the edge of the control. The Width property is located in the Layout section in the Properties window.

The Login control exposes several properties that enable you to control the text that appears on the control. Let's change a couple of things to make the control more customized to the website.

1. Select the Login control if it's not already selected.
2. Press F4 to display the Properties window if it's not already visible.
3. Locate the TitleText property in the Appearance section of the Properties window.
4. Enter `Login to Elite Bits` for the TitleText property.
5. Locate the RememberMeText property. It should be just above the TitleText property.
6. Change the RememberMeText property to `Remember me on this computer`.

After you've made these changes, save the `login.ascx` file. Right-click on the `login.aspx` file in Solution Explorer and select View in Browser to preview the page. Your Login control should look like the one shown in Figure 14.2.

FIGURE 14.2
The Login control has now been customized a bit for the website.

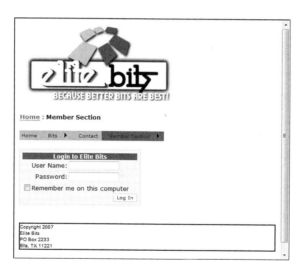

Configuring the Behavior of the Login Control

In addition to the appearance changes already made, you need to make a couple of changes to the behavior of the Login control.

When a login failure occurs, the default behavior for the page containing the Login control is to refresh. In this web application, you want to have the option of displaying the Login control on pages other than the login page. Therefore, if a login failure occurs, it would be better to have the user redirected to the login page because the login page will have links that the user can click if he or she has forgotten a password or if he or she needs to create a new account.

To change the behavior of the Login control so that it will redirect the user to the login page upon an unsuccessful login, follow these steps:

1. Select the Login control.

2. Locate the `FailureAction` property in the Behavior section of the Properties window.

3. Open the drop-down for the `FailureAction` property and set the value to `RedirectToLoginPage`, as shown in Figure 14.3.

FIGURE 14.3

The FailureAction property controls whether the Login control sends a user to the login page when an unsuccessful login takes place.

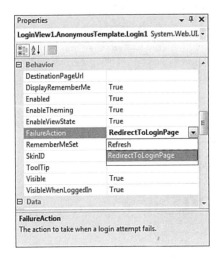

NOTE You can use many other properties of the Login control to control how it behaves and how it appears. For full documentation on the properties of the Login control, see msdn2.microsoft.com/en-us/library/system.web.ui. webcontrols.login_members(VS.90).aspx.

Using the LoginView Control

If you were to describe an interface that allows users to log in to a website, you would likely describe an interface with a space for a username and a space for a password. When the user successfully enters a username and password and gets authenticated to the website, you'd expect that the username and password dialog would no longer be displayed. In its place is often an indicator of who is logged in (frequently displaying a username) and perhaps a link to log out.

ASP.NET enables you to easily create such an interface with the LoginView control. The LoginView control has two views: the AnonymousTemplate view and the LoggedInTemplate view. When no one is logged in, the AnonymousTemplate is displayed, and when a user is logged in, the LoggedInTemplate view is displayed. All of this is automatic and no code is required.

When you inserted a LoginView control into the login.ascx user control in Chapter 10 and then added a Login control to the LoginView control, you added the Login control to the AnonymousTemplate view. We're now going to add some appropriate controls to the LoggedInTemplate view that will be displayed after a user successfully logs in.

1. Open the `login.ascx` file if it's not already open.
2. Select the LoginView control.
3. Click the Smart Tag button for the LoginView control and select the LoggedInTemplate from the Views drop-down, as shown in Figure 14.4.

FIGURE 14.4
You can choose the current view for the LoginView control using the Views dropdown.

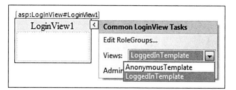

4. Click inside the empty LoggedInTemplate view so that the cursor is blinking inside the LoginView control.
5. Double-click on the LoginName control in the Login section of the toolbox to add a LoginName control to the LoginView control.
6. Click to the right of the LoginName control and press the spacebar to insert a space.
7. Type **Logged In** next to the LoginName control.
8. Press Enter to insert a new line.
9. Double-click on the LoginStatus control to insert it below the LoginName control you inserted in step 5.
10. Click the Smart Tab button for the LoginStatus control and change the view to LoggedIn, as shown in Figure 14.5.

FIGURE 14.5
The LoginStatus control displays a link that enables a user to log off the website.

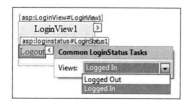

You've just inserted two new controls in the LoggedInTemplate view of the LoginView control. The LoginName control displays the name of the user who is logged in to the website. The LoginStatus control consists of two views: the LoggedOut view and the LoggedIn view. By default, it displays a Login link when the LoggedOut view is displayed and a Logout link when the LoggedIn view is displayed.

After you've completed these steps, you can browse the login.aspx page in your browser and log in to the site, using the user that you created in Chapter 13. When you do, you'll be redirected to the home page (which is Default.aspx in the root of the website) upon a successful login. The default behavior of the Login control is to redirect users to the home page of the website unless the user was directed to the login page because he or she requested a protected page. You can modify that behavior by changing the `DestinationPageUrl` property of the Login control. In this case, just leave it as is for now. As you progress through the application, you'll have an opportunity to test the functionality of the LoginView control.

Creating Accounts Using the CreateUserWizard Control

In Chapter 13, you created a new user using the Web Site Administration Tool. The control that you used to create that new user was actually a CreateUserWizard control. You can insert that same control into one of your pages to allow users to create their own accounts so that they can access your website.

Adding the Create User Page

In this section you add a new page that offers a CreateUserWizard control so that visitors can sign up for their own accounts with your website. You'll also configure the CreateUserWizard control so that users will have to be approved by you before they can log in to the website.

1. Open your website in Visual Web Developer 2008.
2. Right-click on the project name in Solution Explorer and select Add New Item.
3. From the list of templates, select Web Form.
4. Change the name of the Web form to `createuser.aspx`.
5. Check the Place Code in a Separate File check box and the Select Master Page check box.
6. Click Add.
7. Select the MasterPage.master master page, and click OK to create the Web form.
8. Switch to Design view if it's not already selected.

9. Click anywhere inside the `mainContent` Content control and double-click on the CreateUserWizard control in the Login section of the toolbox to add a new CreateUserWizard control to the page.

10. Click the Smart Tag button for the CreateUserWizard control and select the Auto Format link.

11. Select the Professional scheme and click OK to apply it.

12. Save the `createuser.aspx` page.

Your new Web form should look like the one shown in Figure 14.6.

FIGURE 14.6

The createuser.aspx page contains a CreateUserWizard control so that users can create an account for the website.

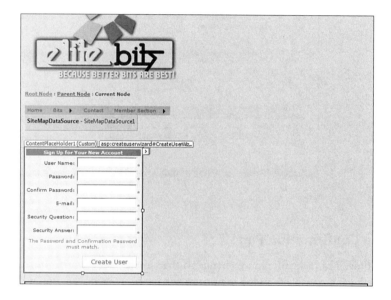

You can now browse to the `createuser.aspx` page and enter in the information to create your own user account. The page is fully functional, but as it stands any user can create an account and view the database data. Because you want more control over who can view your data, you'll change some of the properties of the CreateUserWizard control so that new accounts have to be approved before a user can access the data.

> **NOTE** You'll add a database later that will contain information protected by ASP.NET membership features you've been working on in the past couple of chapters.

1. Select the CreateUserWizard that you just added to the Web form.

2. Locate the `DisableCreatedUser` property in the Behavior section of the Properties window and set it to True.

3. Locate the `LoginCreatedUser` property in the Behavior section of the Properties window and set it to False.

After you make these changes, new user accounts will be disabled and logged out after they are created. To allow a new user to access the website, you'll use the Web Site Administration Tool and check the Active check box for the user, as shown in Figure 14.7.

FIGURE 14.7

The new user, Joe, has not yet been approved. To activate him, check the Active check box shown here.

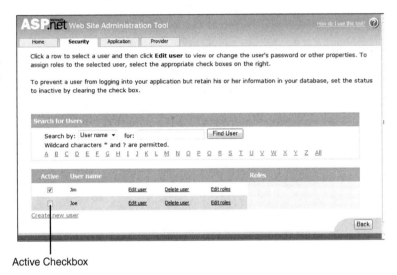

Active Checkbox

Adding a Confirmation Page

You'll need to make one more change to the CreateUserWizard control. Because you are not allowing new users to log in until they have been approved, you want to display a message to users after they register that tells them they will need to be approved before they can log in. To do so, you need to create a simple page that explains your policy, and then you'll configure the CreateUserWizard so that new users are redirected to that page after account creation.

1. Create a new Web form named accountpolicy.aspx. Check the Select Master Page check box and select the MasterPage.master master page.

2. Switch to Design view if necessary.

3. Enter the following text into the `mainContent` Content control: **Thank you for sign-ing up for the website. Before you can log in, your account will have to be approved by our administrator. Your account should be approved within 24 hours.**

4. Save the new Web form.

5. Switch back to the `createuser.aspx` page and select the CreateUserWizard control.

6. Locate the `ContinueDestinationPageUrl` property in the Behavior section of the Properties window.

7. Click the ellipsis button next to the `ContinueDestinationPageUrl` property and select the `accountpolicy.aspx` page in the Select URL dialog.

8. Save the `createuser.aspx` Web form.

You are now ready to test the `createuser.aspx` page. Right-click on the page in Solution Explorer and select View in Browser. When the page appears, enter information for a new user and click the Create User button. When you are informed that your account has been successfully created, click the Continue button and you should be automatically directed to the `accountpolicy.aspx` page, where you'll be politely informed that your account will be activated within 24 hours.

> **TIP** Rather than create a separate page to display the account policy, you could have simply set the `CompleteSuccessText` property of the CreateUserWizard control with the informational text you added to the `accountpolicy.aspx` page. However, many users don't pay much attention to what is displayed in the dialog after clicking Create User, so by making the account policy a separate page, you increase the chances that users will read it.

Resetting Lost Passwords

Anytime you require users to enter a password to access part of your site, you're sure to encounter forgotten passwords as well. If your membership system isn't designed to take care of forgotten passwords, you might find yourself overwhelmed with people contacting you for password resets. Fortunately, ASP.NET allows you to easily enable users to deal with forgotten passwords.

The PasswordRecovery control is designed to allow a user to either retrieve or reset his or her password. By default, ASP.NET stores passwords in a format called a *hash*, which is not human-readable. The process of hashing a password cannot be reversed, and therefore, passwords stored with this method cannot be recovered if they are lost. Instead, the user is required to reset his or her password.

Storing the password in a hashed format is the most secure method because the password that is stored in the database cannot be changed back into a human-readable password. For your purposes, you want to use the most secure method, so you'll use the default configuration.

> **NOTE** If you want to read details on how password hashing works, read aspnet.4guysfromrolla.com/articles/112002-1.aspx.

Creating a page where users can reset a lost password is a two-step process involving the following steps:

1. Create a page containing a PasswordRecovery control.
2. Configure ASP.NET for sending email so that the reset password can be emailed to the user.

Creating the Password Recovery Page

Follow these steps to first create a new page that a user can use to retrieve a forgotten password:

1. Create a new Web form named recoverpassword.aspx and apply the MasterPage.master master page to it.
2. Add a new PasswordRecovery control to the mainContent Content control. The PasswordRecovery control is located in the Login section of the toolbox.
3. Using the Auto Format link, format the PasswordRecovery control, using the Professional scheme.
4. Save the page.

You now need to configure ASP.NET to send email so that the membership provider can send an email to the user with his or her new password.

Configuring ASP.NET for Sending Email

When a user resets his or her password, it is sent to the e-mail on file for the user. By default, ASP.NET doesn't have the information it needs to send email. It needs to know the name of the email server (an *SMTP* mail server) and the username and password you use to authenticate to that server.

> **NOTE** Your SMTP server might not require authentication. If you don't know the information regarding your SMTP server, ask your ISP or your hosting company.

→ For more information on configuring ASP.NET for email, **see** Chapter 23, "Configuring ASP.NET for Email."

To configure ASP.NET to send the email containing the new password, follow these steps:

1. Open the `web.config` file in the root folder of your application.
2. Add the code from Listing 14.1 directly before the opening `<system.web>` element.

Listing 14.1   Configuration Code for ASP.NET Email

```
<system.net>
  <mailSettings>
    <smtp from="you@yourdomain.com">
      <network host="smtp.yourserver.com"
               password="yourpassword"
               userName="yourusername" />
    </smtp>
  </mailSettings>
</system.net>
```

> **NOTE** You need to replace the email authentication information and email address in Listing 14.1 with your own information.

After you've added this code, you can test the `recoverpassword.aspx` page by viewing it in your browser. Enter your name to reset your password. You'll be prompted with the secret question you provided when your account was created. If you supply the correct answer, ASP.NET emails you the new password, as shown in Figure 14.8.

FIGURE 14.8
This email was sent by the PasswordRecovery control. Notice the new (and very strong) password I've been provided.

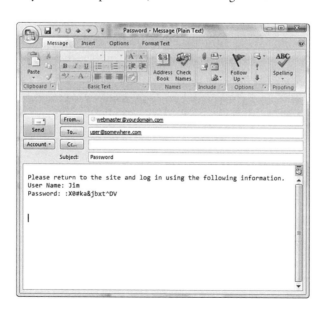

> **TIP** Many of the ASP.NET Login controls require that you actually click the button provided instead of pressing Enter on your keyboard. The PasswordRecovery control is one of those controls. If you simply press Enter, the control does not work. You must click the appropriate button on the control.

Changing Passwords

With these steps you create a new page where a user can change his or her password:

1. Create a new folder at the root of your application and name the folder `members`.
2. Add a new Web form to the `members` folder named `changepassword.aspx`, using the MasterPage.master page.
3. Insert a ChangePassword control into the mainContent Content control.
4. Auto-format the ChangePassword control, using the Professional scheme.
5. Click the ASP.NET Configuration button in Solution Explorer to launch the Web Site Administration Tool.
6. Click the Security tab, and then click the Create Access Rule link.
7. Select the `members` folder, select the Anonymous Users radio button, and select the Deny radio button.
8. Click OK to apply the new access rule.

By creating an access rule on the `members` folder that denies access to anonymous users, you will always be required to log in to the website before accessing any of the files located in that folder. The ChangePassword control requires that you be authenticated to the website to change your password, and your new access rule enforces that requirement nicely.

To test out the new `changepassword.aspx` page, view it in your browser. You'll be automatically redirected to the login page, where you'll be required to enter your credentials. After you are authenticated, you'll automatically be directed to the `changepassword.aspx` page, where you can change your password.

A Few Finishing Touches

Believe it or not, you've almost completely designed your membership system, and you've done it without writing any ASP.NET code at all! However, you need to add a few finishing touches to wrap it all up.

Adding a Link to Reset Password

Users are likely going to expect to be able to reach the `recoverpassword.aspx` page from the login page. The ASP.NET Login control allows you to easily add a link to a password reset page. Let's configure that now.

1. Open the `login.ascx` user control.
2. Switch the LoginView control to the AnonymousTemplate view, if necessary, and click on the Login control to select it.
3. Locate the `PasswordRecoveryText` property in the Links section of the Property window.
4. Change the `PasswordRecoveryText` property to `Forgot Password`.
5. Click the ellipsis button for the `PasswordRecoveryUrl` property and select the `recoverpassword.aspx` page.

The Login control now contains a link that users can click if they have forgotten the password.

Adding a Change Password Link

You should also add a link to the `changepassword.aspx` page to the login user control:

1. Change the LoginView control to the LoggedInTemplate view.
2. Click to the right of the LoginStatus control and press Enter to insert a new line.
3. Add a new ASP.NET Hyperlink control from the Standard section of the toolbox.
4. Change the `Text` property of the Hyperlink control to `Change Password`.
5. Click the ellipsis button for the `NavigateUrl` property and select the `changepassword.aspx` page in the `members` folder.

You can now save the `login.ascx` user control.

> **TIP** We used a Hyperlink control for the Change Password link because ASP.NET will take care of making sure that the hyperlink always points to the correct page, regardless of where the user control is in the site structure.

Fixing the Logo Graphic on the Master Page

You might have noticed that the Elite Bits logo graphic on the master page does not appear on the `changepassword.aspx` page. Instead, there's a broken image placeholder. The reason is that the HTML code for the image works only for pages that are in the root of the website.

To correct the image, you need to modify the HTML code so that ASP.NET is responsible for ensuring that the link always points to the correct image.

1. Open the `MasterPage.master` page in Visual Web Developer 2008.

2. Switch to Design view, if necessary, and click on the Elite Bits logo to select it.

3. Press the Delete key on your keyboard to delete the image.

4. Locate the ASP.NET Image control in the Standard section of the toolbox.

5. Double-click on the Image control to add it to the master page.

6. Change the `ImageUrl` property to point to the `elitebitslogo.jpg` file in the `images` folder.

Now save the master page and the image will always show up correctly.

> **TIP**   There are other ways to ensure that the image shows up, but using an ASP.NET Image control ensures that the image is always visible in the browser and while you design the website. Other methods often break the image in Visual Web Developer 2008.

Checkpoint

You accomplished quite a lot in this chapter. When you started this chapter, the web application had a basic Login control inside the login user control. Now you've got a completely workable membership system, complete with tools that enable users to create user accounts, reset passwords, and change passwords.

Here's what you completed in this chapter:

■ Configured the Login control and LoginView controls

■ Added a page for users to create their own accounts

■ Added a page for users to reset their passwords

■ Added a page for users to change their passwords

■ Created the access rule necessary to protect the membership area

In the next chapter, you'll begin to learn about creating custom forms in ASP.NET. You'll create a new page that will eventually be the contact form page for the web application.

PART V

ASP.NET Forms and Validation

CHAPTER 15

Creating Forms Using ASP.NET

IN THIS CHAPTER

Introduction to ASP.NET Forms

Forms have been a common feature of websites since the early days of the web. Forms are also among the most frustrating web page elements for many people because code has to be processed on the web server for them to be useful.

Expression Web offers form handlers that you can easily use in your website, but these form handlers rely on the FrontPage Server Extensions being installed on the web server hosting your website. As Microsoft begins to phase out the FrontPage Server Extensions (which appears to be inevitable), fewer hosting companies are choosing to offer support for them.

When Expression Web was released, many users found themselves pushed toward using ASP.NET for designing forms, and many of them expressed frustration over the perception of being forced into a new technology. However, as you'll see in the next couple of chapters, ASP.NET forms offer much more power and flexibility than the FrontPage Server Extensions forms.

Because the FrontPage Server Extensions have made form handling so easy over the years, many web designers are familiar with adding form elements such as text boxes and drop-downs to a web page. Users who are new to ASP.NET might find themselves wondering what is different about an ASP.NET form.

The first difference between a regular HTML form and an ASP.NET form is in the appearance of the <form> tag itself while you are designing the page. A typical HTML <form> tag for a FrontPage Server Extensions form might look like this:

```
<form method="post" action="--WEBBOT-SELF--">
```

A typical ASP.NET <form> tag might look like this:

```
<form id="form1" runat="server">
```

As you can see, these two <form> tags are quite different. The FrontPage Server Extensions form contains both a method attribute and an action attribute. Rather than add these attributes when you are designing the form, ASP.NET adds the runat attribute with a value of server. That tells ASP.NET that the <form> tag should be processed on the server before the page is sent down to the visitor's browser. When ASP.NET processes the page on the server, it rewrites the <form> tag to include the method and action attributes.

> **NOTE**   The tag for all ASP.NET controls include a runat attribute set to server so that ASP.NET will know that it should process the tag on the server prior to sending the page to the website's visitor.

Another difference between regular HTML forms and ASP.NET forms is that ASP.NET forms can contain ASP.NET controls, whereas regular HTML forms cannot. Some ASP.NET controls (such as the TextBox and DropDownList) have similar HTML counterparts, but other ASP.NET controls (such as the Calendar control) are complex controls without an HTML equivalent. For that reason, it's easier to create complex forms using the capabilities of ASP.NET.

Adding and Configuring ASP.NET Form Controls

One of the most common forms found on websites is a contact form. A contact form typically includes fields for a user to input contact information and a button to send a message to the website owner. In this chapter, we'll create a contact form on the Contact Us page. In doing so, you'll learn many skills that you can use to create many other types of forms for your website.

Before you start adding controls, it's important to look at the basic requirements for a typical Contact Us page.

Required Elements for the Contact Us Page

The Contact Us page should enable a user to do the following:

- Select either Products or Services from a drop-down.
- Select from a list of products or services based on the selection in the first drop-down.
- Enter a subject for his or her message.
- Enter his or her first name and last name.
- Enter his or her email address.
- Enter a text message no greater than 1,000 characters.
- Submit the form and have an email sent to the website owner.
- Receive a copy of the email sent to the website owner.

In this chapter, you'll add the form controls and set properties for them. As you proceed through the rest of the book, you'll continue to add new functionality to the Contact Us page to completely fulfill the requirements for the page.

Adding Controls to the Contact Us Page

Now that you've clearly defined what the Contact Us page should do, you can go ahead and add the necessary controls to the page.

1. Open the website you've been working on.

2. Add a new Web form named **contactus.aspx** to the website, using masterpage.master for the master page.

3. Click inside the mainContent Content control.

4. Double-click the Label control in the Standard section of the toolbox to add a new Label control to the page.

5. Click on the new Label control to select it.

6. Press F4 to display the Properties window.

7. Locate the Text property in the Appearance section of the Properties window and change it to **Select Topic**.

8. Click on the Label control again and press the right arrow on your keyboard to move the cursor to the right edge of the Label.

9. Press Enter to insert a new line.

10. Double-click DropDownList in the Standard section of the toolbox to add it to the page.

11. Click on the newly added DropDownList to select it, and then change the ID property of the control to **ddlTopic**.

> **TIP** | The ID property is located in the Misc section of the Properties window.

12. Add two new lines after the DropDownList control.

13. Add a new Label control and change the Text property to **Select Subtopic**.

> **NOTE** | We're using Label controls instead of just entering text because you'll use an ASP.NET skin to format these Labels in Chapter 19.

14. Add a new line after the Label control.

15. Add a new DropDownList control and change the ID to **ddlSubtopic**.

16. Add two new lines after the DropDownList control.

17. Add a new Label control and change the Text property to **Subject**.

18. Add a new line after the Label control.

19. Add a new TextBox control and change the ID to **txtSubject**.

20. Change the Width property of the TextBox (located in the Layout section of the Properties window) to **270px**.

21. Add two new lines after the TextBox control and add a new Label control.

22. Change the Label control's Text property to **First Name**.

23. Add a new line and add a new TextBox control.

24. Change the ID property of the TextBox to **txtFirstName**.

25. Add two new lines after the TextBox and add a new Label control.

26. Change the Text property of the Label to **Last Name**.

27. Add a new TextBox under the Label and change the ID property to **txtLastName**.

28. Add two new lines and add a new Label control.

29. Change the Text property of the Label to **E-mail Address**.

30. Add a new line and add a new TextBox control.

31. Change the ID of the TextBox control to **txtEmail** and the Width to **270px**.

32. Add two new lines and add another new Label control.

33. Change the Text property of the Label to **Message (1,000 characters maximum)**.

34. Add a new line after the Label and add a new TextBox control.

35. Set the ID property of the TextBox control to **txtMessage**, the Width property to **400px**, the Height property to **200px**, the MaxLength property to **1000**, and the TextMode property to **MultiLine**.

> **TIP** Both the MaxLength and TextMode properties are located in the Behavior section of the Properties window.

36. Add two new lines and add a new Button control from the Standard section of the Toolbox.

37. Change the ID property of the Button to **btnSend** and the Text property to **Send Message**.

38. Save the contactus.aspx page.

Your form should now look like the one shown in Figure 15.1.

Configuring the Topics DropDownList Control

When the Contact Us page is finished, the Sub Topic drop-down will be populated automatically with ASP.NET Ajax, based on the topic selected in the Topics drop-down. (You'll complete that section of the Contact Us page in Chapter 26.) Because the items in the Topics drop-down are already known, you'll use the ListItem Collection Editor for the DropDownList control to add the topics to the Topics drop-down.

FIGURE 15.1

The Contact Us form now has ASP.NET server controls for collecting informa-tion from site visitors.

To add items to the Topic DropDownList control, follow these steps:

1. Click the Smart Tag button next to the ddlTopic DropDownList control and click the Edit Items link as shown in Figure 15.2.

FIGURE 15.2

The Edit Items link provides easy access to the ListItem Collection Editor.

2. Click the Add button in the ListItem Collection Editor as shown in Figure 15.3.

FIGURE 15.3

The ListItem Collection Editor makes it easy to add items to a DropDownList control at design time.

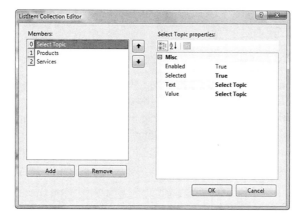

3. Change the Selected property to True.

4. Change the Text property to **Select Topic**.

5. Click the Add button to add a new item.

6. Change the Text property to **Products**.

7. Click the Add button to add a new item.

8. Change the Text property to **Services**.

9. Click OK in the ListItem Collection Editor to add the items to the DropDownList control.

The Topics drop-down now has three items available for selection. When the page loads, Select Topic will be selected. By clicking the drop-down, the user can select either Products or Services.

NOTE | You'll add some ASP.NET server-side code in Chapter 26 that will populate the Sub Topic drop-down, based on the selection in the Topic drop-down.

Processing ASP.NET Forms

Expression Web users are probably familiar with adding a form to a web page. When a typical HTML form is added to a page, it usually contains a Submit button and a Reset button. An ASP.NET form, on the other hand, is typically empty. Instead of having a traditional Submit button, an ASP.NET form can be submitted by various means, based on the configuration of the controls in the form.

TIP | Visual Web Developer automatically adds a form to each ASP.NET page you create.

The AutoPostBack **Property**

Most ASP.NET controls have a property called AutoPostBack that can be set to either True or False and that determines whether or not the control automatically submits the form as the user interacts with the control. For example, if the AutoPostBack property for a TextBox control is set to True, the form is submitted when a user presses Tab or Enter while the cursor is in the TextBox. If the AutoPostBack property for a DropDownList control is set to True, the form is submitted when a selection is made in the DropDownList.

→ For more information on ASP.NET events, **see** Chapter 4, "ASP.NET Events and the Page Lifecycle."

The Button Control

The Button control is a special type of control in that it has no AutoPostBack property, but always submits the form when clicked. Unlike a traditional Submit button, you can have multiple ASP.NET Button controls in a single form.

When a Button control is clicked, it fires off a Click event in server-side code so that you can execute ASP.NET code for that particular button.

NOTE | You'll write ASP.NET code for the Click event of the Button control on the Contact Us page in Chapter 24.

The IsPostBack **Property**

When a traditional HTML (not ASP.NET) form is submitted, the action attribute of the <form> element typically points to a server-side script (perhaps a CGI or ASP script) and the browser is taken to a different page after the submission. ASP.NET forms, on the other hand, are typically submitted back to the same page. ASP.NET provides a property called IsPostBack that enables a developer to determine whether a page is loading for the first time or as the result of a form submission.

When the Contact Us page first loads, all the form fields are empty and the IsPostBack property is False. When a user fills out the form and clicks the Send Message button, the form is submitted and the page loads again. This time, the form fields contain the information the user submitted and the IsPostBack property is True. By checking the value of the IsPostBack property, you can run different code based on whether the page is loading for the first time or as a result of the form being submitted.

The `IsPostBack` property is commonly used to determine whether code should run when a page loads. For example, suppose you have ASP.NET code that runs when your page loads that sets all fields in your form to a default value. If the page is loading because the form has been submitted, you wouldn't want that specific code to run, so you would run your code only if the `IsPostBack` property evaluated to `False`. The following code snippet illustrates this concept:

For C# use the following:

```csharp
protected void Page_Load(object sender, System.EventArgs e)
{
  if(!IsPostBack)
  {
    // run code to set all default values in form
  }
  else
  {
    // process the form data that was submitted
  }
}
```

For Visual Basic use the following:

```vb
Protected Sub Page_Load(ByVal sender As Object, ByVal e As System.EventArgs)
➥Handles Me.Load
  If(Not IsPostBack) Then
    ' run code to set all default values in form
  Else
    ' process the form data that was submitted
  End If
End Sub
```

Displaying a Form Confirmation

Because an ASP.NET page most often posts back to itself, unless you add code to change the appearance of the page, the user sees the page just reload with exactly the same information it previously contained. In the case of the Contact Us page, it would be more appropriate to display a confirmation message of some kind when the user submits the form.

To display a confirmation message when the form is submitted, you need to replace the form elements with a message confirming the submission of the form. To do that, you can use the ASP.NET Panel control. The Panel control provides a convenient means of working with a portion of an ASP.NET page as a single unit. You can place all the form controls inside one Panel and a confirmation message inside another Panel, and you can then choose which Panel to display based on whether the page is loading for the first time.

Placing the Form into a Panel

The first Panel control contains all the form elements on the page. To add the form elements to the Panel, follow these steps:

1. Click on any of the form controls in the Contact Us page and press Ctrl+A to select all the controls.

2. Press Ctrl+X to cut the controls to the Windows clipboard.

3. Locate the Panel control in the Standard section of the toolbox and double-click it to add it to the mainContent Content control.

4. Select the Panel control and change the ID property to **pnlForm**.

5. Remove any values for the Width and Height properties so that the Panel resizes according to the content that's inside it.

6. Click inside the Panel control to place the insertion point inside it.

7. Press Ctrl+V to paste the form controls into the Panel control.

Your page should now look like the one shown in Figure 15.4.

FIGURE 15.4

The form controls now appear within a Panel control.

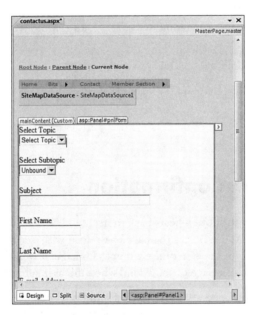

Adding a Confirmation Message

The confirmation message is displayed inside a second Panel. The confirmation panel is invisible when the page first loads. Then when the form is submitted, you can hide the Panel containing the form and show the Panel that contains the confirmation message.

To add the Panel for the confirmation message, follow these steps:

1. Select the `pnlForm` Panel control by clicking on the Quick Tag Selector, as shown in Figure 15.5.

FIGURE 15.5

The Quick Tag Selector is an easy way to select an entire Panel control.

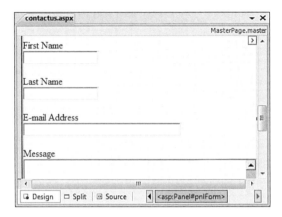

2. Press the right arrow key on your keyboard to move the insertion point to the right of the Panel.

3. Press Enter to insert a new line under the Panel.

4. Add a new Panel control by double-clicking on the Panel control in the toolbox.

5. Change the `ID` property of the new Panel control to **`pnlConfirm`**.

6. Remove any values for the `Width` and `Height` properties.

7. Locate the `Visible` property in the Behavior section of the Properties window and set it to `False` so that the Panel is not displayed when the page first loads.

8. Click inside the new Panel and enter a confirmation message such as **`Thank you for sending your message`**.

When the page loads, the `pnlForm` Panel is displayed and the `pnlConfirm` Panel is hidden. You now need to add some server-side code that will display the `pnlConfirm` Panel and hide the `pnlForm` Panel when the form is submitted.

Adding Server-Side Code

In this section you add some code that determines which Panel control to display, based on the value of the `IsPostBack` property. Double-click on the Elite Bits logo graphic on the `contactus.aspx` page. When you do, an empty `Page_Load` event is added to the page. Add the following code to the `Page_Load` event:

For C# use the following:

```
if (IsPostBack)
{
    pnlForm.Visible = false;
    pnlConfirm.Visible = true;
}
```

For Visual Basic use the following:

```
If IsPostBack Then
    pnlForm.Visible = False
    pnlConfirm.Visible = True
End If
```

If you preview the page in your browser at this point and click the Send Message button, you'll see the form disappear and the confirmation message displayed.

Checkpoint

Here's what you've done so far:

- Created the website
- Created the master page with navigation controls
- Created an external style sheet for CSS styles
- Created the sitemap file to feed navigation structure to navigation controls
- Created the home page attached to the master page
- Added a login user control so that you can easily add a login interface to any web page
- Added a login page containing the login user control
- Created the membership database
- Created a user for the website
- Created two new roles and assigned the user to the Editors role
- Created access rules for the editor folder of the website
- Configured the Login control and LoginView controls
- Added a page for a user to create his or her own account
- Added a page for a user to reset his or her password
- Added a page for a user to change his or her password
- Created the access rule necessary to protect the membership area
- Created a form that will be used as an email contact form
- Added server-side code to display a confirmation message for the contact form

In the next chapter, you'll add validation controls to the contact form so that you can control the information users enter.

CHAPTER 16

Adding Form Field Validation Using ASP.NET

IN THIS CHAPTER

The Necessity of Form Validation

If you're going to offer a form for user input on your website, you should always validate the input that the user provides. There are a couple of reasons why form validation is important. First of all, it ensures that the user provides you with the kind of information you expect. If you are expecting a phone number and a user enters text, you end up with bad data.

Secondly, it ensures that a malicious user doesn't cause problems by entering bad data. For example, suppose you have a form that allows users to enter records into a database and another page that displays the records in the same database. If a malicious user enters some client script into the form, that script executes when the records in the database are displayed. Form validation ensures that you don't run in to such problems.

> **TIP** ASP.NET rejects some types of form information. For example, if a user tries to enter either the < or > character into a form field (characters that are used with script tags,) ASP.NET responds with a "Bad Request" message and does not process the form.

Either client-side code or server-side code can be used to validate a form. Client-side validation provides a better user experience because a user doesn't have to wait for the form to be processed by the server. However, client-side validation can be easily circumvented if client scripting is disabled in the browser. For that reason, the most effective means of validating form fields is to validate on both the client and the server.

ASP.NET provides several validation server controls to aid in form validation, and each of them performs validation on both the client and server. This chapter reviews each of these controls.

ASP.NET Validation Controls

ASP.NET provides six different validation controls that make it easy to validate your form fields without writing any code yourself. Each validation control uses a `ControlToValidate` property that associates it with a particular ASP.NET server control on the page, as shown in Figure 16.1.

The following sections describe the validation controls provided by ASP.NET.

FIGURE 16.1

Use the `ControlToValidate` property of the validation control to associate a validation control with an ASP.NET server control.

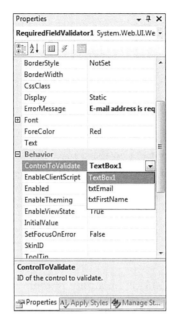

RequiredFieldValidator Control

The RequiredFieldValidator control makes a particular ASP.NET server control a required field. If a control has a RequiredFieldValidator control associated with it, validation will fail if the form is submitted and the value of the associated control differs from the RequiredFieldValidator control's `InitialValue` property.

Suppose you have a form that requires a user to select a value from a DropDownList control. The default value of the DropDownList control is `Select`. If you set the `InitialValue` property of a RequiredFieldValidator control to `Select`, validation fails for the DropDownList unless the user selects a value other than Select.

RangeValidator

The RangeValidator control makes it easy to require that a specific form field value fall within a particular range. The following properties (unique to the RangeValidator control) enable you to control how validation occurs:

- **MaximumValue**—Specifies the maximum value allowed for the control associated with the RangeValidator control.

- **MinimumValue**—Specifies the minimum value allowed for the control associated with the RangeValidator control.

- **Type**—Specifies the data type used for the control associated with the RangeValidator control, as well as for the `MaximumValue` and `MinimumValue` properties. Valid values are `String`, `Integer`, `Double`, `Date`, and `Currency`.

> **NOTE** A discussion of programmatic data types falls outside of the scope of this book. For more information on different data types, see the InformIT network at http://www.informit.com/library/content.asp?b=STY_Csharp_24hours&seqNum=124.

When ASP.NET attempts to validate the control associated with the RangeValidator control, it first attempts to convert the value of the associated control, the value of the `MaximumValue` property, and the value of the `MinimumValue` property to the specified data type. If that conversion fails, validation for the control also fails. As an example, if you specify `Date` for the `Type` property and a value of 1 is specified in the value of the associated control, the value of the `MaximumValue` property, or the value of the `MinimumValue` property, validation fails because it is not possible to convert 1 to a valid date.

RegularExpressionValidator Control

The RegularExpressionValidator control is one of the most powerful validation controls ASP.NET offers because it is incredibly flexible. When you use a RegularExpressionValidator control, you specify a regular expression in the `ValidationExpression` property and the associated control is validated against that regular expression.

Regular expressions are very powerful because they can be used to identify complex patterns. Consider a telephone number as an example. Humans can easily recognize a telephone number in many different formats. You'll likely recognize all the following numerical formats as a phone number:

- 555-1212
- 817-555-1212
- (817) 555-1212
- (817)-555-1212
- 817.555.1212

Although it's easy for you to recognize these patterns as a phone number pattern, teaching a computer to recognize a pattern is extremely difficult. A regular expression makes identifying such patterns possible. In fact, that's precisely why the regular expression syntax was created: to recognize patterns.

A RegularExpressionValidator control would use a regular expression such as the following to validate input as a U.S. phone number:

```
((\(\d{3}\) ?)¦(\d{3}-))?\d{3}-\d{4}
```

Fortunately, you don't have to know how to write regular expressions to take advantage of the RegularExpressionValidator control. Visual Web Developer provides a Regular Expression Editor, complete with many standard regular expressions that you can use, as shown in Figure 16.2.

FIGURE 16.2
The Regular Expression Editor comes complete with many standard regular expressions that you can use in your website.

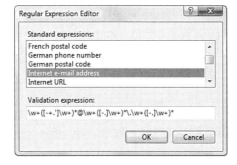

To use the Regular Expression Editor, click the ellipsis button next to the ValidationExpression property in the Visual Web Developer Properties pane, as shown in Figure 16.3.

FIGURE 16.3
The ellipsis button next to the Validation- Expression property provides easy access to the Regular Expression Editor.

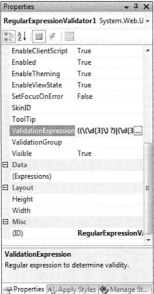

CompareValidator Control

The CompareValidator control enables you to easily compare the value in the associated control with either the value in another control or against a preset value. The following properties are used to configure the CompareValidator control:

- **ControlToCompare**—The value of the control specified in the ControlToCompare property is validated against the value of the control specified in the ControlToValidate property.

- **ValueToCompare**—When specified, the value of the control specified in the ControlToValidate property is compared against this value.

- **Type**—Like the RangeValidator control, the CompareValidator control also has a Type property that can be set to String, Integer, Double, Date, or Currency.

- **Operator**—Specifies the operator used for the comparison. Valid values are Equal, NotEqual, GreaterThan, GreaterThanEqual (greater than or equal to), LessThan, LessThanEqual (less than or equal to), and DataTypeCheck.

The DataTypeCheck operator causes the value for the control specified in the ControlToValidate property to be compared against the data type specified for the Type property. If the value in the control is not of the data type specified for the Type property, validation fails. For example, if you have a field that asks for a user's age, you can use the DataTypeCheck property with Type set to Integer to assure that a number is entered.

CustomValidator Control

In situations where none of the other validation controls are suitable to your needs, you can use the CustomValidator control. The CustomValidator control requires you to write your own client script (if you want to validate on the client) and your own server-side code to validate the form field.

Using the CustomValidator control requires that you write server-side code for the ServerValidate event. You should also write a client script that mirrors the functionality of the server-side code. The ClientValidationFunction property of the CustomValidator control specifies the client-side code function for validation.

Because the use of the CustomValidator control requires a custom-code approach, it is not covered in the context of this book. For more information on using the CustomValidator control, you can review the MSDN documentation at msdn2.microsoft.com/en-us/library/f5db6z8k(vs.90).aspx.

ValidationSummary Control

The ValidationSummary control is designed to display a summary of all validation failures at one place within the page. The following properties are unique to the ValidationSummary control.

- **DisplayMode**—Determines how the summary of validation failures is displayed. Valid values are `List`, `BulletList`, and `SingleParagraph`. `List` and `BulletList` display failures in the same format except that `BulletList` places bullets in front of each failure. `SingleParagraph` places all validation failures in a single paragraph.
- **HeaderText**—Specifies the text to display as the header for validation failures.
- **ShowMessageBox**—A Boolean property that specifies whether or not validation failures are displayed inside a message box with an OK button.
- **ShowSummary**—A Boolean property that specifies whether a summary of validation failures appears on the page. This property is often set to `False` when the `ShowMessageBox` property is `True`.

Common Validation Control Properties

Several properties are common to all validation controls that you're likely to use as you are configuring your form validation. They are described in the following sections.

The `Text` Property

The `Text` property of a validation control specifies the text that is visible when validation has not been performed or when validation succeeds for the control. By default, there is no value for the `Text` property.

> **TIP**
>
> When using RequiredFieldValidator controls, it's common practice to use the `Text` property to indicate that a field is required by specifying "Required Field" or a similar value.

The `Display` Property

The `Display` property controls how a validation error is displayed for a validation control. It has three valid values; `None`, `Static` (the default value), and `Dynamic`.

- When the `Display` property is `None`, validation errors for the control (text that is displayed if validation fails) are not displayed at the location on the page where the validation control exists. This is useful in cases where you are using a ValidationSummary control, as you'll see later in this chapter.
- When the `Display` property is `Static`, space for the validation control's error message is reserved on the page whether a validation error exists.
- When the `Display` property is set to `Dynamic`, space is allocated for the error message only when a validation error occurs.

The best choice for the Display property is often the default setting of Static because it prevents form elements from shifting around when validation error messages are displayed. However, if you are using more than one validation control for a single form field, you'll probably want to set the Display property to Dynamic so that error messages appear next to the control in error.

> **NOTE** When you add validation controls to the Contact Us page later in this chapter, the difference between Static and Dynamic will become clear.

The ErrorMessage **Property**

The ErrorMessage property is used to specify the message that is displayed when a validation error occurs. For example, if a validation control is used to make a particular form field a required field and a user attempts to submit the form without supplying a value for the required field, the text specified in the ErrorMessage property for the validation control is displayed, as shown in Figure 16.4.

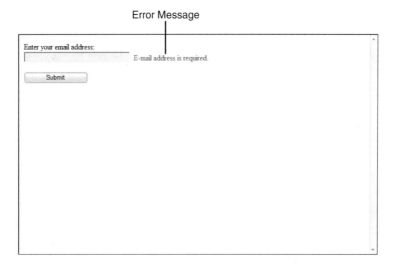

Error Message

FIGURE 16.4

The ErrorMessage property is used to specify the error message text for a validation control.

> **TIP** By default, the ErrorMessage property is set to the type of validation control being used. For example, a RequiredFieldValidator control's default ErrorMessage property is set to RequiredFieldValidator.

The `ControlToValidate` **Property**

The `ControlToValidate` property connects a validation control to a specific ASP.NET server control. For example, if you add a RequiredFieldValidator control to a page to make a TextBox called `txtEmail` a required field, the `ControlToValidate` property of the RequiredFieldValidator control would be set to `txtEmail`.

Visual Web Developer makes it easy to specify the `ControlToValidate` property by allowing you to choose the desired server control from a drop-down that displays the controls on the page, as shown previously in Figure 16.1.

The `EnableClientScript` **Property**

The `EnableClientScript` property is a `Boolean` property (either `True` or `False`) that specifies whether ASP.NET will create the client-side script necessary to validate the control on the client, if the requesting browser is capable of running script. The `EnableClientScript` property is `True` by default.

If the `EnableClientScript` property is set to `False`, ASP.NET performs validation on the server. When the `EnableClientScript` property is `True`, ASP.NET attempts to use the client script to validate the control, assuming the requesting browser is capable. Validation also takes place on the server to protect against users bypassing validation by disabling client scripting in the browser.

> **N O T E** ASP.NET uses the `user-agent` string sent by the browser to determine whether the browser can support the use of client script.

The `SetFocusOnError` **Property**

The `SetFocusOnError` property is also a Boolean property. When `True`, if validation fails for a particular validation control, the control specified in the `ControlToValidate` property obtains the focus so that a user can more easily correct the error. When `False` (the default value), focus is not affected by a validation failure.

If the `SetFocusOnError` property is `True` for more than one validation control that fails validation, focus is set on the first control that failed validation.

The `ValidationGroup` **Property**

The `ValidationGroup` property makes it easy to create a group of validation controls. This property is useful in cases where a form is broken up into sections and you need validation to be performed separately in one or more sections.

Consider the form shown in Figure 16.5. In this form, the user is required to enter a city for a real estate search and then click the Lookup button. A drop-down is then populated with neighborhoods in the city that was entered. The City text box has a validation control associated with it that makes it a required field. Another validation control is associated with the DropDownList control, which requires the user to select a neighborhood.

FIGURE 16.5

This real estate form validates successfully only when the `ValidationGroup` property is used.

If the `ValidationGroup` property is not used, the validation control for the neighborhood drop-down fails when the user attempts to look up a city by clicking the Lookup button. That's obviously not the intended behavior. To correct that problem, the City text box, the validation control associated with the City text box, and the Lookup button all have a `ValidationGroup` property value of `CityLookup`. By giving each of these controls an identical value for the `ValidationGroup` property, validation for those controls occurs separately from the other controls on the page.

CAUTION

If a validation control does not have the same `ValidationGroup` value as the control with which it is associated, it does not correctly validate the associated control.

Adding and Configuring ASP.NET Validation Controls

Now that you have a basic framework of how ASP.NET validation controls work, you can add some validation controls to the Contact Us page.

The first step in adding validation to a form is deciding which form fields you want to validate and what type of input you expect. Table 16.1 lists the validation rules you want to apply to the Contact Us page, along with the type of validation control that's necessary to perform the necessary validation.

Table 16.1   Validation Rules for the Contact Us Page

Control	Rule	Validation Control Required
ddlSubtopic	Entry Required	RequiredFieldValidator
txtSubject	Entry Required	RequiredFieldValidator
txtFirstName	Entry Required	RequiredFieldValidator
txtLastName	Entry Required	RequiredFieldValidator
txtEmail	Entry Required	RequiredFieldValidator
txtEmail	Valid E-mail Address	RegularExpressionValidator
txtMessage	Entry Required	RequiredFieldValidator

Now that you've identified the validation requirements, it's time to add the necessary validation controls to the page:

1. Open the `contactus.aspx` page.
2. Place the insertion point to the right of the ddlSubtopic control.
3. Double-click on the RequiredFieldValidator in the Validation section of the toolbox.
4. Change the `ControlToValidate` property to `ddlSubtopic`.
5. Change the `InitialValue` property to `Select`.
6. Change the `Text` property to `Subtopic Required`.
7. Add a new RequiredFieldValidator to the right of the txtSubject control.
8. Change the `ControlToValidate` property to txtSubject.
9. Change the `Text` property to `Subject Required`.
10. Add a new RequiredFieldValidator to the right of the txtFirstName control.
11. Change the `ControlToValidate` property to txtFirstName.
12. Change the `Text` property to `First Name Required`.
13. Add a new RequiredFieldValidator to the right of the txtLastName control.
14. Change the `ControlToValidate` property to `txtLastName`.
15. Change the `Text` property to `Last Name Required`.
16. Add a new RequiredFieldValidator to the right of the txtEmail control.
17. Change the `Display` property to `Dynamic`.
18. Change the `ControlToValidate` property to `txtEmail`.
19. Change the `Text` property to `Email Required`.

20. Add a new RegularExpressionValidator control to the right of the RequiredFieldValidator control that you added in step 16.

21. Change the `Display` property to `Dynamic`.

> **TIP** The `Display` property for the last two validation controls was set to `Dynamic` so that any error messages appear immediately to the right of the control.

22. Change the `ControlToValidate` property to `txtEmail`.

23. Click the ellipsis button next to the `ValidationExpression` property and select the Internet E-mail Address option, as shown in Figure 16.6.

FIGURE 16.6
Using the Regular Expression Editor, it's easy to configure a regular expression rule for an email address.

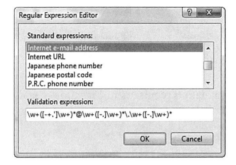

24. Add a new RequiredFieldValidator to the right of the txtMessage control.

25. Change the `Text` property to `Message Required`.

26. Change the `ControlToValidate` property to `txtMessage`.

You can now test the validation for the Contact Us page by browsing to the page and submitting the form. Not only do the necessary fields fail validation unless a value is supplied, but the email address field fails validation unless a valid email address is entered.

Checkpoint

Here's what we did in this chapter:

■ Added form validation controls to the Contact Us page.

In the next few chapters, you'll learn about the new CSS features in Visual Web Developer. You'll start adding styles to your web pages and you'll learn about ASP.NET themes and skins.

PART VI

Styling Web Forms in Visual Web Developer 2008

CHAPTER 17

Creating and Managing CSS Styles

IN THIS CHAPTER

An Introduction to CSS

In Chapter 10, you created a master page for your ASP.NET application to aid in giving the website a consistent appearance. Master pages are a great tool for giving an ASP.NET application a consistent user interface, but the most powerful tool available for ensuring a consistent site appearance is CSS.

> **N O T E** We'll cover the basics of CSS here. If you want to read more detail on CSS, the W3C's recommendation on style sheets is a great resource. You can access it by browsing to www.w3.org/TR/html4/present/styles.html.

CSS is a language that uses rules to define appearance and layout for markup languages, such as HTML. A CSS rule can be applied to a specific HTML tag or to one or more user-defined sections of a page that may contain several different HTML tags.

CSS makes it extremely easy to reformat an entire website. You can reformat a website designed with CSS by making edits to a single CSS file rather than opening each page individually and reformatting individual elements.

> **N O T E** For a great example of CSS formatting in action, visit the Zen Garden website at www.csszengarden.com. You can reformat the entire site with CSS by selecting a design from the list on the right side of the page.

Basic CSS Rules

The following syntax is used to apply a CSS rule:

```
selector: { property: value; }
```

Therefore, to format the <p> tag so that all the text in paragraphs is green in color, you would use the following CSS rule:

```
p: { color: Green; }
```

In the previous example, the CSS selector is the <p> element, the CSS property is `color`, and the CSS value is `green`. When this CSS rule is applied to a page, all text that appears within a <p> tag will be green unless the CSS rule is overridden by another CSS rule or formatting applied directly to the paragraph.

You can combine CSS properties to apply more complex formatting. For example, the following code formats <p> tags with red text that is 12 pixels in size and bolded:

```
p
{
  color: Red;
  font-size: 12px;
  font-weight: bold;
}
```

> **TIP** You don't have to worry about remembering all the CSS properties available to you. As you'll see later, Visual Web Developer provides full IntelliSense for CSS and also a CSS dialog that makes CSS rules easy to create—and you don't have to even look at code.

CSS rules can be applied to a web page using an external style sheet, an embedded style sheet, or an inline style. Styles that are applied using an embedded style sheet override styles in an external style sheet, and styles that are applied using an inline style override an embedded style sheet.

External Style Sheets

External style sheets are created in a separate file with a .css file extension. The code within an external style sheet uses the same formatting that you saw in earlier examples. You can then attach the external style sheet to one or more pages by using the HTML <link> element inside the <head> section of a web page.

The following code attaches a style sheet to an HTML document:

```
<link href="StyleSheet.css" rel="stylesheet" type="text/css" />
```

You can type this HTML code yourself to attach a style sheet and Visual Web Developer will give you IntelliSense as shown in Figure 17.1. However, it's easier to use the Attach Style Sheet menu option in Visual Web Developer.

To use the Attach Style Sheet menu option to attach a style sheet, follow these steps:

1. Create a style sheet and save it as a .css file within your website.
2. Create a new web page or open an existing web page.
3. Make sure you are in Design view and select Format, CSS Styles, Attach Style Sheet from the Visual Web Developer menu.
4. In the Select Style Sheet dialog, select the desired style sheet and click OK, as shown in Figure 17.2.

FIGURE 17.1
Visual Web
Developer provides
full IntelliSense for
adding the <link>
element necessary to
attach a style sheet.

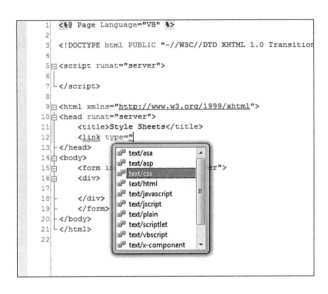

FIGURE 17.2
The Select Style
Sheet dialog makes
adding a link to an
external style sheet
simple.

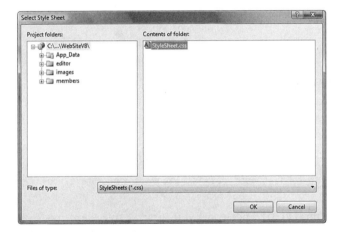

Multiple style sheets can be attached to a single document. For example, you might have some styles defined in a master style sheet that is attached to all your pages and then another style sheet that contains styles specific to a certain section of your website. By attaching both these style sheets to your page, you can take advantage of the styles in each style sheet.

→ For more information on applying CSS styles to a page, **see** Chapter 18, "Applying CSS to Web Forms."

Embedded Style Sheets

An embedded style sheet is like an external style sheet, but rather than use CSS code in an external file, an embedded style sheet uses code that is added directly to the <head> section in a web page.

The following code illustrates a CSS rule defined in an embedded style sheet:

```
<head>
  <title>Sample Web Page</title>
  <style type="text/css">
    div {
      color: Blue;
    }
  </style>
</head>
```

CSS rules that are defined in an embedded style sheet override rules that are defined in an
external style sheet. In other words, if you have a CSS rule defined in an external style sheet
that formats all <p> elements in a green color and then add an embedded style sheet that
formats <p> elements in a red color, the red color overrides the green color defined in the
external style sheet.

Inline CSS Styles

You apply inline CSS styles directly to a specific HTML element by using the HTML `style`
attribute. Inline styles use the same `property: value` format used in the external and embedded style sheets, but because they are applied directly to an HTML element, a selector is
not used with inline styles.

The following code removes the underline from an HTML hyperlink, using an inline CSS
style:

```
<a href="default.aspx" style="text-decoration: none">Home Page</a>
```

You can apply multiple inline styles by separating each with a semicolon. The following code
formats the <p> element as red text that is bolded:

```
<p style="color: Red; font-weight: bold;">Paragraph Text</p>
```

Inline CSS styles override both external and embedded styles. Because inline styles appear
inline with the rest of the web page's HTML code, they can often cause frustration when
you want to style HTML documents. More than once, I've created a style in an external
style sheet that didn't appear to work, only to find after a great deal of frustration that my
new style was being overridden by an inline style buried deep within my page.

NOTE | In the next chapter, you'll learn that Visual Web Developer 2008 contains powerful, new CSS features that alleviate the frustration of using inline styles.

Exploring CSS Classes and IDs

So far, you've seen CSS as it is applied to HTML elements. However, the true power of CSS lies in the use of CSS *classes* and *IDs*.

As you've already seen, the following CSS rule formats all HTML <p> elements in a green color:

```
p { color: Green; }
```

This CSS rule applies to all HTML paragraphs. If you want to apply a CSS rule to a specific paragraph, CSS classes and IDs make that possible.

CSS Classes

CSS classes use the same CSS code that is used in creating rules for HTML elements. However, instead of an HTML element, a custom name (the CSS class name) is used as the selector instead. For example, suppose you want to apply a CSS rule to only those HTML paragraphs that make up the main content area of your web pages. You can accomplish this by creating a CSS class as follows:

```
.Content
{
  color: Black;
  font-family: Arial, Helvetica;
  font-size: 12px;
}
```

This CSS code creates a new CSS class called Content by specifying the class name, appended by a period. This is known as a *class selector*.

To connect the Content CSS class to an HTML paragraph, you use the HTML class attribute. For example, the following HTML code connects the Content CSS class with a specific HTML <p> tag:

```
<p class="Content">Some paragraph text.</p>
```

The Content class can be applied to other HTML elements as well. For example, the following HTML code formats an HTML hyperlink by using the Content class:

```
<a href="default.aspx" class="Content">Home Page</a>
```

This is the simplest example of the use of a CSS class. In fact, the CSS language provides enormous flexibility and power when using CSS classes. For example, suppose you have both <p> tags and <div> tags that make up your content and you need to use a different style for each. By appending an HTML tag to the name of the CSS class, you can easily create a separate CSS class for each HTML element, as shown in the following sample CSS code:

```
p.Content
{
  color: Black;
}

div.Content
{
  color: Gray;
}
```

When the following CSS code is applied in an embedded or external style sheet, the paragraph text becomes black,

```
<p class="Content">This text will be black.</p>
```

and the following div becomes gray:

```
<div class="Content">This text will be gray.</div>
```

This ability to specify that a CSS class applies only to a particular HTML element is extremely powerful when redesigning a website. For example, suppose that your website contains numerous <p> elements and <div> elements and all are formatted with the following CSS class:

```
.Content
{
  font-family: Arial;
  font-size: 12px;
  color: Black;
}
```

Now suppose that you have decided that all the <div> elements should use 18-pixel text that is green instead of black. You could create a new CSS class for the <div> elements and then change all the class attributes on each <div>, but you can accomplish the same thing by simply adding a p selector to the existing Content class selector and creating a new class, using div.Content as the class selector that contains the new formatting.

As powerful as this method is, it's only a hint of the true power behind CSS class selectors. You can also apply logic to your CSS formatting by using CSS class selectors. For example, suppose you create a class that you want applied to <div> elements, but only when they appear immediately after a <p> element. You can accomplish this by using the following CSS rule:

```
p + div
{
  text-indent: 14px;
}
```

You can also use a CSS class as a selector when using the preceding syntax. For example, the following CSS rule formats any <p> tag that follows an element formatted with the CSS class called Content:

```
Content + p { font-family: Arial; font-size: 12px; }
```

> **N O T E** You can apply many other powerful formatting techniques by using selectors in this manner. If you want the full story on using CSS to format your web pages, read *Cascading Style Sheets: Separating Content from Presentation, Second Edition*, from Friends of ED publishing. It's widely considered the best resource on the topic.

CSS IDs

CSS IDs are similar to CSS classes, with one major exception: A CSS ID can be applied to only one element on a page. In Chapter 10, you created a CSS ID for the copyright text on the master page. Here's the CSS code you used for that CSS ID:

```
#Copyright {
  font-family: Arial, Helvetica, sans-serif;
  font-size: x-small;
  border-style: solid;
  border-width: thin;
}
```

Notice that the selector used for this CSS rule is #Copyright. The pound sign that is appended to the selector makes this rule a CSS ID.

To apply a CSS ID to a page element, the id attribute is used. The following line applies the Copyright CSS ID to a paragraph:

```
<p id="Copyright">Copyright 2008, Jimco Books</p>
```

Because this rule is a CSS ID, it can be applied to only one element on the page. If you apply it to another element on the page, Visual Web Developer notifies you as shown in Figure 17.3.

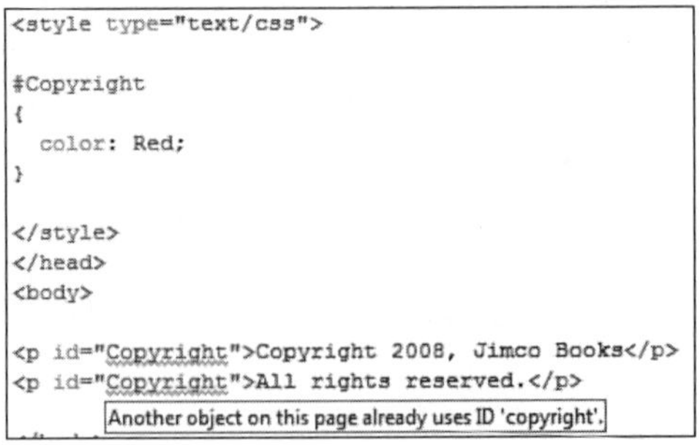

FIGURE 17.3

Visual Web Developer notifies you if you apply a specific CSS ID to more than one element on a page.

```
<style type="text/css">

#Copyright
{
  color: Red;
}

</style>
</head>
<body>

<p id="Copyright">Copyright 2008, Jimco Books</p>
<p id="Copyright">All rights reserved.</p>
        Another object on this page already uses ID 'copyright'.
```

When you define a CSS ID, you can limit it to a particular HTML element just as you can with CSS classes. The following CSS ID can only be applied to a `<div>` element.

```
div#Copyright {
  font-family: Arial, Helvetica, sans-serif;
  font-size: x-small;
  border-style: solid;
  border-width: thin;
}
```

As you can see, CSS is extremely versatile and powerful. However, you may find yourself a little intimidated and overwhelmed by the format and variety of CSS properties. Fortunately, Visual Web Developer offers a convenient user interface for creating styles that removes the burden of having to learn CSS code.

Using the Style Builder Dialog to Create Styles

The Style Builder dialog in Visual Web Developer is one of the Expression Web CSS features that Microsoft incorporated into Visual Web Developer 2008. It's a powerful dialog for creating new CSS styles and editing existing CSS styles.

> **NOTE**
> In this section, we create a style using the Style Builder dialog. Later in this chapter, you'll see how you can edit an existing style with the Style Builder dialog.

Creating a Simple Style

Let's create a new CSS style for use in your web application. Open the web application in Visual Web Developer and follow these steps to create a style for paragraph text:

1. Open the `MasterPage.master` page.

> **TIP**
> A file must be open for you to access the Style Builder.

2. If the page doesn't open in Design view, switch to Design view.
3. Select Format, New Style to open the Style Builder dialog.
4. Select p from the Selector drop-down as shown in Figure 17.4.

FIGURE 17.4

The Selector drop-down is a convenient tool for applying a style to a particular HTML selector.

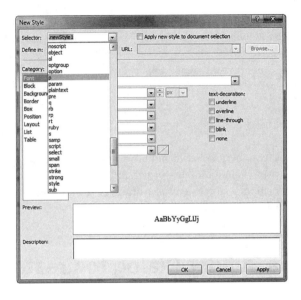

5. Select Existing Style Sheet in the Define In drop-down.

6. Select StyleSheet.css in the URL drop-down so that the new style is added to the StyleSheet.css file.

7. Make sure that Font is selected in the Category list.

8. Select Arial, Helvetica, Sans-serif from the Font-Family drop-down.

9. Select Medium in the Font-Size drop-down. The Style Builder dialog should now look like the one shown in Figure 17.5.

FIGURE 17.5

The new style uses CSS to format paragraphs.

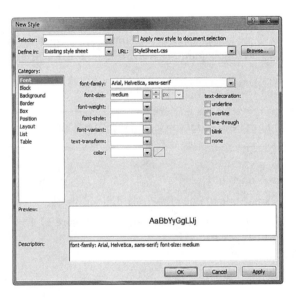

10. Click OK to add the new style to the external style sheet.

When you click OK to add the new style to the `StyleSheet.css` file, Visual Web Developer opens the CSS file and adds the new style to it, but it doesn't automatically save your change to the file. To complete the process, you need to save the `StyleSheet.css` file.

Creating a New CSS Class

Using the Style Builder is also a convenient way to create new CSS classes. Use the following steps to create a new CSS class that you can apply to buttons in the website so that they'll have a customized appearance:

1. Open the MasterPage.master file, if it's not already open, and switch to Design view.

2. Select Format, New Style to access the Style Builder dialog.

3. Select Existing Style Sheet in the Define In drop-down and select StyleSheet.css from the URL drop-down.

4. The Style Builder opens with a new CSS class name already selected. Type **.button** to create a new CSS class, as shown in Figure 17.6.

The button Class Name

FIGURE 17.6

To create a new CSS class, simply type the new name over the default name that Visual Web Developer provides.

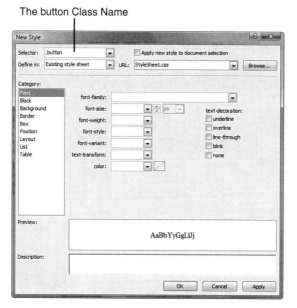

TIP   Make sure that your new CSS class name begins with a period.

5. Make sure that the Font category is selected and select Arial, Helvetica, sans-serif from the Font-Family drop-down.

6. Select Small from the Font-Size drop-down.

7. Select the white color square from the Color drop-down.

8. Select the Border category.

> **TIP** Notice that the Font category appears bolded. A bolded category means that properties have been defined for that category.

9. Make sure that the Same For All check box is checked under the Border-Style column.

10. Select Solid in the Top drop-down. When you do, Solid will be selected and grayed out in the other Border-Style drop-downs.

11. Make sure that the Same For All check box is checked under the Border-Width drop-down and select Thin from the Top drop-down.

12. Make sure that the Same For All check box is checked under the Border-Color drop-down and select the black color square from the Top drop-down.

The Style Builder dialog should now appear like the one shown in Figure 17.7.

FIGURE 17.7

The new button class applies a solid border to the button. This style is applied to a button in the next chapter.

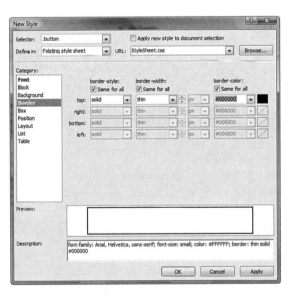

You've now created a CSS class called button. In the next chapter, we'll use that CSS class to apply formatting to a button on your page.

Using the Style Application Toolbar

Everyone has a different approach to designing web pages. I prefer to use the Style Builder dialog to do all my formatting by creating CSS code while I design pages. Others prefer to use the formatting toolbar in Visual Web Developer to select formatting options just as you would with a word processing application.

TIP	The process of applying formatting with the formatting toolbar is called *direct formatting*.

Visual Web Developer provides a special toolbar for controlling the way that direct formatting is applied. The Style Application toolbar (shown in Figure 17.8) gives you control over the formatting code that Visual Web Developer automatically generates.

FIGURE 17.8
The Style Application toolbar provides a means of controlling how Visual Web Developer generates style code.

Two modes of style application are available on the Style Application toolbar: Auto and Manual. (Manual is selected by default.) In both modes, Visual Web Developer creates formatting automatically, either by using inline CSS styles or by creating new CSS classes. However, by selecting Manual mode, you can control how new CSS formatting is applied if you want.

TIP	You might have noticed styles in your web pages called `style1`, `style2`, and so on. These are the CSS classes that Visual Web Developer creates automatically.

Using the Style Application Toolbar to Apply Formatting

The easiest way to understand the Style Application drop-down is to experiment with it. Close your web application if you've got it open so that you can experiment without modifying the application, and then follow these steps:

NOTE	The options in the Style Application toolbar are available only when Manual is selected in the Style Application drop-down.

1. Select File, New File. Select HTML Page and click Open to create a new HTML page.

2. Switch to Design view.

3. If the Style Application toolbar is not visible, select View, Toolbars, Style Application to display it.

4. Make sure that Manual is selected in the Style Application drop-down, and then type some text into the new page so that you can experiment with formatting. Then press Enter.

5. Click inside the text you just entered, so that the insertion point is on the same line as the text, but don't select anything.

6. On the Formatting toolbar, click the Foreground Color button and select a color, as shown in Figure 17.9.

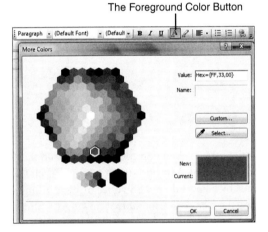

The Foreground Color Button

FIGURE 17.9

The Formatting tool-bar enables you to apply direct format-ting quickly to page elements.

Switch to Source view and examine the code that Visual Web Developer added to your page. You should see that Visual Web Developer has added an inline style to the `<p>` element similar to the following code:

```
<p style="color: #FF3300">
```

Visual Web Developer added an inline style because by default, New Inline Style is selected in the Target Rule drop-down and that inline style is applied to the entire paragraph. The behavior of Visual Web Developer is different when Auto is selected in the Style Application drop-down.

1. Switch back to Design view.

2. Select Auto in the Style Application drop-down.

3. Click inside one of the words in the text you typed but don't select anything.

4. On the Formatting toolbar, click the Foreground Color button and select a different color from the color you chose previously.

Notice that the color you chose is applied to only the word containing the selection point. The rest of the text remains unaffected. If you switch to Source view, you'll see that Visual Web Developer has added a <span> tag and applied formatting to that element, using a new CSS class as follows:

```
This is <span class="style1">some</span> text.</p>
```

> **TIP**   Visual Web Developer defines the `style1` CSS class in the <head> section of the page in an embedded style sheet.

In Manual mode, Visual Web Developer does not add new tags to your page. That's why the formatting you applied when in Manual mode applied to the entire paragraph. To apply the formatting to only one word within a paragraph, Visual Web Developer must insert a new <span> tag. Because new tags are never added to your page when in Manual mode, the formatting applies to the closest tag to the left of the insertion point.

Applying Formatting to Existing Styles

If styles are already applied to your page, Visual Web Developer updates the existing style. However, if you are in Manual mode, you have the option of overriding that behavior if you choose.

Follow these steps to apply a style using the formatting toolbar:

1. If you are still in Source view, switch to Design view.

2. Click inside the paragraph you entered earlier, and then click the Quick Tag Selector for the <span> tag, as shown in Figure 17.10.

FIGURE 17.10

The Quick Tag Selector is a convenient way of selecting a specific page element.

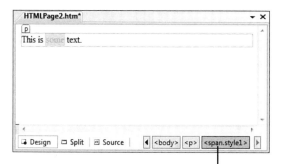

Quick Tag Selector for the <span> Element

3. Click the Foreground Color button and change the color to one that's different than the existing color.

When you select the new color, Visual Web Developer modifies the existing CSS style to reflect the new color. If you are in Manual mode, you also have other options available in the Style Application drop-down on the Style Application toolbar, as shown in Figure 17.11.

FIGURE 17.11

In Manual mode, several options are available for applying formatting changes.

If the New Inline Style option is selected and a style is not already applied to the selection, a new inline style is created to apply the new formatting. If New Auto Class is selected and a style is not already applied to the selection, a new CSS class is generated automatically and added to an embedded style sheet on the page. If the selected formatting is already applied with an existing style, Visual Web Developer modifies the existing style by default, even if you select to create a new style. You can override this behavior by clicking the Reuse Existing Style button, as shown in Figure 17.12.

FIGURE 17.12

The Reuse Existing Style button is selected by default. When the button is active, Visual Web Developer will modify existing style properties when changes are made.

The Reuse Existing Style Button

When the Reuse Existing Style button is not selected, Visual Web Developer always creates a new style. For example, if `style1` specifies a `color` property to `blue` and you change the `color` property to `red`, Visual Web Developer creates a new style to apply the red color if the Reuse Existing Style button is not selected. If the Reuse Existing Style button is selected, the existing `style1` style is updated to reflect the new color.

Managing CSS Styles

You've seen several ways to create new CSS styles. After you've created several styles, managing them can become a burden. Thankfully, Visual Web Developer 2008 borrows the excellent CSS management capabilities from Expression Web.

The Manage Styles Pane

The Manage Styles pane is a powerful way to manage CSS styles. It displays all the styles available to the page that is currently active in Visual Web Developer.

To access the Manage Styles task pane if it's not already visible, select Format, CSS Styles, Manage Styles. As shown in Figure 17.13, the Manage Styles pane shows styles that are not in use on the page as a ball with no outline, styles that are in use as balls with a circular outline, attached or embedded style sheets as a highlighted bar, and a preview of the selected style in a preview window.

FIGURE 17.13
The Manage Styles pane is a powerful way to manage CSS styles.

What you can't see in Figure 17.13 is that the balls that represent styles in the Manage Styles pane are color-coded according to the type of style they represent. CSS IDs are represented by red balls, CSS classes by green balls, and CSS rules applied to HTML elements by blue balls.

As you select elements on a page, the CSS style that applies to that element is automatically selected in the Manage Styles pane. You can also right-click on any style in the Manage Styles pane and choose the Select All x Instance(s) as shown in Figure 17.14 to select all page elements styled with that rule in the active document. This makes it easy to examine which style affects which part of the page.

> **TIP**
> You can use the Manage Styles pane to attach new style sheets by clicking the Attach Style Sheet link.

FIGURE 17.14

You can select all page elements affected by a particular style in the Manage Styles pane.

The Options button enables you to configure the order in which styles are displayed and other display options. The following mutually exclusive categorization options are available when you click the Options button:

- **Categorize by Order**—Displays styles categorized in the order in which they are defined. This is the default setting.
- **Categorize by Element**— Displays styles ordered by HTML element. HTML element styles appear in order at the top of the list. Styles that define CSS IDs and classes appear ordered by type after all HTML element styles.
- **Categorize by Type**—Displays CSS IDs, classes, and HTML element styles in their own collapsible group.

The following mutually exclusive display options are available when you click the Options button:

- **Show All Styles**—This is the default setting and shows all styles available to the active page, regardless of whether they are in use.
- **Show Styles Used in Current Page**—Displays all the styles in use in the current page. Styles that are not in use are not displayed.
- **Show Styles Used on Selection**—Displays only those styles that are used on the currently selected element.

The other two options available are Separate Grouped Selectors and Display Selected Style Preview. The Separate Grouped Selectors option toggles between showing a CSS rule that is applied to multiple selectors on a single line and on separate lines. The Display Selected Style Preview option toggles the display of the CSS preview at the bottom of the Manage Styles pane.

Using the Manage Styles Pane to Add New Styles

The Manage Styles pane offers a convenient way of creating new styles using CSS rules. By either clicking the New Style link shown previously in Figure 17.13 or by right-clicking inside the Manage Styles pane and selecting New Style, you can access the Style Builder dialog and create new styles.

You can also create a new style based on an existing style. Suppose that you have a style defined for the p element and you want to create a style for the div element that builds on that style. If you right-click on the p element in the Manage Styles pane and select New Style Copy, the Style Builder dialog appears configured with all the settings for the p element, enabling you to create a new style based on those settings.

Using the Manage Styles Pane to Modify Styles

Modifying styles is effortless when you use the Manage Styles pane. You can right-click on any style and select Modify Style from the menu to display the Style Builder dialog, where you can make the desired modifications. If you prefer to edit the CSS code for the style, you can select Go To Code after right-clicking a style. Doing so opens the selected CSS code in Visual Web Developer. If the code exists in an external CSS file, Visual Web Developer opens the file if necessary and moves the insertion point to the selected style.

TIP | You can also go to the code that defines a style by double-clicking the style in the Manage Styles pane.

Another powerful feature of the Manage Styles pane is the capability to move a style definition from one location to another. In other words, you can easily drag and drop a style from an embedded style sheet to a linked style sheet or vice versa. Figure 17.15 shows an embedded style in the current page and styles in a linked style sheet. To move the embedded style to the styles.css file, simply drag the navSection style from under the Current Page section and drop it onto the Styles.css banner at the top of the Manage Styles pane.

FIGURE 17.15

You can easily move a style to another style sheet by dragging and dropping the style.

Checkpoint

Here's what you completed in this chapter:

- Created a CSS class that can be applied to a button in the website to improve its appearance.

In the next chapter, you'll learn how to apply styles to your web pages in Visual Web Developer.

CHAPTER 18

Applying CSS to Web Forms

IN THIS CHAPTER

Using the Apply Styles Pane

The Apply Styles pane is another feature that Visual Web Developer 2008 borrowed from Expression Web. The Apply Styles pane is similar to the Manage Styles pane, but its primary purpose is to apply CSS styles to page elements.

> TIP   You cannot drag and drop CSS classes and IDs in the Apply Styles pane as you can in the Manage Styles pane.

As shown in Figure 18.1, the Apply Styles pane uses the same visual representation for CSS styles that is used in the Manage Styles pane. Just as with the Manage Styles pane, the Apply Styles pane uses colored balls to indicate the style type, but the Apply Styles task pane also uses yellow balls to display inline styles.

FIGURE 18.1

The Apply Styles pane uses the same visual cues used by the Manage Styles pane.

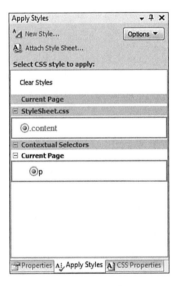

The Apply Styles pane displays only those styles that are relevant to the currently selected page element. Therefore, if a style is defined for the HTML a element, it is displayed in the Apply Styles pane only if a hyperlink or bookmark is selected on the current page.

The Apply Styles pane does not have a style preview section as the Manage Styles pane does. Instead, the name of the style is formatted according to the properties defined in the style. You can change the background color of that preview by clicking the Options button and then selecting Preview Background Color from the menu. This is useful if you use anything other than a CSS style to specify the background color of your page and you want to see what your styles will look like against that color.

To restore the preview background color to the default value of Automatic, click Options and select Preview Background Color. Clear the Value text box, as shown in Figure 18.2.

FIGURE 18.2

By clearing the Value text box, you can restore the background preview color to the default value of Automatic.

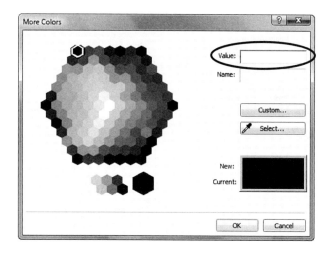

Applying a Style

To apply a style in the Apply Styles pane, select the desired page element and then click on the style in the Apply Styles pane. Alternatively, you can right-click on the style name in the Apply Styles pane and select Apply Style, or you can click the arrow at the right edge of the style and select Apply Style from the menu, as shown in Figure 18.3.

FIGURE 18.3

You can apply styles by clicking the arrow at the right edge of the style and selecting Apply Style from the menu.

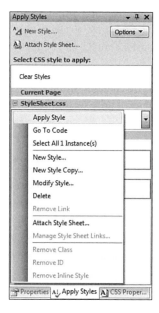

If the applied CSS style is a CSS class or ID, the Quick Tag Selector and the Block Selector display the name of the class or ID. Figure 18.4 shows the Quick Tag Selector and Block Selector of a p element after a CSS class named content is applied to the paragraph.

FIGURE 18.4

Both the Block Selector and the Quick Tag Selector display the name of CSS classes or IDs that are applied to page elements.

Block Selector

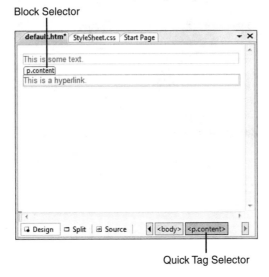

Quick Tag Selector

Removing a Previously Applied CSS Class, CSS ID, or Inline Style

In some cases, you may need to remove an existing style from a page element. For example, Figure 18.5 shows a <p> element surrounded by a <div> element. The style1 CSS class is applied to the <div> element and the style2 CSS class is applied to the <p> element. As you can see in the Apply Styles pane, the style1 class applied to the <div> uses the Arial font-family, but the paragraph is still using the Courier font-family applied by style2.

To force the paragraph to the font-family specified by the style1 CSS class, you can remove the style2 class assignment for the paragraph by clicking inside the paragraph, right-clicking the style2 class in the Apply Styles pane, and selecting Remove Class, as shown in Figure 18.6.

TIP

You can also remove a CSS ID by selecting Remove ID and an inline style by selecting Remove Inline Style.

NOTE

The other options that are available when right-clicking a style in the Apply Styles pane are identical to those that are available in the Manage Styles pane.

→ For more information on the Manage Styles pane, **see** "The Manage Styles Pane," **p. 255**.

FIGURE 18.5

A simple CSS example showing how a CSS class can override properties defined in a higher-level CSS class.

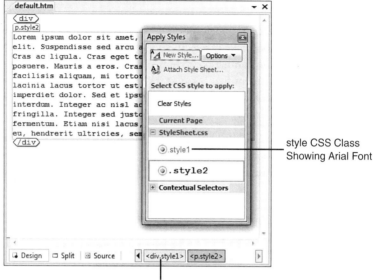

style CSS Class
Showing Arial Font

<div> Formatted with style1 CSS Class

FIGURE 18.6

Removing a CSS class assignment with the Apply Styles pane couldn't be easier.

Using the CSS Properties Pane

Visual Web Developer 2008's new CSS Properties pane (another feature borrowed from Expression Web) is a great way to examine how CSS styles affect a particular page element and also to apply styles to page elements.

Examining CSS Styles

As mentioned earlier, it's not uncommon to apply a style only to find that the properties defined by the style don't take effect. In almost all cases, a conflicting CSS style is at fault. In some cases, locating the conflicting style is easy. For example, the conflict shown previously in Figure 18.5 is easily identified because there are only a few styles. However, as your website grows in complexity, such conflicts become harder to isolate and tracking them down can be a frustrating exercise.

Figure 18.7 shows the CSS Properties pane with the paragraph shown previously in Figure 18.5 selected. CSS properties that are affected by applied CSS rules are shown in bolded blue type, and properties that are overridden by other rules are shown with a line drawn through them.

FIGURE 18.7

The CSS Properties pane is a powerful CSS feature that is new to Visual Web Developer 2008.

Location of Selected Style

Selected Style

Overridden Properties

> **TIP**
>
> If the location of the selected style is an external style sheet such as shown in Figure 18.7, you can click the name of the style sheet to open it in Visual Web Developer.

At the top of the CSS Properties pane, the applied CSS rules are displayed. The location of an applied rule can be an external style sheet or a style defined in the current page. To determine which, select the row for the applied style in which you're interested and the location of that style is displayed.

In Figure 18.7 (shown previously) the `style1` style is selected and the CSS Properties pane shows that this style is defined in `StyleSheet.css`. We also see that the `color`, `font-family`, and `font-size` properties are shown with a line through them, meaning they have been overridden by another CSS rule. To determine what rule is overriding the property, hover the mouse over the overridden property, as shown in Figure 18.8.

FIGURE 18.8
Determining which rule is overriding a particular CSS property couldn't be easier.

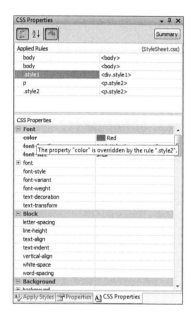

Perhaps the most effective way to determine how CSS styles are affecting a particular page element is to use the Summary view provided by the CSS Properties pane. By clicking the Summary button, you can quickly see which CSS properties are applied to an element and the source of each style. When the Summary button is pressed, as shown in Figure 18.9, only those properties that are impacted by applied CSS rules are displayed.

> **TIP**
> You can also right-click on a property and select Go To Code to view the CSS code for that property, just as you did with the Manage Styles and Apply Styles panes.

Applying CSS Styles

The CSS Properties pane is also a convenient way to apply CSS styles. Because it gives you a complete picture of CSS formatting from many different sources, it's often the most effective way to apply formatting. However, it's also important to use the CSS Properties pane to carefully examine your web pages after CSS changes are made because it's easy to override a property unintentionally.

FIGURE 18.9

The Summary view is an excellent way to understand how CSS rules are applied.

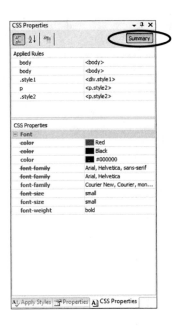

You can modify each CSS property displayed in the CSS Properties pane by entering a value in the column to the right of the property name. You can manually enter the value if desired, but it's often easier to click the arrow at the right edge of the property and select one of the valid values as shown in Figure 18.10.

FIGURE 18.10

The CSS Properties pane allows you to easily enter CSS property values directly.

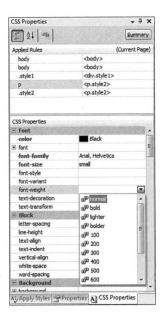

When modifying CSS properties in the CSS Properties pane, it's important to first select the CSS rule that you want to edit from the Applied Rules section of the CSS Properties task pane. After you've made a change to the CSS property, the CSS Properties task pane will give you an immediate indication as to whether or not the newly specified property is over-ridden by another rule. If the property name appears with a line through it after you make a change, it means that the property you just set is overridden by another rule, as shown previously in Figure 18.8.

Because Visual Web Developer allows you to combine the powerful features of the Manage Styles, Apply Styles, and CSS Properties panes, you now have more powerful control over CSS formatting than ever before.

Checkpoint

In this chapter, you learned how to use the powerful CSS features in Visual Web Developer to apply CSS styles to your web pages. In the next chapter, you'll learn how to go one step further by creating skins and themes for your ASP.NET web pages.

CHAPTER 19

Using ASP.NET Themes and Skins

IN THIS CHAPTER

Introduction to ASP.NET Themes

At this point in this book, you've learned two ways to create a consistent appearance for your website: master pages and CSS. In this chapter, we're going to look at yet another method of creating a website with a consistent appearance with ASP.NET themes.

ASP.NET themes were introduced in ASP.NET 2.0 and provide a means of easily controlling the appearance of ASP.NET pages. You can apply a theme to a page or to an entire web application. After a theme is applied to a site, ASP.NET takes care of formatting the page based on the formatting supplied by the theme.

Makeup of a Theme

An ASP.NET theme consists of one or more files called *skins*. A skin is a file that controls the appearance of specific ASP.NET controls. A theme can also contain traditional CSS files. CSS files are useful for controlling the appearance of page elements other than ASP.NET controls. For example, if you want a theme to control the format of regular HTML controls or HTML elements such as the `<body>` element, you need to include a CSS file to format them.

A theme can also contain other file types such as images. Some ASP.NET controls such as the TreeView control allow for images to be used when formatting the control. When those images are included in your theme, your theme can make use of them when formatting your controls.

When images are used in a theme, you should use a path that is relative to the theme's folder. For example, if the SummerBlue theme used images stored in `App_Themes\SummerBlue\images`, you would use the relative path `images\plus.gif` to refer to a GIF image in the `images` folder.

Global Themes and Page Themes

Two types of themes are available in an ASP.NET application: *global themes* and *page themes*. A global theme is available to all ASP.NET applications running on a web server, whereas a page theme is available only to the application containing the folder and files for the theme.

The files for a global theme are stored in the `Microsoft.NET\Framework\vX.X.XXXX\ASP.NETClientFiles\Themes` folder in the Windows folder. Inside the Themes folder is a folder for the theme containing all the files used by that theme. For example, if you are using a theme named CoolTheme, the location for that theme would likely be `c:\Windows\Microsoft.NET\Framework\v2.0.50727\ASP.NETClientFiles\Themes\CoolTheme`.

> **TIP** The `ASP.NETClientFiles` folder does not exist by default. You will have to create the folder and the `Themes` folder in it.

The files for a page theme are stored in a special ASP.NET folder located in the root folder of your website named `App_Themes`. Inside the `App_Themes` folder is another folder that contains the files for each theme. For example, the files for a theme named SummerBlue would be located in the `App_Themes\SummerBlue` folder in the website.

> **TIP** A page theme's name is determined by the name of the folder containing the files that make up the theme.

If you have a global theme and a page theme with the same name, settings applied by the global theme are not overridden by the page theme.

Skin Files

A skin file contains formatting code for ASP.NET controls that is just like the code contained within an ASP.NET web form. For example, the following line of code is a complete skin file that causes ASP.NET Label controls to appear with blue text:

```
<asp:Label runat="server" ForeColor="Blue" Text="Label"></asp:Label>
```

> **TIP** The code in a skin file is exactly like the code for a control that is added to a web form, except that the ID property is not specified in a skin file.

A skin file can contain control properties that define only the appearance of the control. Properties that control the behavior of a control are not valid in a skin file, and if you include such a property, ASP.NET generates an error message in the browser pointing out the problem so that you can correct it.

> **NOTE** There is no comprehensive list of properties that can be themed. If a property defines the appearance of a control, it's safe to assume it is a theme-able property. However, you should always test your theme carefully before using it on a live website.

The best way to fully understand themes is to create one. The next section shows you how to create a simple theme that can be used in the ASP.NET application you're creating.

Creating a Theme

The first step in creating a theme is to create the folder structure for the theme.

Creating the Folder Structure

You can create the App_Themes folder manually, but it's easier to create the folder in Visual Web Developer.

1. Open the web application in Visual Web Developer.
2. Right-click on the application name in Solution Explorer and select Add ASP.NET Folder, Theme as shown in Figure 19.1.

FIGURE 19.1

Visual Web Developer can create any of the special folders used by ASP.NET easily right within Solution Explorer.

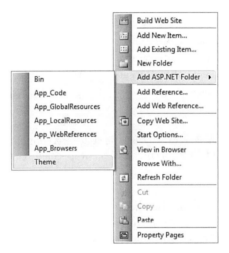

3. Visual Web Developer creates a new folder for your theme called Theme1. Change the name of the Theme1 folder to **CoolTheme**.

Solution Explorer should now appear like Figure 19.2.

Creating a Skin File

As mentioned previously, a skin file is used to format the appearance of ASP.NET controls. You can use any number of skin files for your theme. In other words, you can place all your skinning code in one skin file or you can use multiple skin files.

The easiest way to create a skin file is to use the user interface elements provided by Visual Web Developer to format the control you want to skin. You can then copy the code that Visual Web Developer creates and paste it into your skin file after making minor modifications to the code.

FIGURE 19.2

The folder structure for the CoolTheme theme as seen in Solution Explorer.

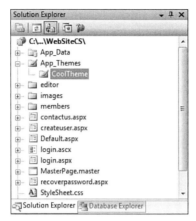

Because the theme you're creating will be applied to the contact form you created earlier in the book, the theme will need to format the appearance of the controls that appear on that page. The contact form contains the following controls:

- DropDownList
- Label
- TextBox
- RequiredFieldValidator
- RegularExpressionValidator

Some developers prefer to use one skin file for each control type or group controls into multiple skin files, but these steps use one skin file because there are only a few controls to skin:

1. Select the CoolTheme folder in the web application.
2. Select File, New File, and select Skin File.
3. Accept the default name of SkinFile.skin or change it to the name of your choice and click Add.

If you selected the CoolTheme folder in step 1, the new skin file is automatically added to your theme's folder. If you didn't select the CoolTheme folder before adding the new skin file, Visual Web Developer asks you whether you want to add the skin file to the App_Themes folder, as shown in Figure 19.3.

FIGURE 19.3

If a theme folder is not selected when a skin file is added, Visual Web Developer prompts you to add the file to the App_Themes folder.

If you select Yes in the dialog shown in Figure 19.3, Visual Web Developer creates a new theme folder that uses the name of your skin file and places the new skin file into that folder. In that case, you'll need to move the skin file into the CoolTheme folder manually.

Generating Formatting Code for Controls

Now that you've got a new skin file, you can generate some formatting code to use in the skin file. You do that by adding each control type to a blank page, formatting them the way you want them formatted by the CoolTheme theme, and then transferring that formatting code into the skin file.

1. Create a new ASP.NET web form, using any name you choose.

> **TIP** The web form is only a temporary file so that you can generate the formatting code for the controls, so the name of the file doesn't matter. However, you may want to take note of the file name so that you can delete the file after you've created your skin.

2. Switch to Design view and add a new DropDownList, Label, TextBox, RequiredFieldValidator, and RegularExpressionValidator to the page. Your page should now look similar to the one shown in Figure 19.4.

FIGURE 19.4
This temporary web form will be used to apply the formatting for your theme's skin file.

3. Select the DropDownList control you just added.
4. If the Properties window is not visible, press F4 to display it.
5. Change the BackColor property to **#99CCFF**.

6. Click the plus sign next to Font in the Properties window.

7. Change the `Name` property to **Arial**.

8. Change the `Size` property to **Small**.

9. Select the Label control you added in step 2.

10. Click the plus sign next to the `Font` property.

11. Change the `Name` property to **Arial** and the `Size` property to **Small**.

12. Change the `ForeColor` property to **#006699**.

13. Select the TextBox control you added in step 2 and set the following properties:

    - Change the `BorderColor` property to **Black**.
    - Change the `BorderStyle` property to **Solid**.
    - Change the `BorderWidth` property to **1px**.
    - Change the `ForeColor` property to **#006699**.

14. Select each of the validation controls that remain and configure the Font property by setting the Name property to **Arial** and the Size property to **Small**.

Your web form should now look like the one shown in Figure 19.5.

FIGURE 19.5

The completed temporary web form is now formatted as desired for the theme.

Transferring Formatting Code to the Skin File

By making property changes to the appearance of these controls in the Properties window, you've generated the code for your skin file. All that's necessary at this point is to move the code into the skin file and do a small amount of cleanup.

1. Switch to Source view.

2. Select all the server control code and copy it to the Windows clipboard.

CAUTION
> Make sure you select only the server control code and not any of the HTML tags such as <div> or <br> tags; otherwise, you'll get an error when ASP.NET tries to apply your skin.

3. Open the skin file you created earlier and paste the code you copied in step 2 into the skin file at the bottom of the file.

TIP
> The skin file contains a comment block at the top that is delimited by the <% and %> characters. You should paste the code into the skin file at the bottom of the file after the comment block.

The last step in the process is to make a few code modifications:

1. Remove the ID property from each control.
2. Remove the Text property from the Label control.
3. Remove the ErrorMessage property from the RequiredFieldValidator control and the RegularExpressionValidator control.

After you make these code modifications, your skin file should contain the code that you see in Listing 19.1.

Listing 19.1   The Skin File

```
<asp:DropDownList runat="server" BackColor="#99CCFF"
    Font-Names="Arial" Font-Size="Small"></asp:DropDownList>
<asp:Label runat="server" Font-Names="Arial" Font-Size="Small"
    ForeColor="#006699"></asp:Label>
<asp:TextBox runat="server" BorderColor="Black" BorderStyle="Solid"
    BorderWidth="1px" Font-Names="Arial" Font-Size="Small"
    ForeColor="#006699"></asp:TextBox>
<asp:RequiredFieldValidator runat="server" Font-Names="Arial"
    Font-Size="Small"></asp:RequiredFieldValidator>
<asp:RegularExpressionValidator runat="server" Font-Names="Arial"
    Font-Size="Small"></asp:RegularExpressionValidator>
```

Save your skin file and your theme is now ready to be applied to one or more of your pages. To complete the process, you learn in the next section how to apply the theme to the con-tactus.aspx web form.

Applying a Theme

To apply your theme to the `contactus.aspx` web form, you need to change the `Theme` property for the page. To do so, follow these steps:

1. Open the `contactus.aspx` web form and switch to Design view.
2. Click the Object Name drop-down at the top of the Properties window and select DOCUMENT, as shown in Figure 19.6.

FIGURE 19.6

The Object Name drop-down is a convenient way of selecting the open document and making changes to page properties.

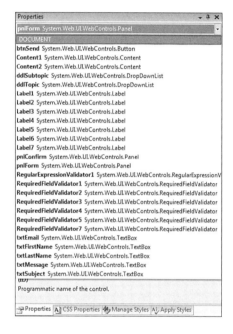

3. Change the `Theme` property of the page to **CoolTheme** as shown in Figure 19.7.

> **TIP**
>
> If you set the `EnableTheming` property of any control to `false`, that control will never be affected by a theme's formatting.

The `contactus.aspx` web form now uses the CoolTheme theme and the skin file that you created earlier. However, you may have noticed that the appearance of the page has not changed in Visual Web Developer's designer. Formatting applied by themes is not visible in the designer. To view a page as formatted by a theme, you must preview the page in your browser because ASP.NET has to process the page to apply the theme.

FIGURE 19.7

The ThemeName property of the page configures the theme that is used for the page.

Preview the contactus.aspx page in your browser now and you should see the theme applied to the page, as shown in Figure 19.8.

FIGURE 19.8

The Contact Us page with the CoolTheme theme applied.

NOTE | The steps for applying the page theme are no different for global themes.

Default Skins and Named Skins

Within a particular theme, there are two possible types of skin files: default skins (such as the skin created for the CoolTheme theme) and named skins. The difference between the two is the SkinID property.

When you created the skin file earlier in this chapter, you created a default skin. The default skin is automatically applied to any page that uses the CoolTheme theme. A named skin is just like a default skin, but a named skin uses the SkinID property in the skin file and on the web form to specify a particular skin.

The CoolTheme theme that you created earlier formats a TextBox control with a thin, black border and a white background. Suppose that you decide to create your skin so that TextBox controls that require data entry are formatted with a light blue background and a black border. A named skin is the perfect solution for this.

These next steps show you how to create a named skin called RequiredText that you can apply to the TextBox control.

Open the skin file you created earlier in this chapter and add the following code to the bottom of the file:

```
<asp:TextBox runat="server" BorderColor="Black"
    BorderStyle="Solid" BorderWidth="1px" Font-Names="Arial" Font-Size="Small"
    ForeColor="#006699" BackColor="#CCFFFF" SkinID="RequiredText">
</asp:TextBox>
```

Notice that you added the BackColor property to specify the light blue color and the SkinID property to specify the name of the named skin.

After you create the code for the named skin, you can apply it to a specific TextBox control by setting the SkinID property of a TextBox control that uses CoolTheme to **CoolTheme**.

Open the contactus.aspx page and select the txtSubject TextBox control. Locate the SkinID property in the Behavior section of the Properties window and set the SkinID property to **RequiredText**, as shown in Figure 19.9.

Go ahead and set the SkinID property of all the other TextBox controls to **RequiredText**.

A named skin enables you to create one or more skins that can be assigned to individual server controls, as opposed to a skin that is assigned to all controls of a specific type. You can create any number of named skins so that you can customize the appearance of your website exactly as you wish.

FIGURE 19.9

After a name skin has been created, you can assign it to a control in the drop-down in the Properties window, as shown here.

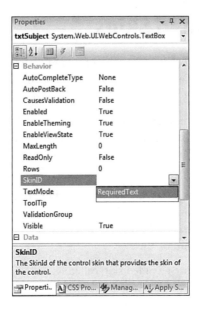

Using a Theme with CSS Files

As I mentioned earlier, you can use a CSS file in your theme to format page elements other than ASP.NET controls. However, you may also have CSS files outside your theme, such as the StyleSheet.css file that is applied to the web application created here. In those cases, if you apply a theme as you did in this chapter, the theme overrides any formatting in the CSS file.

If you want to ensure that any CSS files in your website are always applied, you can apply the theme by using the StyleSheetTheme property instead of the Theme property. When you use the StyleSheetTheme property, ASP.NET does not allow the theme to override a local CSS file.

When you use the StyleSheetTheme property, the value is specified just as when using the Theme property. In other words, to use the CoolTheme theme by using the StyleSheetTheme property, you would set the property value to **CoolTheme**.

NOTE   In this case, there aren't any CSS styles that interfere with the CoolTheme theme, so it doesn't matter whether you use the StyleSheetTheme property or the Theme property.

Checkpoint

As you've seen in this chapter, ASP.NET themes are another powerful tool to making sure that a website has a consistent appearance. Here's what you completed in this chapter:

- Created a default skin for the application.
- Created a named skin for required text controls.

As you progress through the next few chapters, you'll learn how to connect the ASP.NET application to a database.

PART VII

Data Access with ASP.NET

CHAPTER 20

ASP.NET Data Controls

IN THIS CHAPTER

Accessing Data in ASP.NET 3.5

Database access used to be a feature only for large, enterprise websites. That is certainly no longer the case. On today's Web, databases are used for many purposes, from displaying data to users to storing page content for content management systems. Suffice it to say that if you are going to learn to build websites for today's Internet, you need to understand how to use data access.

Fortunately, data access is no longer just the realm of programmers. Microsoft has put substantial effort into making ASP.NET a robust tool for creating data access with minimal code, and often with no code at all. Much of this is possible because of the inclusion of data providers and new controls to facilitate easy connectivity to databases.

> **NOTE**   If you want to read the technical details of the data providers available in the .NET Framework 3.5, read msdn2.microsoft.com/en-us/library/a6cd7c08(vs.90).aspx.

In many cases, displaying data in ASP.NET is as easy as dropping a data source control onto your page, pointing it to your database, and then dropping a data control onto your page and pointing it to the data source control. In fact, as you'll see later in this chapter, ASP.NET enables you to create very powerful data-enabled interfaces without writing any code at all.

The first step in making a website data-enabled is to add a data source control to the page. Let's look at the data source controls available to ASP.NET and how they are configured.

ASP.NET Data Source Controls

A data source control is a special control in ASP.NET that provides powerful capabilities to your page when connecting it to a database. Data source controls are not visible when a page is browsed in a browser. Their sole purpose is to make a connection and communicate with a database.

Visual Web Developer 2008 comes with six different data source controls. The data source controls available are as follows:

- SqlDataSource
- AccessDataSource
- LinqDataSource
- ObjectDataSource

- XmlDataSource
- SiteMapDataSource

SqlDataSource Control

The SqlDataSource control is used to connect to any database that is supported by the .NET Framework data engine. You can use the SqlDataSource control to connect to SQL Server databases, Microsoft Access databases, Oracle databases, and many other database types. However, the SqlDataSource control is optimized for use with SQL Server.

> **NOTE** By saying that the control is optimized for SQL Server, I don't mean to imply that it's not a robust solution for other database types. I simply mean that if you are using a SQL Server database, you should use the SqlDataSource control if possible.

To use a SqlDataSource control, simply drag it from the Data section of the toolbox to your web form. When you drop it onto a page, the Common SqlDataSource Tasks popup appears, as shown in Figure 20.1. To configure the data source, click the Configure Data Source link.

FIGURE 20.1

The Common SqlDataSource Tasks popup provides a link to make configuring the data source a simple task.

→ For more on configuring a data source control, **see** "Configuring a Data Source Control," **p. 289**.

AccessDataSource Control

The AccessDataSource control provides simple data connectivity to an Access database located within your web application. The AccessDataSource control does not allow you to specify a password, so as mentioned earlier, if your database requires a password, you need to use the SqlDataSource control to connect to it.

LinqDataSource Control

The LinqDataSource control is the only data source control that is new to Visual Web Developer 2008. LINQ is a new technology available in the .NET Framework 3.5. LINQ stands for Language Integrated Queries. Essentially, it's a powerful method of querying data directly using VB or C#, rather than using the traditional Structured Query Language (SQL) queries.

LINQ is an advanced programming topic that we don't cover in this book, but you can read plenty of information on using LINQ at msdn2.microsoft.com/en-us/netframework/ aa904594.aspx. Another great website for LINQ information is Hooked on LINQ, available at www.hookedonlinq.com.

ObjectDataSource Control

The ObjectDataSource control allows you to use a *business object* to query a data source. A business object can be a DLL or a class that is defined in the App_Code folder of your website.

→ For more information on the App_Code folder and other special ASP.NET folders, **see** "Special Folders in an ASP.NET Application," **p. 116**.

Using a business object to query data enables you to build a multi-tiered application that provides a layer of abstraction between your ASP.NET application and your data source so that the ASP.NET code is not reliant on the structure of the data source being used. For example, if you are not using a business object and you choose to move your data from a SQL Server database into an XML file, you have to make changes to any ASP.NET page that accesses that data to avoid breaking your website. However, if you use a business object, you have to only change the code in the business object so that it queries against the new data source and all pages that use that business object will continue to work normally.

For more information on the ObjectDataSource control, see msdn2.microsoft.com/ en-us/library/9a4kyhcx(vs.90).aspx.

XmlDataSource Control

The XmlDataSource control connects your ASP.NET application to XML data. You can also configure an XML transform and specify an XPath query so that only certain data is returned.

XML files used by the XmlDataSource control should be located in your web application.

For more information on the XmlDataSource control, see msdn2.microsoft.com/en-us/library/51ew3eby.aspx.

SiteMapDataSource Control

The SiteMapDataSource is used with the ASP.NET navigation controls. By default, the SiteMapDataSource automatically uses the `web.sitemap` XML file in the root of your web application.

→ For more information on the web.sitemap file and using the ASP.NET navigation controls, **see** "Creating a Sitemap File," **p. 156**.

Configuring a Data Source Control

You configure data source controls by using the Configure Data Source link on the Common Tasks popup that is displayed for the control.

> TIP   The SiteMapDataSource is the only data source control that does not provide a link for configuration. It is configured automatically for navigation controls.

Let's have a look at how the SqlDataSource control is configured because it will give you a good idea of how all data source controls are configured. When you click the Configure Data Source link, you are presented with the Configure Data Source dialog, as shown in Figure 20.2.

If you have a connection string already defined in your `web.config` file, it will be available in the drop-down. If you don't already have a connection string configured, you can click the New Connection String button to create a connection to your database.

→ For more information on the web.config file, **see** "ASP.NET Configuration Files," **p. 66**.

FIGURE 20.2
The Configure Data
Source dialog makes
configuring a data
source control as
simple as clicking a
mouse.

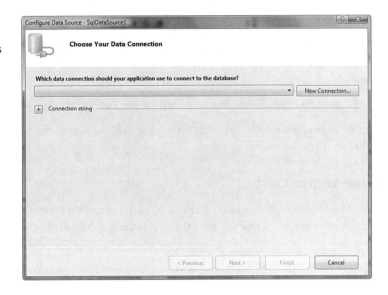

When you click the New Connection String button, the Choose Data Source dialog is displayed and you are asked to select the type of database to which you are connecting. When you make a choice of database type, you can also choose from a list of data providers applicable to the selected database type, as shown in Figure 20.3.

FIGURE 20.3
The data provider
drop-down is popu-
lated with a list of
valid data providers
automatically.

TIP

The best choice of providers is going to be the one that is chosen by default.
It's best not to change it unless you know that you need to for some reason.

When you click Continue in the Choose Data Source dialog, as shown previously in Figure 20.3, the Add Connection dialog is displayed. The appearance and options available in this dialog depend upon which type of database you are configuring and which provider you chose. Figure 20.4 shows the Add Connection dialog for a SQL Server connection, whereas Figure 20.5 shows the Add Connection for an Access database.

FIGURE 20.4

The Add Connection dialog, when connecting to a SQL Server dialog, contains options specific to that type of connection.

FIGURE 20.5

The Add Connection dialog, when connecting to an Access database, enables you to select the database file to which you'd like to connect.

TIP

You might be wondering why you'd use the SqlDataSource to connect to Access instead of the AccessDataSource. The primary reason is because the SqlDataSource enables you to specify a username and password and the AccessDataSource does not.

If your Access database is password protected, you'll want to use the SqlDataSource control to connect to it instead of the AccessDataSource.

After you enter all the necessary information for connecting to your preferred database, click the Next button in the SqlDataSource control to move to the next step. If you created a new connection string for your database, you are asked whether you want to save the connection string as shown in Figure 20.6. If you choose to save the connection string, Visual Web Developer saves it into the web.config file for your application.

FIGURE 20.6

You can save your connection string so that it can be used easily on other pages or for other data source controls.

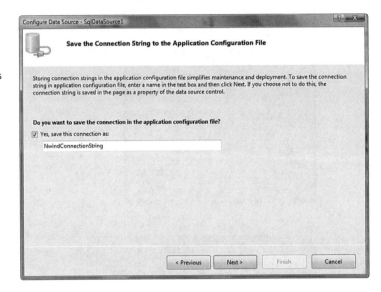

When you click Next to go to the next step, the true power of the data source control becomes apparent. As shown in Figure 20.7, the next step enables you to create a query against your database or to specify a stored procedure that has already been created.

FIGURE 20.7

The true power of the data source controls lies in the capability to create complex queries from within a user-friendly user interface.

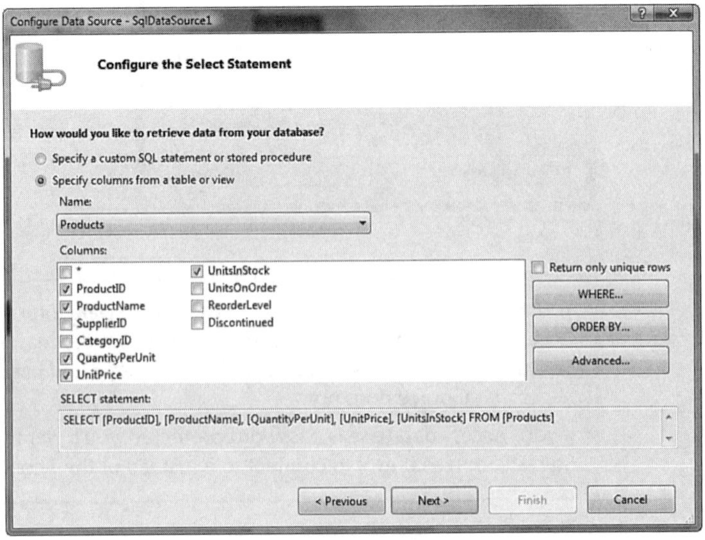

> **N O T E** We go into the details of how to build queries and retrieve data using the data source controls in Chapter 21, "Displaying Data from a Database."

The final step of the configuration enables you to test your query. You can now click Finish to close the dialog and you are ready to use one of the ASP.NET data controls to display the data that the data source control provides.

Other ASP.NET Data Controls

The data source controls are responsible for getting data to and from a data source. The other data controls are responsible for displaying data and for presenting a user interface that allows you to modify that data.

Seven data controls are available to you in Visual Web Developer 2008:

- GridView
- DataList
- DetailsView
- FormView
- ListView (new to Visual Web Developer 2008)
- Repeater
- DataPager (new to Visual Web Developer 2008)

This chapter provides an overview of each of these controls. In Chapter 21, you'll find details on how you can display data from a database with the ASP.NET data controls.

GridView Control

The GridView control (shown in Figure 20.8) is arguably the most powerful and feature-rich data control available in Visual Web Developer. At its most basic level, it displays data from a data source in tabular form. However, it is extremely flexible and provides powerful features such as paging and sorting without requiring you to write code.

To configure the GridView control, use the Common GridView Tasks pop-up, which becomes available when you click the Smart Tag button. From the Common GridView Tasks pop-up, you can enable paging, sorting, and many other features of the GridView control, as shown in Figure 20.9.

FIGURE 20.8

The GridView is an
extremely powerful
and flexible control.

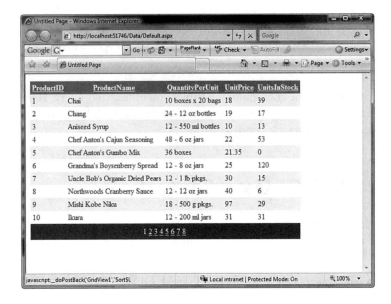

FIGURE 20.9

Configuring the
GridView control is
made easy by the
Common GridView
Tasks popup.

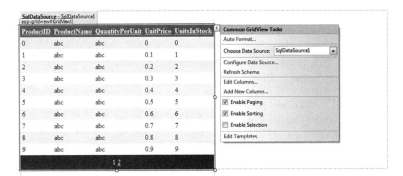

DataList Control

The DataList control (shown in Figure 20.10) displays a list of data returned by the data
source control connected to it.

Unlike the GridView control, the DataList control displays all the data in each cell. If you
want to change the format of the data being displayed, you can use templates that are provided by the DataList control.

NOTE   Chapter 21 discusses the use of templates in data controls as well.

FIGURE 20.10
The DataList displays
each record from the
data source in a list
format.

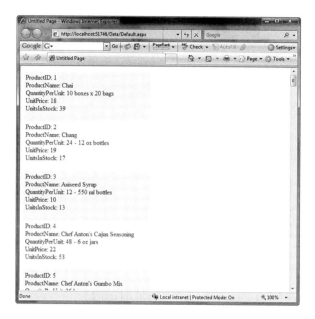

FIGURE 20.10
The DataList displays each record from the data source in a list format.

DetailsView Control

The DetailsView is designed to display a single record. Although you can certainly use a DetailsView alone on a page, it's best used in conjunction with another data source control such as the GridView control.

Figure 20.11 shows a DetailsView control showing the details of a record selected in a GridView control. Notice that the GridView control displays only a couple of fields. The DetailsView is used to display the details of the record that is selected in the GridView.

NOTE   Chapter 21 shows you how to create a page like the one shown in Figure 20.11.

FormView Control

By default, the FormView control appears to be similar to the DetailsView control. However, the FormView control can be configured easily so that you can use it to add new records to a database.

Figure 20.12 shows a FormView using the default settings. Figure 20.13 shows the same control after it has been switched to a template that is used for editing records.

FIGURE 20.11

The DetailsView is the perfect choice when creating a master/details interface.

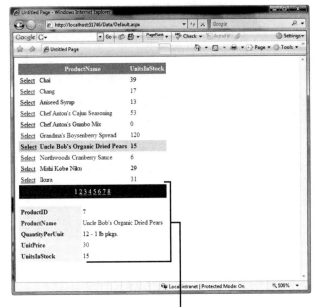

DetailsView Control

FIGURE 20.12

The FormView with the default settings looks just like the DetailsView.

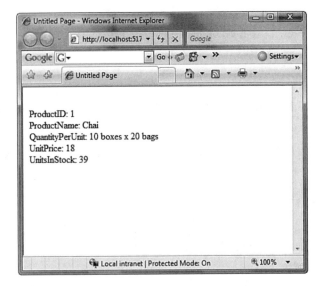

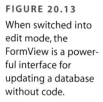

FIGURE 20.13

When switched into edit mode, the FormView is a powerful interface for updating a database without code.

➔ For more information on using the FormView control to insert items into a database and edit existing records, **see** Chapter 22, "Adding, Editing, and Deleting Records."

ListView Control

The ListView control is an extremely flexible control that enables you to configure the way you want your data displayed. Although not as simple to use as some of the other data controls, the ListView does make it possible to design your data presentation exactly the way you wish. It also can provide editing, insertion, and other advanced data features.

You'll see more on the ListView control in the next chapter.

Repeater Control

The Repeater control does not render its own interface. Instead, it is specifically designed to loop through all the records returned by a data source. When using the Repeater control, you format the layout of a single returned record, using other ASP.NET controls or HTML code, and then the Repeater control takes care of looping through the records.

DataPager Control

The DataPager control is new to Visual Web Developer 2008. The DataPager provides paging capabilities to the ListView control. The DataPager control displays the interface to page through records (such as a Next Record button, Previous Record button, and so on) and it controls the paging for you. You can also control the number of records that are displayed on each page.

NOTE | In the current version of Visual Web Developer, the DataPager control works only with the ListView control.

As you've seen, Visual Web Developer 2008 contains several powerful and flexible controls to make it easy to connect your website to a database. However, these controls are not the only controls that can be bound to data from a data source. Chapter 21 looks at the process of actually displaying data from a database, and it will become clear just how easy it is to connect any ASP.NET control to a data source control.

Checkpoint

In this chapter, you learned the basics of the data controls available to you in Visual Web Developer 2008. You've also learned how you can use combinations of these data controls to add powerful interactivity to your website. In the next chapter, you'll have an opportunity to use what you've learned to create data-enabled pages.

CHAPTER 21

Displaying Data from a Database

IN THIS CHAPTER

Configuring the Data Source

The preceding chapter presented an overview of data access in ASP.NET. In this chapter, you'll put that knowledge into practice and create a new web form that will be used to display data from a Microsoft Access database.

> **NOTE** To work through the examples in this chapter, download the sample project for this chapter at the Que Publishing website at www.quepublishing.com.

The data we'll be working with is located in the `products.mdb` Access database located in the App_Data folder of the sample web application. If you don't want to use the sample database, you can use your own database, but you'll need to make the necessary changes yourself to accommodate your specific database.

Adding an AccessDataSource Control

The first things you need to do are add a new web form and add a new AccessDataSource control to the page.

1. Open the web application in Visual Web Developer.
2. Right-click on the `members` folder and select Add New Item.
3. Add a new web form and name it **productlist.aspx**.
4. Check the Select Master Page check box and select the `MasterPage.master` master page, and then click Add.
5. Switch to Design view, if necessary.
6. Drag an AccessDataSource control from the Data section of the toolbox to the mainContent Content control on the page.

Your page should now look like the one shown in Figure 21.1.

> **TIP** If you're using your own database and that database requires a password, use a SqlDataSource control instead.

Configuring the AccessDataSource Control

As I mentioned in the last chapter, the data source control is responsible for connecting to the database and retrieving data from it. It then feeds that data to the data controls that present the data to your users.

FIGURE 21.1

The AccessDataSource control inside the mainContent Content control.

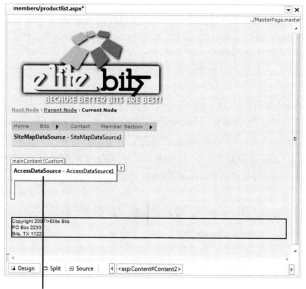

The AccessDataSource Control

To configure the AccessDataSource control, complete the following steps:

1. Click the Smart Tag button to display the Common AccessDataSource Tasks pop-up as shown in Figure 21.2.

FIGURE 21.2

The Common AccessDataSource Tasks pop-up provides a convenient link for configuring the data source.

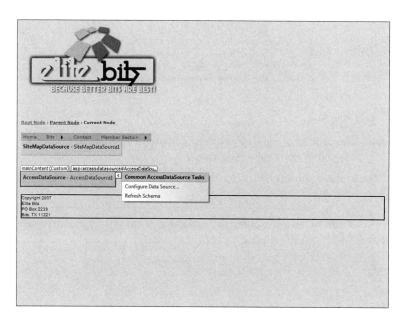

CAUTION | Make sure that you don't click the Smart Tag button for the Content control instead of the AccessDataSource control. If in doubt, select the AccessDataSource control first, using the Quick Tag Selector.

2. Click the Configure Data Source link.

3. Click the Browse button and browse to the products.mdb file located in the App_Data folder of the web application.

4. Select the products.mdb file and click OK to select it. The Configure Data Source dialog should now look like the one shown in Figure 21.3.

FIGURE 21.3

Notice that the path to the Access database is entered relative to the root of the web application.

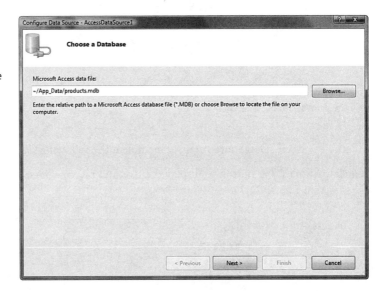

5. Click Next.

6. The products.mdb database has only one table, named Products, and it's already selected in the Name drop-down.

7. In the Columns list, check the * check box, as shown in Figure 21.4.

TIP | In a SQL query, the * character means that all columns will be returned.

FIGURE 21.4

The Configure Data Source dialog is a powerful mechanism for configuring a database query.

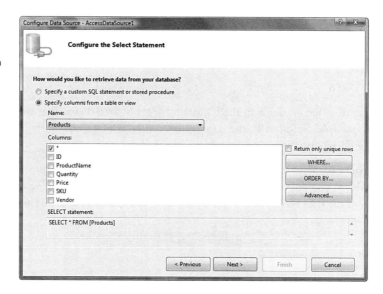

8. Click the Advanced button.

9. Make sure that the Generate INSERT, UPDATE, and DELETE Statements check box is unchecked, as shown in Figure 21.5.

FIGURE 21.5

The Generate INSERT, UPDATE, and DELETE Statements check box causes Visual Web Developer to generate code to support editing a database. You'll add that functionality in the next chapter.

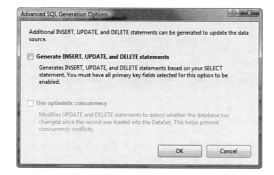

NOTE   The Use Optimistic Concurrency check box shown in Figure 21.5 causes Visual Web Developer to add additional code to your page to prevent multiple users from overwriting each other's modifications to data. We won't use that feature in this example.

10. Click OK.

11. Click Next, and then click Finish to finish the configuration of the data source.

Ordering Data

More options are available in the Configure Data Source dialog that we're not going to use in this example. Specifically, the data source can be configured to retrieve data in a particular order and can also filter data for you.

To retrieve the data in a specific order, click the Order By button shown previously in Figure 21.4. When you do, you are presented with a dialog where you can select the order in which you want the data retrieved from the database, as shown in Figure 21.6.

FIGURE 21.6
Configuring the order in which items are retrieved from a database is made easy with the Add ORDER BY Clause.

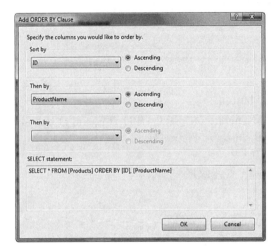

Filtering Data

You can also specify the option of retrieving only those records that match specific criteria. To specify these options, click the WHERE button shown previously in Figure 21.4. When you do, you are presented with the Add WHERE Clause dialog, as shown in Figure 21.7.

The Column drop-down contains all the columns in the data source. The Operator drop-down contains a list of common operators to use in your filter. The Source drop-down adds a considerable degree of flexibility to your query. The following options are available:

- **None**—Enables you to specify an explicit value.
- **Control**—Enables you to use a value from an ASP.NET server control.
- **Cookie**—Reads the value of an HTTP cookie and uses that value for filtering the data.
- **Form**—Reads the value from a form field for filtering data.
- **Profile**—Reads a specific value from the user profile for use in the query.

FIGURE 21.7

The Add WHERE Clause dialog is a convenient means of filtering data returned from a database.

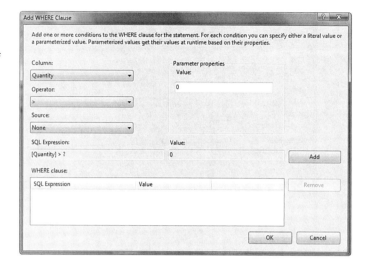

N O T E   For more information on ASP.NET profiles, read my book *Special Edition Using Microsoft Expression Web* from Que Publishing.

- **QueryString**—Reads a `querystring` value from a URL and uses it to filter the data.
- **Session**—Reads a Session variable and uses that value for filtering the data.

Suppose you have a TextBox control named `txtProductName` on your web form and you would like to allow users to enter a product name or part of a product name into that TextBox and retrieve all products that match that input. To add that functionality, you would complete the following steps after clicking the WHERE button shown previously in Figure 21.4.

1. Select ProductName in the Column drop-down.
2. Select the desired operator in the Operator drop-down. The LIKE operator would be appropriate for this example.
3. Select Control in the Source drop-down.
4. Select the ID of the TextBox in the Control ID drop-down, as shown in Figure 21.8.
5. Click Add to add the new clause.

After a WHERE clause has been added, you cannot edit it. If you want to modify the clause, you must remove it and add a new WHERE clause using the desired settings.

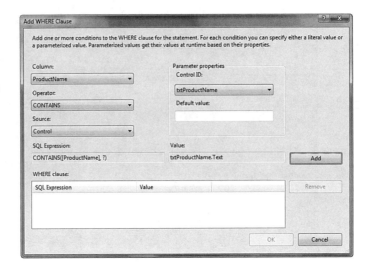

NOTE We use a WHERE clause later in this chapter.

The AccessDataSource is now configured to connect to the products.mdb database and to retrieve data, insert new records, update existing records, and delete existing records. As you'll see as you progress through the rest of this chapter and through the next chapter, literally nothing else is required to provide powerful data access. The data source control provides all the power for you.

Using Data Controls to Display Data

The first step in adding data controls for data access is deciding what kind of functionality you want and how you want it to be presented. In this case, the object is to display a list of products in a grid. We want to create an interface that allows users to see a small amount of data inside that grid. By selecting a row, the user can view details on the selected record.

NOTE This chapter focuses entirely on displaying data. Chapter 22 covers inserting, updating, and deleting data.

Adding a GridView Control

Because we want to display data in a tabular form, the GridView is the perfect choice. The GridView also adds many advanced features that can be used for building an interface.

NOTE | If you used previous versions of ASP.NET, you might be familiar with the DataGrid control. The GridView control is the next generation of the DataGrid control.

To add a GridView control to the `productlist.aspx` web form, follow these steps:

1. Open the `productlist.aspx` web form, if necessary, and switch to Design view.
2. Add a new GridView control to the page from the Data section of the toolbox.

TIP | The location of the GridView control relative to the AccessDataSource control doesn't matter. When the page is browsed, the AccessDataSource control will not be visible.

3. If the Common GridView Tasks pop-up is not visible, click the Smart Tag button on the GridView to display it.
4. In the Choose Data Source drop-down of the Common GridView Tasks pop-up, select AccessDataSource1, as shown in Figure 21.9.

FIGURE 21.9
To connect the GridView to the AccessDataSource control, select the AccessDataSource control in the Choose Data Source drop-down.

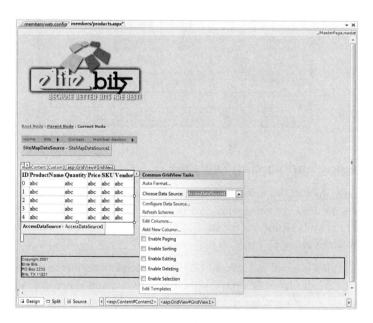

Believe it or not, what you've just done is all that's necessary to retrieve and display data from the database. To test the page, browse to the `productlist.aspx` page by selecting File, View in Browser.

| **TIP** | In Chapter 14, the `members` folder was configured so that only authenticated users can access it. Therefore, you have to enter a username and password to view the `productlist.aspx` web page. If you'd prefer to test the page without bothering with a password, simply rename the `web.config` file to `web.config.temp` while testing. Just remember to name it back! |

When you browse to the `productlist.aspx` page, you'll see a page like the one shown in Figure 21.10.

FIGURE 21.10

The GridView control, displaying data from the Access database.

Adding Paging and Sorting Features

By default, the GridView displays all the records in the database on one page. The `products.mdb` database contains only 12 records at this point, so displaying all the records on one page is not cumbersome. As the database grows, however, it can become unwieldy to display all the records at once.

The GridView control has the capability to implement paging so that only a certain number of records are displayed at a time. If the database contains more than the number of records specified, an interface is added to the page that enables users to move between pages of data to display all the records.

| **NOTE** | By default, the GridView control displays 10 records at a time when paging is enabled. |

To enable paging on the `productlist.aspx` web form, follow these steps:

1. Click the Smart Tag button on the GridView control to display the Common GridView Tasks pop-up.

2. In the Common GridView Tasks pop-up, check the Enable Paging check box, as shown in Figure 21.11.

3. Save the page.

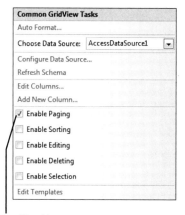

Enable Paging Checkbox

When you enabled paging, the GridView control displays links to each page at the bottom of the control. You can move between pages by clicking the link to the desired page. However, by using the Properties window, you can change the settings of the GridView control's pager. For example, if you'd like to provide a Next button and Previous button for paging instead of numerals, you can change the Mode property of the GridView control's Pager settings, as shown in Figure 21.12.

When sorting is enabled, a user can sort the GridView by clicking on a column header. Enabling sorting for the GridView control is just as easy as enabling paging. To enable sorting, check the Enable Sorting check box in the Common GridView Tasks pop-up.

When paging is enabled, each column header is displayed as a hyperlink. Clicking the column header sorts the GridView by that column. Clicking the same column header again reverses the sort order.

FIGURE 21.12

Many properties can be configured for the GridView control's pager.

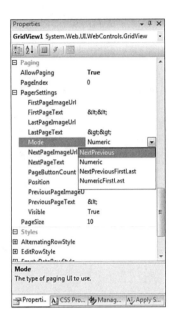

Creating a Master/Detail View

The Products database used for this example contains only a few columns. In a real-world environment, a database might have dozens of columns, too many to display in a GridView control. In such situations, a master/detail view enables you to display only a few columns in your grid. When a row in the grid is selected, the details of that record are displayed.

To create a master/detail view for the productlist.aspx web form, you add a new control below the GridView control to display the detailed view. You then need to configure the GridView control so that it displays only a few columns instead of all the columns in the database.

Configuring the GridView Control

Let's configure the GridView control so that only a few columns are displayed instead of all of them.

1. Click the Edit Columns link in the Common GridView Tasks pop-up, as shown previously in Figure 21.11.
2. In the Selected Fields section of the Fields dialog, select the ID field.
3. Change the Visible property of the ID field to **False**, as shown in Figure 21.13.
4. Select the Quantity field in the Selected Fields section and click the red X button to delete that field.
5. Delete the SKU and Vendor fields so that only the ID, Product Name, and Price fields are selected, as shown in Figure 21.14.

FIGURE 21.13
The ID field is made
invisible so that it
isn't displayed.

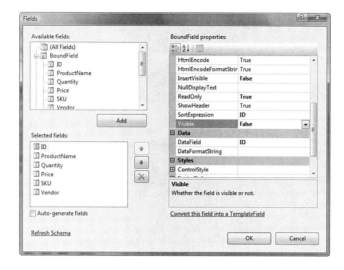

FIGURE 21.14
Only the ID, Product
Name, and Price
fields are utilized by
the GridView control.

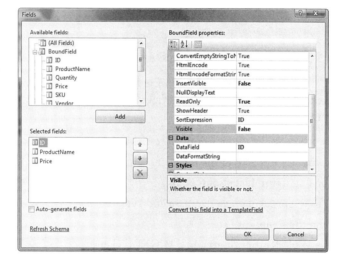

NOTE   In a real-world application, you would likely want to configure the data source
control to retrieve data for only the fields you want to display. However, for this
example, I wanted to show you how you can edit the columns and fields of the
control if desired.

The last step of configuring the GridView control is to configure it to allow users to select a
particular row. To do that, check the Enable Selection check box in the Common GridView
Tasks pop-up shown previously in Figure 21.11. Checking the Enable Selection check box
adds a new column to the GridView control that contains a link to allow for selection of a
specific row, as shown in Figure 21.15.

FIGURE 21.15

Checking the Enable
Selection check box
adds a column of
links that enable a
user to select a row
in the GridView.

Adding a Data Source Control for the DetailsView

To display the details of a selected record in the DetailsView control, you need to add a new
data source control that is configured to retrieve only the record that is selected in the
GridView control.

1. Add a new AccessDataSource control to the web form.

2. Change the ID property of the new data source control to **DetailsDataSource**.

3. Click the Configure Data Source link.

4. Browse to the products.mdb database and click Next.

5. Select * in the Columns list.

6. Click the WHERE button to add a WHERE clause.

7. Select ID in the Column drop-down.

8. Select = in the Operator drop-down.

9. Select Control in the Source drop-down.

10. Select GridView1 in the Control ID drop-down. The Add WHERE Clause dialog
    should now look like the one shown in Figure 21.16.

11. Click the Add button to add the new WHERE clause.

12. Click OK, then click Next and Finish to complete the configuration of the data source.

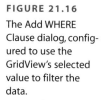

FIGURE 21.16
The Add WHERE Clause dialog, configured to use the GridView's selected value to filter the data.

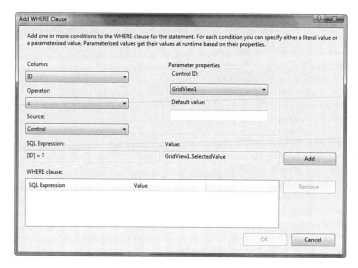

Adding and Configuring the DetailsView Control

The DetailsView control is specifically designed for displaying details on a specific record in a database. Let's add a DetailsView control to the `productlist.aspx` web form to display details of the row that is selected in the GridView control.

1. Select the GridView control and then press the right arrow key on your keyboard to move the selection point to the right of the GridView.

2. Press Enter twice to add two new rows.

3. Add a new DetailsView from the Data section of the tool box.

4. In the Common DetailsView Tasks pop-up, select the `DetailsDataSource` control from the Select Data Source drop-down.

Your page should now appear like the one shown in Figure 21.17.

You can now test the `productlist.aspx` page by viewing it in your browser. Click the Select link in the GridView to display details on the selected record in the DetailsView control. You can also click the link to move between pages of data. Because of the ASP.NET data source control, it was possible to add all this functionality to your page without writing a single line of code.

> **TIP**
> If you would like to configure the page so that it doesn't scroll back to the top of the page each time you click a link, see the sidebar that follows, titled "Maintaining Scroll Position."

FIGURE 21.17

The DetailsView control is the perfect interface for displaying details on a selected record.

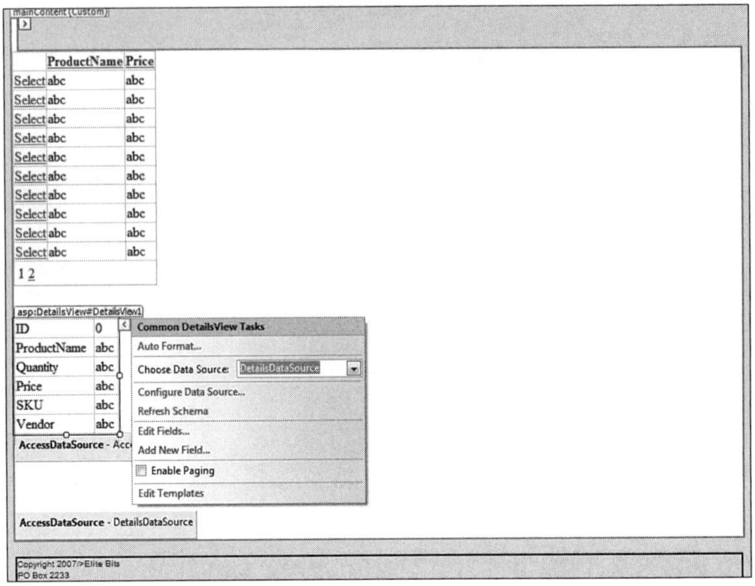

Maintaining Scroll Position

If your screen size doesn't allow the entire page to fit without scrolling down, you'll find that the page scrolls back to the top each time you select a new record. ASP.NET provides a `MaintainScrollPosition` property for the page that forces the page to remain at the current scroll position when you select a row.

To set the `MaintainScrollPosition` property for the page, switch to Source view and locate the @ Page directive at the top of the page. Click just inside the closing bracket at the end of the @ Page directive and add the following property setting just before the closing bracket:

```
MaintainScrollPosition="true"
```

After this change is made, selecting a record in the GridView will no longer cause the page to scroll back to the top.

Checkpoint

Here's what you completed in this chapter:

- Created a user interface for browsing products in the Products database.
- Configured a master/detail view for the Products database.

In the next chapter, you'll create the interface for inserting new records, editing existing records, and deleting records from the database.

CHAPTER 22

Adding, Editing, and Deleting Records

Creating the Editing Interface

In the previous chapter, you saw how to create an interface for retrieving records from a database. This chapter shows you how to create a similar interface, but you will add the abilities to add, edit, and delete records with the FormView control.

Adding and Configuring a GridView Control

In Chapter 13 we created an ASP.NET role called Editors and gave that role the capability to browse files in the editor folder of the web application. In this chapter you add a web form to the editor folder that will provide the interface for editing the database.

Right-click on the editor folder and select Add New Item. Add a new web form named **editdata.aspx** and attach it to the MasterPage.master master page. Add an AccessDataSource control to the page and change the ID property of the AccessDataSource to **GridDataSource**. Configure the GridDataSource control by following these steps:

1. Click the Configure Data Source link in the Common AccessDataSource Tasks pop-up.
2. Click Browse and select the products.mdb database and click Next.
3. In the Columns list, select the ID, ProductName, and Price fields.
4. Click Next and then Finish to complete the configuration of the data source.

Now add a new GridView control. Choose GridDataSource for the GridView's data source. Edit the columns of the GridView and make set the ID field's Visible property to **False**, just as you did in Chapter 21.

The final step in configuring the GridView control is to check the Enable Paging, Enable Sorting, and Enable Selection check boxes in the Common GridView Tasks pop-up, as shown in Figure 22.1.

FIGURE 22.1

Enable paging, sorting, and selection support for the GridView using the Common GridView Tasks pop-up as shown here.

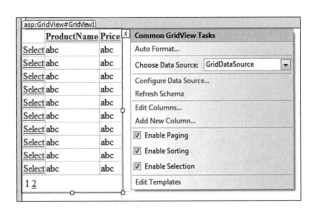

If you check the Enable Editing check box shown previously in Figure 22.1, the GridView displays a link to allow for inline editing of data, as shown in Figure 22.2.

FIGURE 22.2
The GridView supports inline editing of database records.

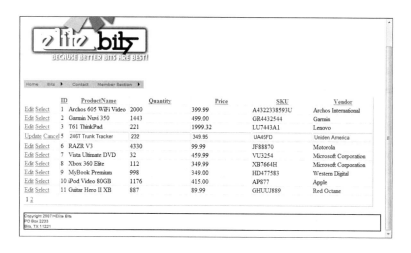

No code is required to add editing capabilities to the GridView (simply checking the Enable Editing checkbox is sufficient,) but it makes sense to allow for editing in the GridView itself only if you are displaying all fields of the database. In this case, we're displaying only a couple of fields, so we'll use a FormView control to edit the data.

➔ For additional detail on the GridView Control, **see** "Using Data Controls to Display Data," **p. 306**.

Adding and Configuring a New Data Source

Just as you did in Chapter 21, you need to add a separate data source control to provide data connectivity for the control used to display details of the selected record.

Add a new AccessDataSource control to the page and change the ID property to `EditDataSource`. Click the Configure Data Source link and configure it by following these steps:

1. Click Browse and select the `products.mdb` database. Click Next.
2. Select the `*` check box in the Columns list.
3. Click the WHERE button to add a new WHERE clause.
4. Select `ID` in the Column drop-down, = in the Operator drop-down, and `Control` in the Source drop-down.
5. Select `GridView1` from the Control ID drop-down and click Add to add the new WHERE clause.
6. Click OK.

7. Click the Advanced button and check the Generate INSERT, UPDATE, and DELETE Statements check box.

8. Click OK, and then click Next and Finish to complete the configuration of the data source control.

Add a new FormView control to the page under the GridView control you added earlier and choose the EditDataSource from the Choose Data Source drop-down in the Common FormView Tasks pop-up.

Adding and Configuring the FormView Control

As I mentioned in Chapter 20, the FormView control is used to display a single database record and allows for the editing, insertion, or deleting of records. A FormView control is similar to the DetailsView control you used in Chapter 21, but a FormView uses templates to work with the data and is more suitable for adding an interface for adding, editing, and deleting data.

→ For more detail on using templates, **see** "Modifying Templates," **p. 323**.

Notice that the FormView control you added earlier automatically provides a link for editing the record, deleting the record, or for adding a new record, as shown in Figure 22.3.

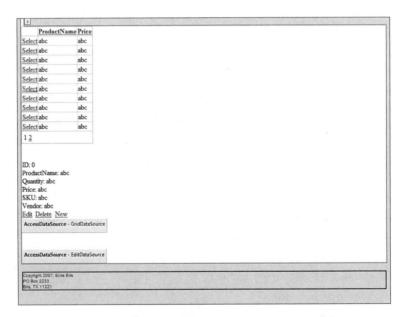

FIGURE 22.3

The FormView control provides links for editing, deleting, and adding new records to your database.

The interface for editing the database is now complete. Let's move on to completing the steps necessary to make the editor fully functional.

Configuring the Functionality of the Editor

The functionality of the editor is already almost finished. However, a few small modifications are still needed to make it all work correctly.

Adding New Records

When the `editdata.aspx` page is displayed and a product is selected, the FormView control is displayed, as shown in Figure 22.4.

FIGURE 22.4
The FormView control is displayed when a product is selected.

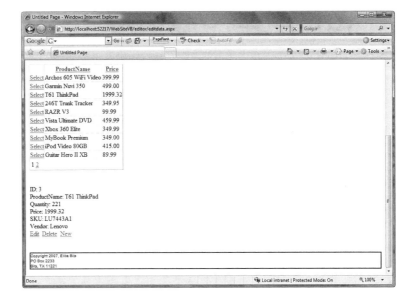

By clicking the New link at the bottom of the FormView control, you can display the interface for adding a new record, as shown in Figure 22.5.

However, if you attempt to add a new record, you'll see an error in your browser as shown in Figure 22.6.

This error is displayed because the code that Visual Web Developer generated for the INSERT statement that supports adding records expects you to supply a value for the ID field in the database. However, the value for the ID field is automatically generated by Microsoft Access when new records are added and is not being provided by the user. Therefore, for you to add new records to the database, you need to make a small modification so that the data source doesn't expect you to provide a value for the ID.

FIGURE 22.5

By clicking the New link on the FormView control, you can easily add a new record to the database as shown here.

FIGURE 22.6

Adding a new record at this point generates an error message.

Switch to Source view for the editdata.aspx page and locate the code for the EditDataSource control. A few lines below the opening tag for the control, you'll see the following code:

```
InsertCommand="INSERT INTO [Products] ([ID], [ProductName], [Quantity],
➡[Price], [SKU], [Vendor]) VALUES (?, ?, ?, ?, ?, ?)"
```

You need to remove the ID field from the code here. You also need to remove the first question mark because it represents the value that is supplied for the ID. Change the code to the following:

```
InsertCommand="INSERT INTO [Products] ([ProductName], [Quantity], [Price],
➡[SKU], [Vendor]) VALUES (?, ?, ?, ?, ?)"
```

The last step is to remove the ID from the parameters that Visual Web Developer added for the InsertCommand you just edited. If you scroll down several lines in the page, you'll see code that looks like the following:

```
<InsertParameters>
            <asp:parameter Name="ID" Type="Int32" />
            <asp:parameter Name="ProductName" Type="String" />
            <asp:parameter Name="Quantity" Type="String" />
            <asp:parameter Name="Price" Type="String" />
            <asp:parameter Name="SKU" Type="String" />
            <asp:parameter Name="Vendor" Type="String" />
</InsertParameters>
```

To fix this section of code, remove the following line:

```
<asp:parameter Name="ID" Type="Int32" />
```

The capability to add new records to the database is almost finished. If you browse to the editdata.aspx page and add a new record now, the record will be added to the database, but the GridView will not be updated with the new data. To fix that problem, you need to add one line of server-side code that refreshes the GridView control when a new item is added.

1. Switch to Design view and select the FormView control.
2. Click the Events button in the Properties window.
3. Double-click on the ItemInserted event.
4. Add the following code, based on the language you are using:

C#

```
GridView1.DataBind();
```

Visual Basic

```
GridView1.DataBind()
```

You can now save the page and preview it in your browser. When you add a new record to the database, it is added to the GridView control as well.

TIP — New records are added to the last page of the GridView control.

Right now, a user has to select a record before a new record can be added. It would be more user-friendly to allow a user to click a link to add a new record without selecting a record first. You can do that easily by using the ASP.NET LinkButton control.

Complete the following steps to add a link to add a new record:

1. Add a new ASP.NET LinkButton control above the existing GridView control.
2. Change the ID property of the LinkButton control to `lnkAddRecord`.
3. Change the Text property of the LinkButton control to `Add New Record`.
4. With the LinkButton selected, click the Events button on the Properties window.
5. Double-click on the Click event and add the following code, based on the language you are using:

C#

```
FormView1.ChangeMode(FormViewMode.Insert);
```

Visual Basic

```
FormView1.ChangeMode(FormViewMode.Insert)
```

Now save the page and preview it in your browser. By clicking the Add New Record link as shown in Figure 22.7, you can add a new record easily, without having to select an existing record first.

FIGURE 22.7

Adding a link to add a new record makes the interface more user-friendly.

Editing Records

The capability to edit records is fully functional at this point, but to force the GridView control to update with the new data, you need to add a single line of server-side code to the `ItemUpdated` event of the FormView control.

Select the FormView control and click the Events button in the Properties window. Double-click on the `ItemUpdated` event and add the following code, based on the language you are using:

C#

```
GridView1.DataBind();
```

Visual Basic

```
GridView1.DataBind()
```

The capability to edit existing data is now complete. Browse to the `editdata.aspx` page and select a record. Click the Edit link, make a change, and then click Update. The GridView and the database will be updated with your new data.

Deleting Records

The capability to delete records is also complete. However, as you may have surmised, you need to add the code necessary to update the GridView control.

Select the FormView control, click the Events button, and double-click on the `ItemDeleted` event. Add the same code that you've added to the other events to force the GridView to update when items are deleted.

You have now completed the interface for adding new records, updating records, and deleting records. Now let's look at modifying templates so that you can make the interface of the FormView control a bit more polished.

Modifying Templates

The FormView control is a *templated control*. That means that it uses a series of views called *templates* that can be modified in the Visual Web Developer designer.

To edit the templates of the FormView control, click the Edit Templates link on the Common FormView Tasks pop-up, as shown in Figure 22.8.

FIGURE 22.8

The Edit Templates link provides an interface for modifying the templates of the FormView control.

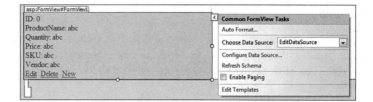

When you change into Edit Templates mode, the Common FormView Tasks pop-up displays a drop-down with a list of the templates available for the control, as shown in Figure 22.9. When you select a template, the template is displayed in the interface for the control so that you can modify it if you wish.

FIGURE 22.9

A list of templates is available in Edit Templates mode so that you can modify a template if you wish.

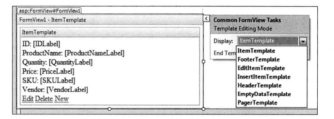

The following templates are available for the FormView control:

- **ItemTemplate**—Displayed when an item is displayed in a non-editable format.
- **FooterTemplate**—Displayed at the bottom of the FormView control. The FooterTemplate is empty by default.
- **EditItemTemplate**—Displayed when the FormView control is in edit mode.
- **InsertItemTemplate**—Displayed when the FormView is in insert mode.
- **HeaderTemplate**—Displayed at the top of the FormView control. The HeaderTemplate is empty by default.
- **EmptyDataTemplate**—Displayed when the FormView control is not data-bound to any data. This is the template that is displayed when the editdata.aspx page is first loaded before a record is selected.
- **PagerTemplate**—Displayed when paging is enabled for the FormView control.

Let's make a small modification to the InsertItemTemplate and the EmptyDataTemplate.

Modifying the InsertItemTemplate

Click the Edit Templates link on the FormView's Common FormView Tasks pop-up, as shown previously in Figure 22.8. Select the InsertItemTemplate from the list of templates, as shown previously in Figure 22.9. When you do, the FormView changes into Insert mode, as shown in Figure 22.10.

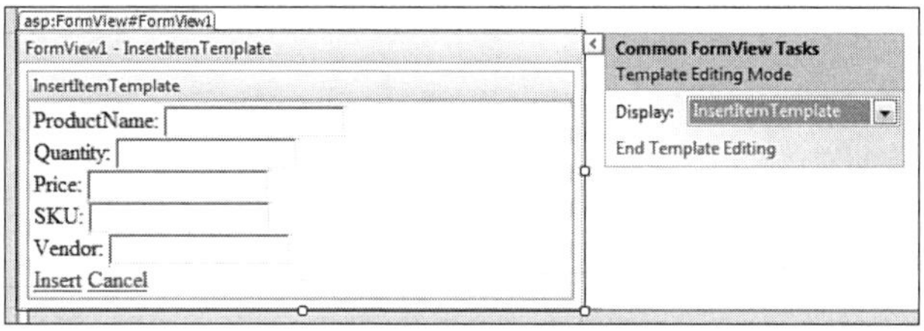

FIGURE 22.10

This FormView control is in Insert mode so that you can edit the template that is displayed when new records are added.

Add a line break between each field name and TextBox control in the InsertItemTemplate, as shown in Figure 22.11. This small modification gives the FormView control's appearance a sense of polish that it didn't have otherwise when new records are added.

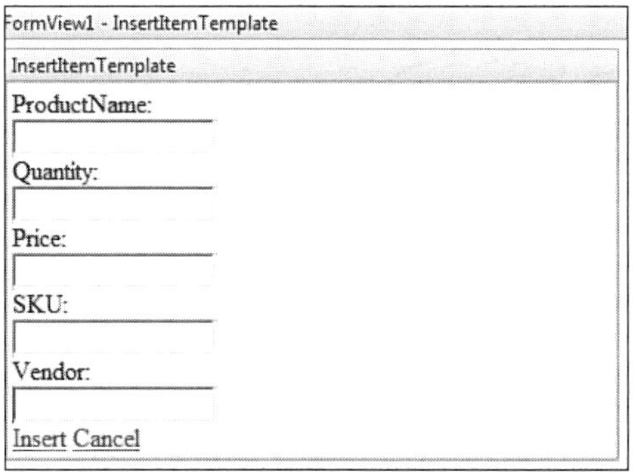

FIGURE 22.11

The FormView now has a more polished appearance when new records are added.

Modifying the EmptyDataTemplate

By default, the EmptyDataTemplate is empty. Therefore, when you first browse the `editdata.aspx` page, the FormView control does not display anything. It would be a good idea to modify that template so that an informational message is displayed to the user.

Select the EmptyDataTemplate in the Display drop-down. Click inside the EmptyDataTemplate and enter the following text:

```
Click Add New Record to add a new record.
Select a record to view details, edit, or delete a record.
```

When you browse the `editdata.aspx` page after making that change, the user is greeted with an informational message, as shown in Figure 22.12.

FIGURE 22.12

An informational message in the EmptyDataTemplate gives the user has a better idea of how to use the interface you've provided.

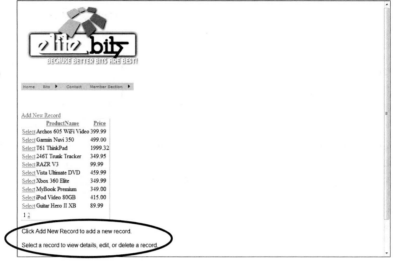

Templated controls are extremely flexible and powerful. For example, suppose that the fictional Elite Bits company has an approved list of vendors and you want to prevent users adding new records that specify a vendor who is not on the approved list. By editing the InsertItemTemplate and replacing the TextBox with a DropDownList containing approved vendors, you can easily enforce such a constraint.

Checkpoint

Here is what you completed in this chapter:

- Built an interface for adding new records, editing existing records, and deleting records.
- Configured the templates in the FormView control to provide a more user-friendly and attractive interface.

In the next couple of chapters, you'll learn how to send email from an ASP.NET application and you'll complete the functionality of the contact form you began earlier.

PART VIII

Sending Email with ASP.NET

CHAPTER 23

Configuring ASP.NET for Email

IN THIS CHAPTER

How ASP.NET Sends Mail

One of the most common uses of forms in a website is to send email. Sending email from a website used to be a complex and difficult task, but as with so many other tasks that used to be complex, ASP.NET makes sending email easy.

In this chapter you'll see two different classes from the .NET Framework used to send email with ASP.NET; the `System.Net.SmtpClient` class and the `System.Net.MailMessage` class.

The `System.Net.SmtpClient` Class

The `SmtpClient` class facilitates the sending of email with the *Simple Mail Transfer Protocol* or *SMTP*. The `SmtpClient` class is used to connect your ASP.NET application to the network (either the Internet or another network) and to authenticate you (if necessary) to the SMTP mail server.

We will use a few properties of the `SmtpClient` class to connect to the SMTP server on the network:

- **`Host` Property**—The `Host` property is used to specify the name of the SMTP server to which you are connecting.

- **`Port` Property**—Every connection on a network takes place over a specific channel on the network called a *port*. SMTP communication takes place on port 25 by default. The `Port` property defaults to a value of 25, but if your SMTP server requires a different port, you can specify that by using the `Port` property.

> **TIP**
>
> It's uncommon for an SMTP server to not use port 25. Ask your network administrator, ISP, or hosting company if you're not sure what port your SMTP server uses.

- **`Credentials` Property**—Most SMTP servers require that you provide a username and password or otherwise authenticate yourself before you can send email.

    Some SMTP servers (usually on corporate networks) allow you to use the credentials of the account running your ASP.NET code. In those cases, you can specify to use the default credentials, but in this web application, we'll specify a username and password.

The `System.Net.MailMessage` Class

The `MailMessage` class (as you've likely guessed) represents the actual message that is sent. The following list shows some of the properties of the `MailMessage` class, all of which should be self-explanatory:

- **To**—The destination email address(es) for the message.
- **From**—The email address of the sender.
- **Cc**—The email address(es) that appear on the CC line.
- **Bcc**—The email address(es) that appear on the BCC line.
- **Subject**—The email's subject.
- **Attachments**—A list of file attachments included with the email.
- **IsBodyHtml**—A Boolean property that specifies whether or not the Body property uses HTML code.
- **Body**—The body of the email being sent. This is the actual text of the email message.

After you set the properties of the MailMessage class, you call the Send method and the SmtpClient class is used to send the message.

> **NOTE** In the next chapter, we'll write the code necessary to send an email from the contact form created earlier.

Modifying the Configuration File for Email

In a real-world ASP.NET application, you may be sending email from many pages in your application. If the SMTP properties (such as server name, username, password, and so on) change, it's not efficient to have to make changes on each page that sends email.

Fortunately, many of the properties of the SmtpClient class can be specified in the configuration file for your ASP.NET application. If you specify properties in the configuration file, you have to modify only the configuration file if any of those properties change, and all pages that send email will automatically use the new settings.

> **TIP** If you specify a setting in your server-side code that's already been specified in your configuration file, the setting that you specify in code overrides the setting in the configuration file.

> **NOTE** If you added the email configuration settings to your web.config file in Chapter 14, you can skip doing it now. Otherwise, you should add these settings into your web.config now.

Adding Email Configuration to the `web.config` **File**

Mail configuration is specified in the `<system.net>` section of the `web.config` file. The `web.config` file doesn't contain a `<system.net>` section by default, so you need to add one.

Open the web application and then open the `web.config` file in Visual Web Developer. Add the following code to the `web.config` file directly before the opening `<system.web>` element:

```
<system.net>
    <mailSettings>
        <smtp>
            <network host="smtp.yourServer.com"
                     password="yourPassword"
                     userName="yourUsername" />
        </smtp>
    </mailSettings>
</system.net>
```

> **TIP**
>
> The settings you specify for your SMTP server are often the same settings you use in your email client for the outgoing mail server for your domain. Your hosting company probably has instructions for setting up email clients on their website that you can use to find settings for your configuration file.

Using the Web Site Administration Tool

You can also use the Web Site Administration Tool to configure your SMTP settings. The Web Site Administration Tool enables you to add and edit SMTP settings while minimizing the possibility of errors due to incorrect configuration or typographical errors.

→ For more information on using the Web Site Administration Tool, **see** "The Website Administration Tool," **p. 68**.

> **TIP**
>
> When using the Web Site Administration Tool to configure SMTP settings, all entries are optional. If you don't provide a value for a required property in the configuration file, you need to provide it in your ASP.NET server-side code.

To use the Web Site Administration Tool to configure your SMTP settings, follow these steps:

1. Open your website and click the ASP.NET Configuration button at the top of the Solution Explorer window, as shown in Figure 23.1.

FIGURE 23.1

The ASP.NET Configuration button in Solution Explorer is a quick way to access the Web Site Administration Tool.

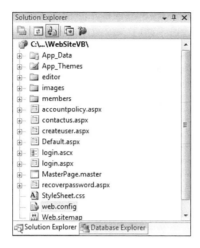

2. Click the Application tab or the Application Configuration link in the Web Site Administration Tool.

3. Click the Configure SMTP Email Settings link on the Application page of the Web Site Administration Tool.

4. Enter your SMTP server name, as shown in Figure 23.2.

FIGURE 23.2

SMTP configuration can be modified on the Application tab of the Web Site Administration Tool.

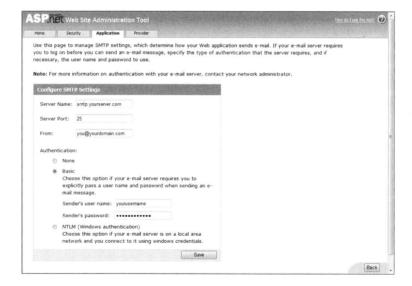

5. Enter the port if necessary. In most cases, the default value of 25 should not be changed.

6. Enter an email address in the From text box if desired. The email address you enter here will show up as the sender of the email that ASP.NET sends.

7. Select an authentication method. Choose None if your SMTP server doesn't require authentication. Choose Basic if your SMTP server requires authentication that differs from the credentials of the account that your ASP.NET code is using. Choose NTLM if you want to use the credentials of the account running your ASP.NET code.

> **NOTE** You can use impersonation to change the account used to run ASP.NET code. However, that topic is outside the scope of this book.
>
> For detailed information on implementing impersonation in an ASP.NET application, see support.microsoft.com/kb/306158.

8. Click Save to save the configuration settings to the web.config file in your application.

After you click Save, the Web Site Administration Tool automatically updates your web.config file with the changes, and they take effect immediately.

> **TIP** For details on what happens when you save settings to the web.config file, see the sidebar What Happens When a Configuration File is Saved.

What Happens When a Configuration File Is Saved

Every ASP.NET application runs inside a special area set aside in memory called an *application domain*. The purpose of the application domain is to provide isolation between different ASP.NET applications. The application domain ensures that one ASP.NET application doesn't access protected areas of another ASP.NET application.

When an application domain starts up, ASP.NET reads the information in the configuration file to set up the application domain. It then begins monitoring certain folders and files within the application for any changes. If a change is detected, ASP.NET shuts down the application domain and restarts it again so that any changes will take effect.

When you make a modification to the application's web.config file (whether by directly modifying the file or by modifying it indirectly with a tool such as the Web Site Administration Tool), ASP.NET immediately recycles the application pool so that the new configuration applies immediately to the application.

Checkpoint

In this chapter, you learned about how ASP.NET sends email and configured the SMTP settings for your website. You are now ready to write the ASP.NET server-side code necessary to send the email. You'll do that in the next chapter.

CHAPTER 24

Sending Form Results to Email

IN THIS CHAPTER

Adding Server-Side Code to Send Email

After making the configuration entries in the last chapter, the ASP.NET application is configured to send email. In this chapter, you're going to write code that sends an email when a user submits the contact form created in Chapter 15.

Reviewing the Contact Form

It's been a while since you last worked with the contact form, so here's a quick review of the controls that exist in it. Table 24.1 lists each control and the data that each control supplies to the email you'll be sending.

Table 24.1   Controls in the Contact Form

Control ID	Purpose of Control
ddlTopic	Contains either Products or Services based upon the user's choice.
ddlSubtopic	Contains the product name or service name.
txtSubject	Contains the subject of the email.
txtFirstName	Contains the user's first name.
txtLastName	Contains the user's last name.
txtEmail	Contains the user's email address.
txtMessage	Contains the text of the user's message.

Adding the Code

To add the code that sends an email to the Page_Load event of the contact page, open the contact page. Right-click anywhere inside the Content control in the contactus.aspx page and select View Code, as shown in Figure 24.1.

When the server-side code for the page is displayed, you'll see the code that you added in Chapter 15, as follows:

Existing C# Code

```
if (IsPostBack)
{
    pnlForm.Visible = false;
    pnlConfirm.Visible = true;
}
```

Existing Visual Basic Code

```
If IsPostBack Then
    pnlForm.Visible = False
    pnlConfirm.Visible = True
End If
```

FIGURE 24.1

Right-click on the page and select View Code to access the server-side code for the Contact page.

To send email when the contact form is submitted, you need to add some new server-side code immediately after the first line of code that was added in Chapter 15.

Adding C# Code

If you're using C#, first add the following code to the top of the code file:

```
using System.Net.Mail;
using System.Text;
```

Adding these using statements to your code makes it easier to add the rest of the code. Add the new code before the existing two lines in the Page_Load event. After adding the new code, the code in your Page_Load event should look like the code shown in Listing 24.1. (Line numbers are provided for reference only.)

Listing 24.1   C# Code to Send Email

```
1   SmtpClient sc = new SmtpClient();
2   StringBuilder sb = new StringBuilder();
3   MailMessage msg = null;
4
5   sb.Append("Email from: " + txtFirstName.Text + " "
    ➥+ txtLastName.Text + "\n");
6   sb.Append("Reference : " + ddlSubtopic.SelectedItem.Text + "\n");
7   sb.Append("Message    : " + txtMessage.Text + "\n");
8
9   msg = new MailMessage(txtEmail.Text, "you@yourdomain.com", txtSubject.Text,
    ➥sb.ToString());
10  sc.Send(msg);
11  msg.Dispose();
12  pnlForm.Visible = false;
13  pnlConfirm.Visible = true;
```

Adding Visual Basic Code

If you're using Visual Basic, add the following code to the top of the code file.

```
Imports System.Net.Mail
Imports System.Text
```

Now add the code to send the email so that the code in your Page_Load event looks like the code shown in Listing 24.2. (Line numbers were added for reference only.)

Listing 24.2   Visual Basic Code to Send Email

```
1   Dim sc As SmtpClient = New SmtpClient()
2   Dim sb As StringBuilder = New StringBuilder()
3   Dim msg As MailMessage = Nothing
4
5   sb.Append("Email from: " + txtFirstName.Text + " " + txtLastName.Text
    ➥+ vbCrLf)
6   sb.Append("Reference : " + ddlSubtopic.SelectedItem.Text + vbCrLf)
7   sb.Append("Message   : " + txtMessage.Text + vbCrLf)

8   msg = New MailMessage(txtEmail.Text, "yourEmail@domain.com",
    ➥txtSubject.Text, sb.ToString())
9
10  sc.Send(msg)
11  msg.Dispose()
12  pnlForm.Visible = False
13  pnlConfirm.Visible = True
```

Explaining the Code

Line 1 creates a new SmtpClient object to be used to send the email. Notice that the code doesn't explicitly set any properties of the SmtpClient object that you create because all the properties are configured in the web.config file.

Line 2 creates a StringBuilder object that is used to build the message body. The StringBuilder is a specialized class in the .NET Framework that is specifically designed for creating a long string by appending two or more smaller strings together. The StringBuilder is used because it's much more efficient in its memory usage than just appending regular strings together.

Line 3 creates a variable called msg and specifies that the variable will eventually hold an instance of the MailMessage class. This new variable is set to null in C# and Nothing in Visual Basic to avoid warnings when the website is executed.

Lines 5 through line 7 are used to build the body of the message. Notice that the body contains information obtained from the user, such as the first and last name, the final item that was selected in the ddlSubtopic drop-down, and the message that was entered by the user.

Line 8 creates a new `MailMessage` object and assigns it to the `msg` variable created in line 3. When the `MailMessage` is created, several properties of the `MailMessage` are specified. Values for these properties are specified inside the parenthesis in line 8. The first value (`txtEmail.Text`) sets the `From` property; the second (your email address) specifies the email address that is to receive the email; the third (`txtSubject.Text`) specifies the subject of the email; and the fourth specifies the body, using the `StringBuilder` object created on line 2.

Line 10 sends the email by calling the Send method for the `SmtpClient` class. After the email has been sent, line 11 calls the Dispose method on the `SmtpClient` class. The Dispose method cleans up any resources that the `SmtpClient` class used when sending the mail message.

> **NOTE** If you save the page, preview it in your browser, and submit the form at this point, you'll get an error because you haven't yet written the code that populates the ddlSubtopic drop-down. That portion of the application is finished in Chapter 25, "Creating and Testing an ASP.NET Web Service."

Sending HTML Emails

The code that you've just added to the `contactus.aspx` page sends a plain text email. However, there may be times when you might want to send an HTML email. For example, if you want your email to contain hyperlinks or images, you'll need to use HTML.

An HTML email is one that uses HTML markup for the message body. However, to successfully send an HTML email, you must configure the `MailMessage` object so that it will understand the HTML code. You do that by using the `IsBodyHtml` property. The code that follows demonstrates how to send an email when using HTML:

```
StringBuilder sb = new StringBuilder();
SmtpClient sc = new SmtpClient();
MailMessage msg = new MailMessage(txtEmail.Text, "jim@jimcobooks.com");
msg.Subject = "HTML Email Message";
sb.Append("<h1>Mail Message</h1><p>This is an HTML message.</p>");
sb.Append("<p>Check out <a href=\"http://www.jimcobooks.com\">my website</a>.
➥</p>");
msg.Body = sb.ToString();
msg.IsBodyHtml = true;
sc.Send(msg);
```

> **TIP** When using HTML to send emails, keep in mind that the recipient of the email should have an email client that is capable of understanding HTML messages. Otherwise, the recipient will not see the intended formatting.

Sending Emails with Attachments

Allowing a user to include an attachment with an email can be extremely convenient. For example, suppose you are a software developer and your customer has generated a log of errors they are encountering with your product. By creating your contact form to allow for attachments, you give the user the option of sending the log along with the information they fill out in the form.

The ASP.NET FileUpload control renders an HTML file input control. When a user clicks the Browse button, he or she has the opportunity to select a file on the local computer. When the file is selected, the local path to the file is added to the text box portion of the FileUpload control, as shown in Figure 24.2.

FIGURE 24.2
The ASP.NET FileUpload control facilitates the upload of files to the web server.

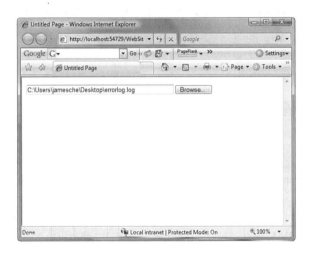

When the user submits the form that contains the FileUpload control, ASP.NET automatically takes care of uploading the file to the web server. You can then access that file in server-side code by using the `PostedFile` property of the `FileUpload` class. After you have access to the file, you can use the `Attachments` property of the `MailMessage` class to attach it to the email message.

The `Attachments` property contains a collection of attachments, each represented as an `Attachment` object. To create a new attachment, use the `Add` method of the `Attachments` property.

The following code shows an ASP.NET FileUpload control added to a page:

```
<asp:FileUpload ID="fuAttach" runat="server" />
```

To attach the file that a user selects in the fuAttach FileUpload control, you would use the following syntax. (In this example, msg represents a `MailMessage` object.)

```
msg.Attachments.Add(new Attachment(fuFile.PostedFile.InputStream,
➥fuFile.FileName);
```

When adding the new attachment, I've used two properties of the `FileUpload` control as parameters of the new attachment: `PostedFile.InputStream` and `FileName`. `PostedFile.InputStream` provides you with access to the file that was uploaded. The `FileName` property is a string that contains the name of the file that was uploaded.

> **NOTE**   For more details on the `Attachment` class, see msdn2.microsoft.com/en-us/library/system.net.mail.attachment(vs.90).aspx.

Using the methods outlined in this chapter, you can use ASP.NET to send emails for just about any purpose. The power of the mail classes that are provided by the .NET Framework make it easy to do something that used to take a considerable amount of programming code and effort.

Checkpoint

In this chapter, you added the server-side code necessary to send email from the contact form. In the next two chapters, you'll add more complex functionality to the contact form, using ASP.NET web services and ASP.NET Ajax.

PART IX

Ajax and Web Services

CHAPTER 25

Creating and Testing an ASP.NET Web Service

IN THIS CHAPTER

An Explanation of ASP.NET Web Services

Many ASP.NET web applications use data from a database on some portion of the website. In most cases, that data is not specific to any particular page. In other words, not only is that data suitable for use on many pages, but also for many different applications. For example, you might want to use price list information from your database in multiple pages. You might also want to allow your vendors to easily access the price list from their applications as well. ASP.NET Web services make such tasks easy.

A Web service does not display a user interface. Instead, it is designed to provide information in XML format that can be used by an application. The data that is returned by a Web service is in XML format so that is can be used easily by an application.

> **TIP** Web services can be used by any kind of application, not just web applications.

The Structure of a Web Service

When you create an ASP.NET Web service, Visual Web Developer creates a file with an `.asmx` file extension and, if you chose to include the code in a separate file, a code file in the `App_Code` folder. The `.asmx` file is actually an empty file, except for a single line that contains the @ `WebService` directive, similar to the following:

```
<%@ WebService Language="C#" CodeBehind="~/App_Code/ProductService.cs"
➡Class="ProductService" %>
```

→ For more information on ASP.NET directives, **see** "ASP.NET Directives," **p. 22**.

The code file contains the server-side code for the Web service. Unlike a web form, a Web service does not have events. Instead, it uses one or more functions called *web methods* that return data to the calling application. A web method can also accept one or more input parameters. For example, a Web service that provides a weather forecast to applications might accept a ZIP code as an input parameter and return the forecast for that particular ZIP code in XML.

> **TIP** The transfer of data between an application and a Web service uses the *SOAP*. SOAP is a means of transferring data between applications in XML format.
>
> SOAP used to stand for Simple Object Access Protocol, but because of the growing scope of SOAP and how it's used, it is now simply called SOAP.

The WSDL Document

To use a Web service, an application needs to have some way of discovering what web methods are available, the input parameters that are accepted (if any), and what the application can expect as a response. To obtain that information, applications use the Web service's *WSDL (Web Services Description Language) document*. The WSDL document is in XML format and describes the Web service in detail.

To access a Web service's WSDL document, simply append ?WSDL to the URL of the .asmx file. For example, if the URL of the Web service you're using is

```
http://www.weatherwebservice.com/weather.asmx
```

the WSDL document would be available when you browsed to the following URL:

```
http://www.weatherwebservice.com/weather.asmx?WSDL
```

> **TIP** Visual Web Developer automatically creates the WSDL file for you when you reference a Web service in your application. It's not necessary for you to understand the syntax of a WSDL file to use a Web service.

Because Web services are so different from other web applications you've probably created, let's create and run a simple Web service so that you can get a better idea of how they work.

Creating an ASP.NET Web Service

An ASP.NET Web service can exist as a separate application or as a class within an existing web application. This example uses a new class inside the existing application.

> **NOTE** In a real-world scenario, you would not typically create a Web service inside your ASP.NET application. We're using that method here because it makes it easier to package the web application into one project in Visual Web Developer for the purposes of this book.
>
> In most cases, you would create a Web service as a separate project in Visual Web Developer or you would add a reference to an existing Web service provided by a third party.

Follow these steps to create a new Web service:

1. Open the web application.
2. Right-click on the project in Solution Explorer and select Add New Item.
3. Choose Web Service from the list of templates and enter **ProductService.asmx** for the Web service name.

NOTE   We'll enhance this Web service later in the chapter so that it returns a list of products and services that populate a drop-down.

4. Check the Place Code in Separate File check box, as shown in Figure 25.1, and click Add to add the Web service to the web application.

FIGURE 25.1
To add a new Web service, use the Web Service template provided by Visual Web Developer.

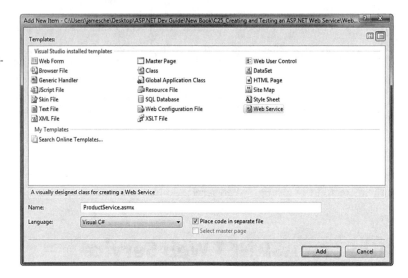

When you create a new Web service in Visual Web Developer, one web method is created for you automatically. That web method is called `HelloWorld`, and it returns a string that says `"Hello World."` The following code shows you what that web method looks like in a C# Web service:

```
[WebMethod]
public string HelloWorld()
{
    return "Hello World";
}
```

TIP   Any function that uses the `WebMethod` attribute should be declared with the `public` keyword so that it is available to any application using the Web service.

Invoking a Web Service Directly

To invoke the new Web service you just created, simply browse to the `ProductService.asmx` file. When you do, you'll see the page shown in Figure 25.2, and a list of all web methods provided by the Web service is shown at the top of the page.

Invoking a Web Service Directly | 349

Web Method

FIGURE 25.2
Browsing to the
.asmx file provides
you with a list of web
methods that the
Web service pro-
vides.

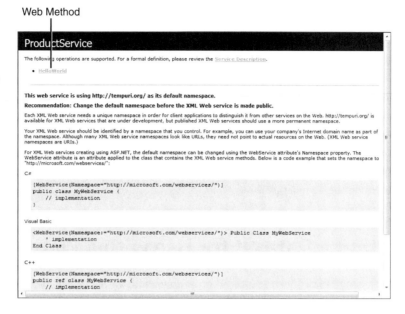

TIP   You can view the Web service's WSDL document by clicking the Service
       Description link at the top of the page.

From this page, you can test a web method by simply clicking on it. If you click the link for
the HelloWorld web method, you see the page shown in Figure 25.3. To test the Web service, click the Invoke button.

FIGURE 25.3
You can test web
methods by clicking
the link for the web
method you want to
test and then clicking
the Invoke button.

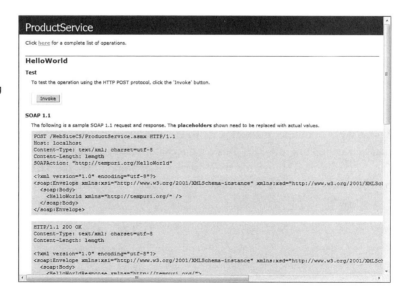

When you click the Invoke button for the `HelloWorld` web method, the response that is displayed contains the following XML:

```
<?xml version="1.0" encoding="utf-8" ?>
<string xmlns="http://tempuri.org/">Hello World</string>
```

In the case of the `HelloWorld` web method, the response is a string. Therefore, the response can be used as a string in the application that is using the Web service. For example, you could use the response to populate the `Text` property of a Label control.

Obviously, a response from a real web method would be more complex. Let's modify the Web service that you just created so that you can use it to populate the `ddlSubtopic` drop-down on the Contact page.

Creating a Dataset for Use with a Web Service

You can populate the `ddlSubtopic` drop-down with an ASP.NET Web service in a couple of different ways. One way would be to write all the server-side code in the Web service's code file to connect to the database and pull out the data you need. Then you would still need to write more server-side code in the `contactus.aspx` page to connect to the Web service and retrieve the data. However, that method is far too complex for my taste when Visual Web Developer can make the whole process much easier by using a Dataset.

NOTE
> Before you complete the rest of this chapter, you should download the sample website for this chapter from this book's website at www.quepublishing.com. This chapter uses a new database that contains additional information to support the Web service you'll create.

A *Dataset* is simply a representation of your data that resides in memory and contains one or more sets of data in tabular format called *DataTables*. A DataTable has rows and columns of data just like a table in a database, but it's contained in memory instead of inside a database.

Figure 25.4 shows a representation of a Dataset that contains two different DataTables.

Visual Web Developer makes it easy to create a Dataset that contains the data from the database containing the Elite Bits products and services. We'll use a Web service to retrieve the data from the Dataset and then use that data to populate the `ddlSubtopic` drop-down based upon whether the user selects Products or Services from the `ddlTopic` drop-down.

FIGURE 25.4

A Dataset containing two DataTables.

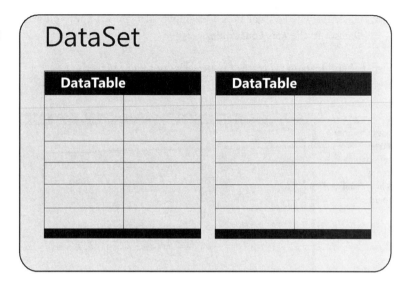

Creating the Dataset

Follow these steps to create a new Dataset:

1. Open the web application.
2. Right-click on the project name and select Add New Item.
3. In the Add New Item dialog, select DataSet from the list of templates.
4. Type **ProdServDS** in the Name text box, as shown in Figure 25.5, and click Add to add the new Dataset to your project.

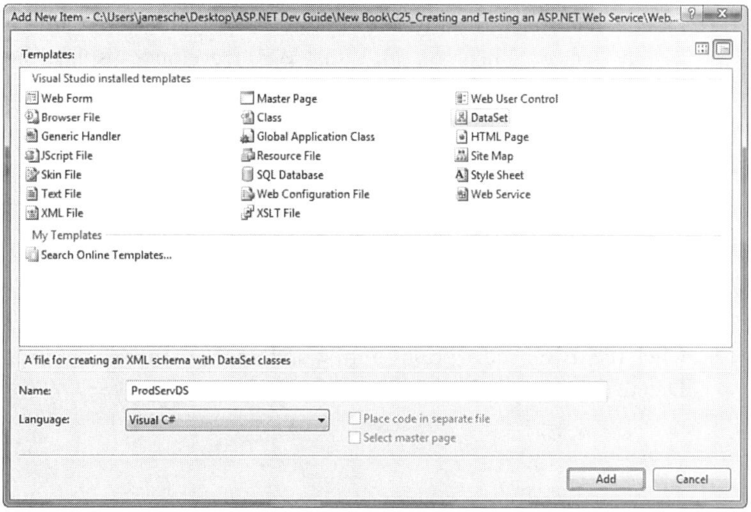

FIGURE 25.5

Adding a new Dataset to your application with Visual Web Developer is a simple process.

5. Click Yes when Visual Web Developer asks you whether you want to save the new Dataset in the App_Code folder.

Visual Web Developer creates the new Dataset and opens the Dataset designer as shown in Figure 25.6.

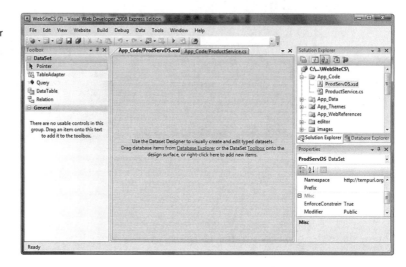

Connecting to the Database

To connect the new Dataset to your database, Visual Web Developer provides a powerful control called the TableAdapter. Follow these steps to add a TableAdapter and connect to the database:

1. Drag a TableAdapter control from the toolbox and drop it anywhere on the Dataset's design surface. When you do, Visual Web Developer displays the TableAdapter Configuration Wizard.

2. Select the EliteBits.mdb database from the drop-down in the TableAdapter Configuration Wizard, as shown in Figure 25.7, and click Next.

3. By default, the database connection string is stored in the application's web.config file, as shown in Figure 25.8. Accept these settings and click Next.

4. The only option available in the next step is to use SQL statements, so click Next to continue.

5. Click the Advanced Options button and uncheck the Generate Insert, Update, and Delete Statements check boxes. Click OK.

FIGURE 25.7

Select the `EliteBits.mdb` database in the TableAdapter Configuration Wizard to connect to the database.

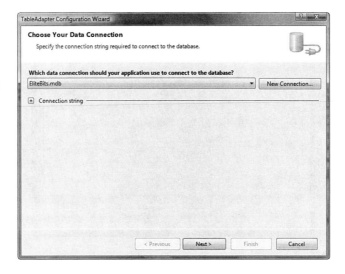

FIGURE 25.8

If you save the connection string in the configuration file, it is easier to manage if a change is required later.

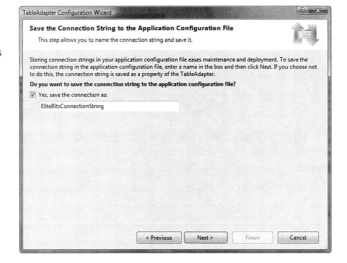

6. Click the Query Builder button.

7. In the Add Table dialog, select ProdServ and click Add as shown in Figure 25.9.

8. Click Close.

9. In the Query Builder dialog, check the * (All Columns) check box, as shown in Figure 25.10.

FIGURE 25.9

Add the ProdServ table to the query, using the Add Table dialog.

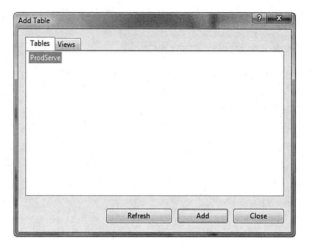

FIGURE 25.10

By selecting the * (All Columns) check box, you ensure that all fields from the table are returned by your query.

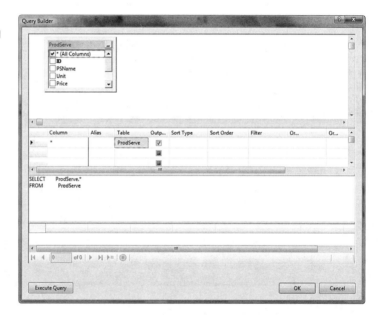

10. In the section of the dialog where the SQL query is displayed, add the following to the SQL query, as shown in Figure 25.11:
    ```
    WHERE (Type = @Type)
    ```

11. Click OK. Visual Web Developer warns you that the SQL query cannot be parsed. Click Ignore to ignore the error.

12. Click Next.

13. Uncheck the Fill a DataTable check box.

14. Under the Return a DataTable check box, change the method name to **GetProdServByType**, as shown in Figure 25.12.

FIGURE 25.11

To make it possible to pass in a parameter for the Type column, you need to manually edit the SQL query.

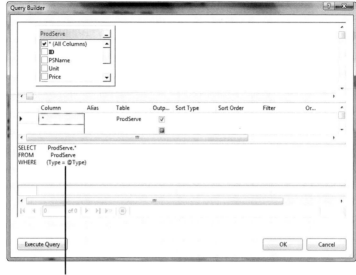

Edited SQL Query

FIGURE 25.12

Change the method name to GetProdServByType.

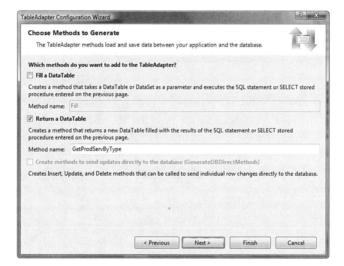

15. Click Next, and then click Finish. Visual Web Developer warns you again in the final step that the query cannot be parsed, but you can safely ignore that.

Adding a Parameter

The query that you've just created expects you to pass a parameter to it that will be used to return data based on what's in the Type column of the database. The parameter contains either Service or Product, based upon the item selected in the `ddlTopic` drop-down.

To add a new parameter to the query, follow these steps:

1. Select the GetProdServByType query in the TableAdapter.

2. In the Properties pane, click the ellipse button next to the `Parameters` property, as shown in Figure 25.13.

FIGURE 25.13

The Parameters property of the Fill query is a simple way to add new parameters to a query.

3. In the Parameter Collections Editor dialog, click the Add button.

4. Change the `Parameter Name` property in the Parameters Collection Editor to **Type** as shown in Figure 25.14.

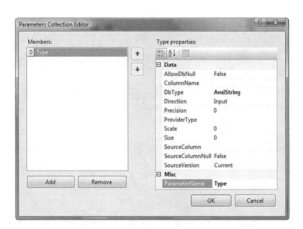

FIGURE 25.14

Change the parameter name to Type. This is the same name used in the SQL query.

5. Click OK to finish adding the new parameter.

Now that the TableAdapter has been configured, change the name of the DataTable that it will return by selecting the DataTable name (currently DataTable1) and changing the Name property in the Properties pane to **ProdServ** as shown in Figure 25.15.

Click here, and then change the Name property

FIGURE 25.15
Change the name of the DataTable to ProdServ to make it easier to refer to it in your Web service's code.

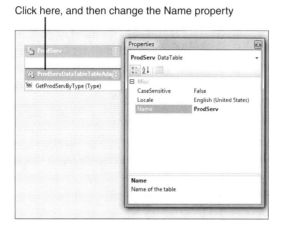

Using a Dataset with a Web Service

As you saw earlier, when you created your Web service, Visual Web Developer added a web method called HelloWorld. You need to make some modifications to that web method to use it for the Contact page.

Open the code file for the Web service (ProductService.cs or ProductService.vb) and change the code for the HelloWorld method to the following code based on your language.

For C#

```
[WebMethod]
public ProdServDS.ProdServDataTable GetProdServ(string psType) {
    ProdServDSTableAdapters.ProdServTableAdapter ProdServTA = new
    ➥ProdServDSTableAdapters.ProdServTableAdapter();
    return ProdServTA.GetProdServByType(psType);
}
```

For Visual Basic

```
<WebMethod()> _
Public Function GetProdServ(ByVal psType As String) As
➥ProdServDS.ProdServDataTable
    Dim ProdServTA As ProdServDSTableAdapters.ProdServTableAdapter =
    ➥New ProdServDSTableAdapters.ProdServTableAdapter()
    Return ProdServTA.GetProdServByType(psType)
End Function
```

The first change made is to the web method, so that instead of returning a string, it returns a `ProdServDS.ProdServDataTable`. The web method has been modified so that it accepts a string parameter called `psType`. The `ddlTopic` drop-down passes either "Service" or "Product" to the `GetProdServ` web method.

The web method also creates a new instance of `ProdServDSTableAdapters.ProdServTableAdapter`. This instance contains the DataTable returned by the query created earlier. You can run that query by calling it as a method of the `ProdServTableAdapter` instance and passing in either `Service` or `Product` for the type parameter. The result is a DataTable that contains the records from the database that meet the specific type passed to it.

> **NOTE** I realize that this chapter is throwing a lot at you. Don't worry if you're a little confused at this point. After you finish the chapter, it should all come together.

Testing the Web Service

Now it's important to test the Web service and make sure that everything's working as you expect. Browse the `ProductService.asmx` file in your browser and click the GetProdServ link. When you do, you'll see a page like the one shown in Figure 25.16.

FIGURE 25.16

The `GetProdServ` web method requires a parameter that specifies whether you would like to see products or services.

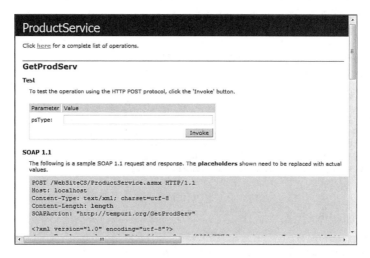

Type **service** in the textbox and click Invoke. When you do, you should see an XML file returned that contains only services from the database, as shown in Figure 25.17.

FIGURE 25.17
This XML result contains only services from the database.

Now it's time to connect the Web service to the Contact page.

Using a Web Service in a Web Form

Now that you've confirmed the Web service is working as you expect, you can take the steps necessary to use that Web service to populate the drop-down on the Contact page. The first step in that process is to add a reference to the Web service.

Adding a Reference to the Web Service

As discussed in the beginning of this chapter, for an application to use a Web service, it must first discover the methods that are available in the Web service and also how the Web service expects those methods to be called. To do that, you add a *web reference* to the Web service from your ASP.NET application. When you do, Visual Web Developer automatically accesses the WSDL document for the Web service and takes the steps necessary to support that Web service.

To add a new web reference to the ProductService Web service, follow these steps:

1. Right-click the project name in Solution Explorer and select Add Web Reference to display the Add Web Reference dialog, as shown in Figure 25.18.

FIGURE 25.18

The Add Web
Reference dialog is a
fast and easy way to
add a reference to a
Web service.

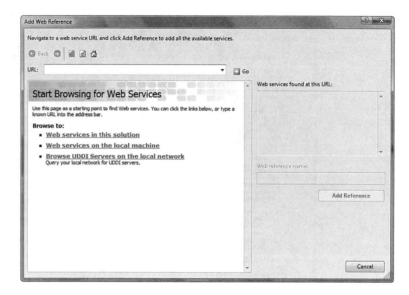

2. Click the Web Services in This Solution link, as shown in Figure 25.18.

3. Click the link to the ProductService Web service, as shown in Figure 25.19. Doing so populates the URL textbox with the URL to the Web service.

FIGURE 25.19

Click the link to the
Web service to popu-
late the URL text box
with the link to the
Web service.

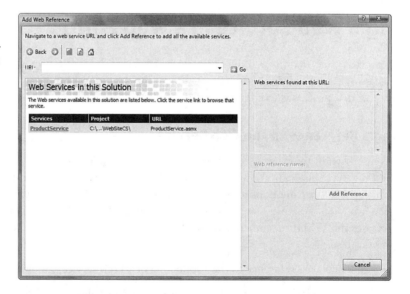

4. Click the Add Reference button, as shown in Figure 25.20, to add the web reference.

FIGURE 25.20

The Add Reference button adds the web reference to the project.

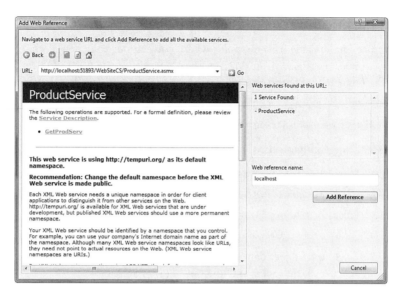

Visual Web Developer adds the web reference to the App_WebReferences folder in your application, as shown in Figure 25.21. Inside that folder is a folder corresponding to the server name of the Web service (localhost in this case), and inside that folder are all the files necessary for Visual Web Developer to understand the web methods made available by the Web service.

FIGURE 25.21

The files necessary for Visual Web Developer to support the Web service are added to your project automatically.

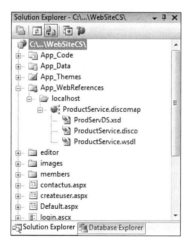

NOTE

In addition to the WSDL document, other files are in the web reference folder. We don't cover all the details of those files in this book. If you're interested in more details, read *Sams Teach Yourself Web Services in 24 Hours* from Sams Publishing.

Adding a Data Source for the DropDownList Control

You've finally made it to the point where you can put your new Web service to use. To connect the ddlSubtopic drop-down to the Web service, we use an ObjectDataSource control. The ObjectDataSource control is used when data is accessed using a separate component. In this case, the component is the TableAdapter created earlier.

→ For more information on the ObjectDataSource control, **see** "ObjectDataSource Control," **p. 288**.

To add and configure the ObjectDataSource control, follow these steps:

1. Open the contactus.aspx page and switch to Design view if necessary.
2. Click the Smart Tag button to display the Common DropDownList Tasks pop-up.
3. Click the Choose Data Source link in the Common DropDownList Tasks pop-up.
4. Select <New Data Source> from the Select a Data Source drop-down.
5. Select the Object data source from the list of data sources and change the ID to **ProdServDataSource**, as shown in Figure 25.22.

FIGURE 25.22

Select the Object option from the list of data sources and change the name to ProdServData-Source as shown here.

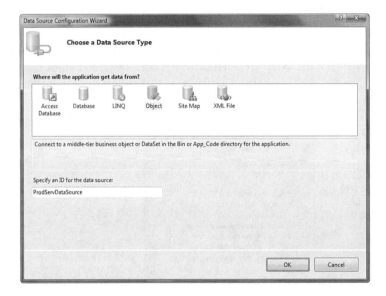

6. Click OK.
7. Select ProdServDSTableAdapters.ProdServTableAdapter from the Choose Your Business Object drop-down, as shown in Figure 25.23.

FIGURE 25.23

The Configure Data Source dialog box provides a list of business objects, one of which is your Dataset's TableAdapter you created earlier.

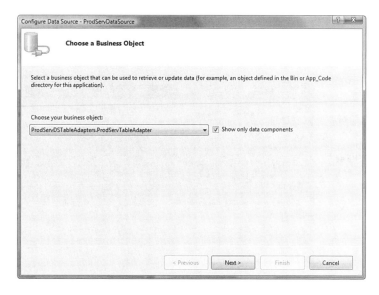

8. Click Next.

9. Only one method is available for your business object, so click Next to proceed to the next step.

10. In the Define Parameters portion of the Configure Data Source wizard, select Control in the Parameter Source drop-down and select ddlTopic from the ControlID drop-down, as shown in Figure 25.24.

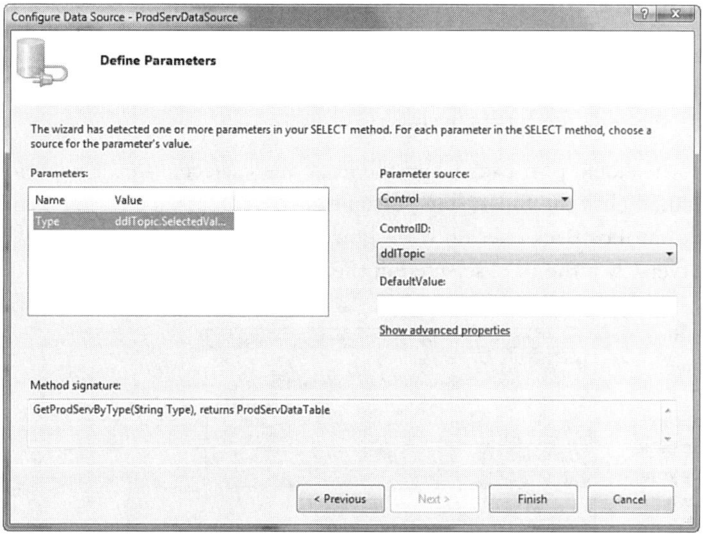

FIGURE 25.24

The Define Parameters portion of the Configure Data Source wizard configures the selected value of the ddlTopic drop-down as the parameter of the Web service's web method.

11. Click Finish.

12. Enter **PSName** to both drop-downs in the Choose a Data Source portion of the Data Source Configuration Wizard, as shown in Figure 25.25.

FIGURE 25.25

Because we want to display the name of the product or service in the drop-down, enter **PSName** in both drop-downs, as shown here.

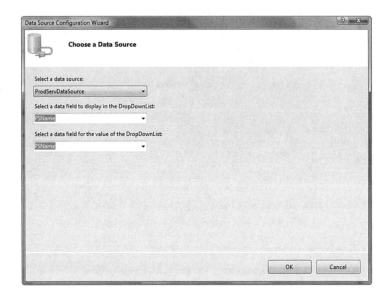

13. Click OK to complete the configuration of the ObjectDataSource control.

Completing the Configuration of the Web Form

To finish the configuration of the web form, you need to change the postback behavior of the ddlTopic control, make a small modification to the items in the ddlTopic control, and modify the code file for the web form.

The form should post back when the item that's selected in the ddlTopic control is changed. To do that, click the Smart Tag button on the ddlTopic control and check the EnableAutoPostBack check box as shown in Figure 25.26. The page will now post back to the server when the item selected in the drop-down changes.

FIGURE 25.26

By checking the EnableAutoPostBack check box, you can ensure that the page is processed by your ASP.NET code when the user changes the selection in the drop-down.

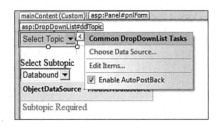

When we added items to the ddlTopic dropdown to the web form in Chapter 15, we used the default settings. Therefore, we need to remove the final *s* in each Value property for both items in the drop-down to match the data in the Type field in the database.

NOTE

When an item in the ddlTopic drop-down is selected, the Value property for the selected item is passed to the SQL query you created earlier.

Click the Smart Tag button on the ddlTopic drop-down and click the Edit Items link. Select the Products item and change the Value property to **Product**. Select the Services item and change the Value property to **Service** as shown in Figure 25.27.

The new Value property without the trailing "s"

FIGURE 25.27
Change the Value property by removing the trailing "s" for each item in the drop-down.

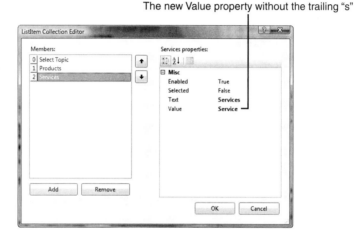

Finally, the code that's in the Page_Load event of the contactus.aspx web form needs to be moved. Because the AutoPostBack property of the ddlTopic drop-down is enabled, each time a new item is selected, the Page_Load event fires and the code in it runs. Because that code is currently configured to send an email, an error will occur in the application.

To resolve that issue, the code in Page_Load needs to be moved into a Click event for the btnSend control so that it will only run when the button is clicked. To do that, follow these steps:

1. Select the btnSend control.
2. Click the Events button in the Properties pane.
3. Double-click on the Click event to add the signature for the event.
4. Move the code from the Page_Load event into the new btnSend_Click event.
5. Remove the code that checks for postback from the btnSend_Click event.

The code for the btnSend_Click event should now look like the code that follows, depending on your language.

For C#

```csharp
protected void btnSend_Click(object sender, EventArgs e)
{
    SmtpClient sc = new SmtpClient();
    StringBuilder sb = new StringBuilder();
    MailMessage msg = null;

    sb.Append("Email from: " + txtFirstName.Text + " " + txtLastName.Text
    + "\n");
    sb.Append("Reference : " + ddlSubtopic.SelectedItem.Text + "\n");
    sb.Append("Message   : " + txtMessage.Text + "\n");

    msg = new MailMessage(txtEmail.Text, "email@domain.com",
    txtSubject.Text, sb.ToString());
    sc.Send(msg);
    msg.Dispose();
    pnlForm.Visible = false;
    pnlConfirm.Visible = true;
}
```

For Visual Basic

```vb
Protected Sub btnSend_Click(ByVal sender As Object, ByVal e As
System.EventArgs) Handles btnSend.Click
    Dim sc As SmtpClient = New SmtpClient()
    Dim sb As StringBuilder = New StringBuilder()
    Dim msg As MailMessage = Nothing

    sb.Append("Email from: " + txtFirstName.Text + " " + txtLastName.Text
    + vbCrLf)
    sb.Append("Reference : " + ddlSubtopic.SelectedItem.Text + vbCrLf)
    sb.Append("Message   : " + txtMessage.Text + vbCrLf)

    msg = New MailMessage(txtEmail.Text, "email@domain.com",
    txtSubject.Text, sb.ToString())
    sc.Send(msg)
    msg.Dispose()

    pnlForm.Visible = False
    pnlConfirm.Visible = True
End Sub
```

Save the contactus.aspx page and preview it in your browser. Select either Products or Services from the first drop-down and the second drop-down will be populated with data from the database based on your selection.

The Web service used here is a local Web service, so the postback occurs quickly. However, if this Web service were on a remote server, it might take several seconds for the Web service call to complete. In such a scenario, the page would be blank during that postback and the user experience would not be as good as you would like. In the next chapter, Ajax features are added to the Contact form to improve the user experience.

Checkpoint

Here's what you completed in this chapter:

- Created a Web service that retrieves data from a database.
- Created a Dataset to connect the Web service to a database.
- Databound a DropDownList control to the Web service.

In the next chapter, the Contact page is extended with the addition of Ajax features.

CHAPTER 26

Adding Ajax Functionality

IN THIS CHAPTER

What Is Ajax?

The underlying architecture of web applications has always posed a problem with usability. Whenever a user performs an action on a web page that requires a postback to the web server, data from all form fields is sent over the network, the page goes blank, and the browser sits in limbo waiting for the web server to send the response. In a typical ASP.NET scenario, where a postback reloads the same page after the server processes the data, the speed of the application can be sacrificed because the entire page has to reload each time it's posted back.

Ajax (Asynchronous JavaScript and XML) is well suited to providing a user experience that doesn't suffer from such problems. When a web page uses Ajax to post back to the server, only the applicable form data is sent to the server in a process known as a *partial postback*. After the server processes that data, it responds with data that the web page uses to dynamically update the page as necessary. During this process, the web page remains visible in the browser. The result is a user experience very much like a Windows application instead of a typical browser-based experience.

The technology that Ajax uses is called XMLHttp. *XMLHttp* is a standardized method of exchanging data between an application and a web server. Almost all browsers support XMLHttp, and the latest Opera mobile browser allows for support of Ajax functionality from mobile devices and smart phones.

Microsoft's ASP.NET AJAX

Microsoft's implementation of Ajax is called ASP.NET AJAX. It includes the AJAX Library (client-side libraries,) the ASP.NET AJAX Extensions (the server-side components of ASP.NET AJAX,) and the ASP.NET AJAX Control Toolkit, a collection of Ajax controls complete with source code that you can use any way you want.

> **NOTE** ASP.NET AJAX underwent extensive beta testing under the code name Atlas.

Microsoft AJAX Library

The Microsoft AJAX Library consists of client scripts and libraries that can be used to add Ajax functionality to any web page. The AJAX Library is the perfect choice, for example, for PHP developers who want to use Microsoft's implementation to add Ajax functionality to a PHP application. In fact, one of Microsoft's employees has developed PHP for Microsoft AJAX Library that does just that, and you can download it from codeplex.com/phpmsajax.

NOTE	We'll use the AJAX Library in the "Using the AJAX Library" section of this chapter, but I won't be able to go into as much detail on it in this book as you might want. If you're interested in reading more about it, read *Beginning Ajax with ASP.NET* from Wrox. It's an excellent book on Ajax.

Microsoft ASP.NET AJAX Extensions

The Microsoft AJAX Extensions consist of a series of .NET Framework assemblies that include not only server-side functionality, but also ASP.NET controls that make using Ajax in an ASP.NET page a drag-and-drop endeavor. The following Ajax controls are included with Visual Web Developer 2008:

- **ScriptManager**—The ScriptManager control is required on any web form that uses the AJAX Extensions. It provides the capability of dynamically including client-side scripts used in Ajax functionality.

TIP	Any web form that uses Ajax must have exactly one ScriptManager control and it must appear above any control that uses Ajax. Otherwise an error will occur.

- **ScriptManagerProxy**—The ScriptManagerProxy control is used most often in content pages that use ASP.NET master pages. We'll look at this control in more detail in the "Using the AJAX Library" section later in this chapter.
- **Timer**—The Timer control allows you to easily perform postbacks of a page (both synchronous and asynchronous) at a regular interval.
- **UpdatePanel**—The UpdatePanel control is a container for any control on a web form that takes part in an Ajax partial postback. We use an UpdatePanel later in this chapter.
- **UpdateProgress**—The UpdateProgress control is designed to display a message or some other indicator when an UpdatePanel is performing a partial postback.

Microsoft AJAX ASP.NET Control Toolkit

The AJAX ASP.NET Control Toolkit (which can be viewed and downloaded from www.asp.net/ajax/control-toolkit/) is a set of Ajax controls developed by Microsoft that includes full source code. Microsoft released these controls to encourage developers to use Microsoft's AJAX Extensions to create their own Ajax controls, and some of the coolest Ajax controls are included in the toolkit.

Developing new Ajax controls and extenders is an advanced programming topic and I don't cover it in this book, but Microsoft has provided plenty of excellent documentation on the AJAX ASP.NET Control Toolkit website.

Adding Ajax Functionality to a Web Form

In the previous chapter, you created an ASP.NET web service that accesses data from a database to populate the ddlSubtopic drop-down, based on the user's choice in the ddlTopic drop-down. The postback that occurs when the user changes the selection in the ddlTopic drop-down causes the page to go blank while the page is processed, and when the page reloads, it scrolls back to the top of the page. You can greatly improve the user experience by using Ajax to post the choice in the ddlTopic drop-down and dynamically populate the ddlSubtopic drop-down.

Targeting the .NET Framework 3.5

Before you can use Microsoft AJAX in your ASP.NET application, you need to configure your project to use the .NET Framework version 3.5. Version 3.5 of the .NET Framework contains enhancements that run on top of ASP.NET 2.0. One of those enhancements is Microsoft AJAX.

When you open a project for the first time with Visual Web Developer 2008, you will be asked whether you want to configure your application to target the .NET Framework version 3.5, as shown in Figure 26.1.

FIGURE 26.1

The first time you open an ASP.NET 2.0 application in Visual Web Developer 2008, you'll be asked whether you want to configure it to target the 3.5 .NET Framework.

If you see this dialog when you open your web application, click Yes to configure the project. Otherwise, you need to manually configure the project to target the 3.5 Framework after you've opened it. Follow these steps to manually configure the project:

1. Right-click on the project name in Solution Explorer and select Property Pages from the menu.
2. In the Properties dialog, click the Build option from the list on the left.
3. Select .NET Framework 3.5 in the Target Framework drop-down, as shown in Figure 26.2, and click OK.

After you've configured the web application for the 3.5 Framework, open the contactus.aspx page and switch to Design view. You should see an AJAX Extensions section in the toolbox, as shown in Figure 26.3.

FIGURE 26.2
You can use the Properties dialog for the project to configure your project to target the .NET Framework 3.5 version.

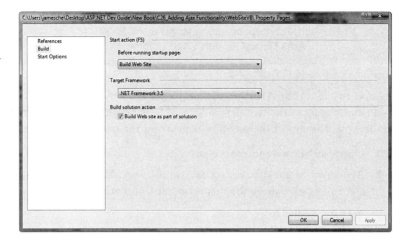

FIGURE 26.3
The AJAX Extensions section of the toolbox is visible after you configure your project to target the .NET Framework 3.5.

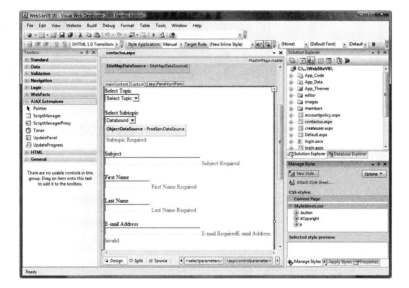

Adding a ScriptManager Control

As I mentioned earlier, any page that uses Microsoft's AJAX Extensions must have exactly one ScriptManager control on the page. The ScriptManager control must also be added to the page above any control that uses Ajax. Otherwise an error will occur.

The ScriptManager control is used by Ajax to load the necessary client scripts to support partial postbacks. However, you can add your own scripts as well. For example, you may have client-side code that you've written with the Microsoft AJAX Client Library. By adding that script to the ScriptManager's Scripts collection, you can utilize it in your Ajax pages.

> **NOTE** The concept of adding scripts to the ScriptManager is covered in the "Using the AJAX Library" section of this chapter.

It's time to add a ScriptManager control to the `MasterPage.master` master page. (When using master pages, it's often desirable to add the ScriptManager control to the master page so that you can support the use of Ajax in any of the content pages that use the master page.)

1. Open the `MasterPage.master` page.
2. Add a new ScriptManager control on the page. Make sure that the ScriptManager control appears above the mainContent ContentPlaceHolder control.
3. Save the master page.

Your master page should now look similar to the one shown in Figure 26.4.

FIGURE 26.4

The master page with the newly added ScriptManager control. Notice that the ScriptManager control is placed above the ContentPlaceHolder control on the page.

Adding an UpdatePanel Control

The UpdatePanel control is an extremely powerful control. Any control that is placed within an UpdatePanel control automatically becomes an Ajax-enabled control. In the case of the `contactus.aspx` page, the two drop-down controls should be Ajax enabled so that when an item is selected in the first, the second is updated with new items via Ajax. I can promise you that doing that is going to be a lot easier than you might think.

We need to add a new UpdatePanel control that contains both drop-downs. To do that, add the UpdatePanel and then cut and paste the DropDownList controls into it, as follows:

1. Click to the left of the Label control that says Select Topic and press Enter to insert a new line above the Label.

2. Add a new UpdatePanel control from the AJAX Extensions section of the toolbox.

3. Select the Label controls and two DropDownList controls, and then select Edit, Cut to remove them and place them on the Windows Clipboard.

4. Click inside the new UpdatePanel control and select Edit, Paste to paste the controls inside the UpdatePanel control.

Believe it or not, you have just finished Ajax-enabling the Contact page. If you preview the page in your browser and select an item in the Topic drop-down, ASP.NET AJAX will be used to populate the Subtopic drop-down with the appropriate items.

Using the AJAX Library

The AJAX Library enables you to write client-side scripts that interact with your ASP.NET application. Suppose the web service call that populates the `ddlSubtopic` drop-down had a possibility of taking a few seconds to complete. In such a scenario, displaying a message to the user is a good practice, and the AJAX Library makes it easy to do.

> **NOTE** You can use the UpdateProgress control to display a message, but it's a good idea to know how to take advantage of the AJAX Library in case you want a more customized solution.

In this section, we add a `<div>` element to the contact form and use the AJAX Library to change the text displayed in that `<div>` while the Ajax request executes.

Adding Controls to the Web Form

We need to add a `<div>` element and a ScriptManagerProxy to the `contactus.aspx` page. The `<div>` element will be used to display the status message. The ScriptManagerProxy is used to add the client script that implements the AJAX Library to the page.

Remember that there can be only one ScriptManager control on a page. Because a ScriptManager has already been added to the master page, it automatically becomes part of the `contactus.aspx` page as well.

You could add the client-side script used for the `contactus.aspx` page to the ScriptManager control on the master page, but if you do that, every page that uses the master page will have to download that script, adding to the total size of each page. The ScriptManagerProxy enables you to add scripts to a specific page in a scenario where a ScriptManager control is already included from another page.

To add the `<div>` element, follow these steps:

1. Open the `contactus.aspx` page.
2. Click to the right of the `ddlSubTopic` DropDownList control and press Enter to add a new line.
3. Add a new Div control to the new line from the HTML section of the toolbox.
4. Change the `Id` property of the Div to **WaitIndicator**.

Next, add a ScriptManagerProxy control to the page above the two DropDownList controls. After you finish the client-side script, you add it to the Scripts collection for the ScriptManagerProxy control.

Creating the Client Library

The client library is a JavaScript file that is used to interact with the page during an Ajax partial postback. To create the client library, follow these steps:

1. Right-click on the project in Solution Explorer and select Add New Item.
2. Choose AJAX Client Library from the list of templates, as shown in Figure 26.5.

FIGURE 26.5

The AJAX Client Library template creates a new JavaScript file for use with Ajax.

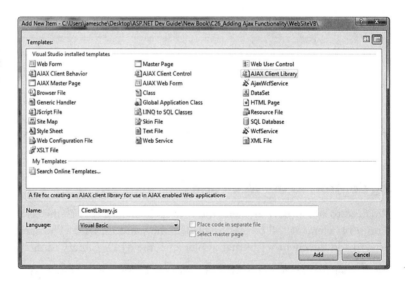

3. Use the default name of `ClientLibrary.js` and click Add to add the file to the project.

Open the new JavaScript file and add the following code to it:

```
Sys.Net.WebRequestManager.add_invokingRequest(App_InvokeRequest);
Sys.Net.WebRequestManager.add_completedRequest(App_CompleteRequest);
```

```
function App_InvokeRequest(sender, eventArgs)
{

    var waitDiv = $get("WaitIndicator");
    waitDiv.innerHTML = "Please wait...";


}

function App_CompleteRequest(sender, eventArgs)
{
    var waitDiv = $get("WaitIndicator");
    waitDiv.innerHTML = "";


}
```

The first couple of lines of code add the event handlers that fire when the Ajax request begins (the `invokingRequest` event) and ends (the `completedRequest` event.) The `App_InvokeRequest` and `App_CompletedRequest` functions set the `innerHTML` property of the `<div>` that you added earlier using the `$get` method that the AJAX Library provides. The `$get` method returns a reference to the control whose ID is passed to it.

Adding the Client Script to the ScriptManagerProxy

The final step is to add the `ClientLibrary.js` file to the ScriptManagerProxy's Scripts collection:

1. Select the ScriptManagerProxy control.
2. Click the ellipse button for the `Scripts` property.
3. Click the Add button in the ScriptReference Collection Editor.
4. Change the Path property of the new ScriptReference to **ClientLibrary.js**.
5. Click OK and save the page.

When the `contactus.aspx` page is browsed, the ScriptManagerProxy loads the ClientLibrary.js script for you.

If you browse to the page right now, the added script displays a message that says `Please wait...` while the Ajax request is being processed. However, because the Ajax request is almost instantaneous in the test application, you need to build in a delay so that you can see the effect.

Open the code file for the `contactus.aspx` page and add the following code to the `Page_Load` event, based on the language you are using:

For C#

```
if (IsPostBack) System.Threading.Thread.Sleep(5000);
```

For Visual Basic

```
If IsPostBack Then System.Threading.Thread.Sleep(5000)
```

After you add this code, the Ajax request takes five seconds to complete and you'll be able to see the Please wait... message during that time.

As you've seen in this chapter, Microsoft's Ajax implementation makes it extremely easy to incorporate this powerful feature into your applications. With only a small modification to your website, you can make the user's experience much more robust and user-friendly.

Checkpoint

In this chapter, you added Ajax capabilities to the contactus.aspx page. You also added a small amount of client-side code and server-side code. Anytime you add code to a page, there's always a possibility of introducing a bug. In the next chapter, you'll learn how to debug an application and track down any problems in code.

PART X

Debugging and Troubleshooting ASP.NET

CHAPTER 27

Debugging ASP.NET Applications

IN THIS CHAPTER

The Basics of Debugging

Any developer will tell you that one thing is certain when writing computer code: bugs. As hard as you try to avoid bugs, you're going to introduce them anytime you write code. The human brain is not wired to work the way a computer works, and because of the disparity between humans and the pure logic of the computer, we'll have software bugs until computers start writing software. Your job as a developer is to avoid bugs where possible and to track down bugs if you've introduced them into your code.

There are generally two reasons why you would need to debug an application. The first reason is that an error message is displayed and you need to find out why. These kinds of problems are usually the easiest to track down because you've got an indicator of where in your code something went wrong.

The second reason why you might need to debug your application is when the data used by your application is not what you expect it to be. These kinds of problems are often difficult to troubleshoot because the symptoms can be subtle and the code that's causing the problem is often not the code that is executing when the problem is noticed.

> **NOTE** Debugging your code also provides peace of mind in knowing that your code works the way that you expect it to.

The process of debugging involves stopping the execution of an application at a particular point and investigating the application's state. An application is debugged by an application called a *debugger* that's designed to peek into an application while it's running. The debugger has access to the memory that the application is using and can therefore determine the value of the application's variables and so on.

The debugger can also identify the name of the file containing the source code that is executing, and the line of code in that file that is executing at the time of the error. To identify the name of the file and the line that is executing, the debugger must load a special file called a *symbol file*.

> **NOTE** The symbol file is created when the application that's being debugged is built into an executable file.

You might find all that marginally interesting, but in fact, a good debugger prevents you from having to bother with how it works. Visual Web Developer is just such a debugger. Configuration is almost always trouble free, and the powerful debugging tools available to you make it much easier to track down problems in your code.

Enabling and Configuring Debugging for an ASP.NET Application

To debug an ASP.NET application in Visual Web Developer, you have to enable the project for debugging. After the project is enabled for debugging, Visual Web Developer can debug it according to the configuration options you've configured for the project.

Enabling Debugging

You enable debugging by using the `<compilation>` element in the `web.config` file in the root of your application, and it's disabled by default. To enable debugging, the following line needs to be added to the `web.config` file:

```
<compilation debug="true" />
```

→ For more information on the web.config file, **see** "ASP.NET Configuration Files," **p. 66**.

Fortunately, you don't have to know how to manually enable debugging because Visual Web Developer does it for you automatically when you first attempt to debug your application. If debugging is not enabled when you start debugging your project, Visual Web Developer prompts you with the dialog shown in Figure 27.1. Click Yes to add the `<compilation>` element to the `web.config` file and enable debugging.

FIGURE 27.1
Visual Web Developer enables debugging for you automatically when it's not already enabled.

> T I P   For details on why you should always disable debugging before moving your application to the live server, see the sidebar titled "Why You Should Disable Debugging on a Live Site."

You also need to make sure that ASP.NET debugging is enabled in the project's Start options. as detailed in the next section.

Why You Should Disable Debugging on a Live Site

You might have noticed that the dialog shown in Figure 27.1 warns you that you should always disable debugging in a production application. There are several reasons for that, but I think two are most important.

First of all, when you have debugging enabled, Visual Web Developer creates one DLL file for every page in your application. These DLL files get loaded into the memory your application is using, but they aren't loaded into any particular location in memory. Therefore, you end up with DLL files sprinkled all over the memory space of your application.

The reason why it's bad to have so many DLLs loaded into memory in this fashion is because they end up decreasing the amount of contiguous memory available to your application. When an ASP.NET application runs, the Common Language Runtime uses large blocks (up to 64 megabytes) of memory at a time, and all this memory has to be contiguous. If the Common Language Runtime can't find enough contiguous memory, it generates an error in the form of an `OutOfMemoryException`. When you run your application with debugging disabled, ASP.NET creates one DLL for each folder in your application, thereby greatly reducing the number of DLL files.

The second major problem with running an application in debug mode is that ASP.NET prevents requests from timing out when you are running in debug mode. Therefore, if you are running your live site in debug mode, and a user requests a page that contacts a database server when there's a problem with the database server, the page sits and waits for a very long time, rather than eventually timing out as it normally would. (For all intents and purposes, it will wait forever.) This is a bad situation, not only because your users get no feedback that anything's wrong, but also because that page could be holding onto resources in memory and will continue to do so, until you recycle your application.

If you want to read more on this topic, Tess Fernandez, one of my colleagues in Sweden, has a great blog entry on it at blogs.msdn.com/tess/archive/2006/04/13/575364.aspx. I highly recommend Tess's blog, but I warn you that it's very technical. However, it will give you an interesting glimpse into the life of an escalation engineer at Microsoft.

Configuring Debugging

To configure debugging, use the Start Options for the project. Right-click on the project and select Property Pages to access the Property Pages for the project. Click the Start Options item in the list on the left side of the dialog to display the Start Options, as shown in Figure 27.2.

By checking the ASP.NET check box in the Debuggers section of the Start Options, you configure the project for ASP.NET debugging. When ASP.NET debugging is enabled, Visual Web Developer communicates with the web server to obtain the information necessary to debug the server-side code in your application.

> **NOTE**   Unlike the `debug` attribute mentioned earlier, ASP.NET debugging in the Property Pages is enabled by default.

FIGURE 27.2

Configure ASP.NET debugging by using the property's Start Options in the Property Pages for the project.

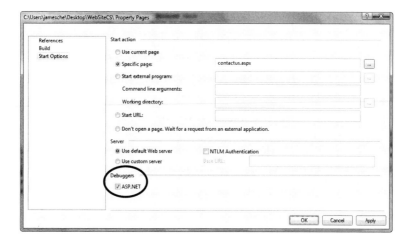

TIP

You can debug client-side script even if ASP.NET debugging is disabled.

→ For more information on configuring Start Options in Visual Web Developer, **see** "Start Options in Visual Web Developer," **p. 124**.

Debugging Server-Side Code

Before you can debug your server-side ASP.NET code, you need to specify a page that will be run automatically when you start debugging. This page is called the *start page*.

NOTE

As indicated previously, other start options are available in the project's property pages, but the start page option is the default because it is most often used for debugging ASP.NET applications.

After you specify a start page, press F5 or select Debug, Start Debugging to begin debugging your application. Doing so launches your start page in the browser and attaches the debugger to enable you to debug your application. At this point, the application will run normally until either an error occurs that your code doesn't account for, or until the debugger encounters a location in your code called a breakpoint.

NOTE

When you first start debugging, you may be informed that script debugging is disabled in your browser. If you see this prompt, it's safe to continue. This is covered in more detail in the "Debugging Client-Side Scripts" section later in this chapter.

Setting a Breakpoint

A *breakpoint* is an indicator to the debugger that code execution should be temporarily halted. The most basic kind of breakpoint is added to a specific line of code. When code execution reaches the line of code where the breakpoint is specified, the debugger stops the execution of the program and waits for your input.

To illustrate this concept, let's set a breakpoint on the contactus.aspx page. Right-click on the contactus.aspx page in Solution Explorer and select Set as Start Page. Then right-click on the page again and select View Code to view the server-side code. Add the breakpoint by right-clicking on the Page_Load event and selecting Breakpoint, Insert Breakpoint as shown in Figure 27.3.

FIGURE 27.3

Add a breakpoint by right-clicking on a line of code and selecting Breakpoint, Insert Breakpoint.

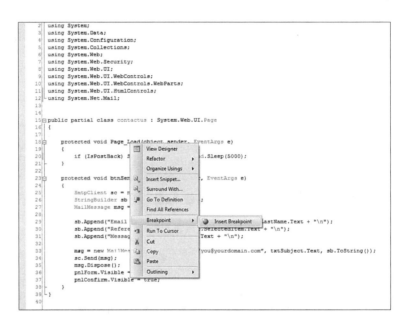

Visual Web Developer displays a red ball in the left margin at the line where the breakpoint was inserted, as shown in Figure 27.4.

You can use any of three methods to start debugging: Press F5; select Start, Start Debugging; or click the Start Debugging button on the main toolbar, as shown in Figure 27.5.

FIGURE 27.4

A red ball is placed in the left margin at the line where the breakpoint is set.

```
14
15 ⊟ public partial class contactus : System.Web.UI.Page
16 | {
17
18 ⊟     protected void Page_Load(object sender, EventArgs e)
19 |     {
20          if (IsPostBack) System.Threading.Thread.Sleep(5000);
21 |-    }
22
23 ⊟     protected void btnSend_Click(object sender, EventArgs e)
24 |     {
25          SmtpClient sc = new SmtpClient();
26          StringBuilder sb = new StringBuilder();
27          MailMessage msg = null;
28
29          sb.Append("Email from: " + txtFirstName.Text + " " + t
30          sb.Append("Reference : " + ddlSubtopic.SelectedItem.Te
31          sb.Append("Message   : " + txtMessage.Text + "\n");
```

Start Debugging Button

FIGURE 27.5

Clicking the Start Debugging button on the main toolbar is a convenient way to activate the debug process in an application.

NOTE   As previously mentioned, you might see a dialog informing you that script debugging is disabled when you begin debugging. You can safely ignore this dialog for now and just click Yes to continue debugging.

After you start debugging, Visual Web Developer launches your browser and halts execution of the application when it gets to the Page_Load event. Visual Web Developer then displays a yellow arrow in the left margin next to the next line of code that will be executed, as shown in Figure 27.6.

FIGURE 27.6

A yellow arrow is displayed in the left margin at the line of code that will be executed next.

```
12 └ using System.Net.Mail;
13
14
15 ⊟ public partial class contactus : System.Web.UI.Page
16 | {
17
18 ⊟     protected void Page_Load(object sender, EventArgs e)
19       {
20           if (IsPostBack) System.Threading.Thread.Sleep(5000);
21 |-      }
22
23 ⊟     protected void btnSend_Click(object sender, EventArgs e)
24 |     {
25          SmtpClient sc = new SmtpClient();
26          StringBuilder sb = new StringBuilder();
27          MailMessage msg = null;
28
29          sb.Append("Email from: " + txtFirstName.Text + " " + txtLastName.Text + "\n");
30          sb.Append("Reference : " + ddlSubtopic.SelectedItem.Text + "\n");
31          sb.Append("Message   : " + txtMessage.Text + "\n");
32
33          msg = new MailMessage(txtEmail.Text, "you@yourdomain.com", txtSubject.Text, sb.ToS
34          sc.Send(msg);
35          msg.Dispose();
36          pnlForm.Visible = false;
37          pnlConfirm.Visible = true;
38 |-      }
39 └ }
```

After code execution has stopped, you have the following options:

- **Select Debug, Continue (F5)**—Continues execution of the application until another breakpoint is hit or an application error is encountered.
- **Select Debug, Step Into (F11)**—Executes the current line of code and stops on the next line of code to be executed. If the current line of code calls another method, the debugger stops on the first line of the new method.
- **Select Debug, Step Over (F10)**—Executes the current line of code and stops on the next line of code to be executed. If the current line of code calls another method, the debugger executes the entire method and stops on the line in the original method immediately after the line that calls the new method.
- **Select Debug, Step Out (Shift+F11)**—Executes the current line of code. If the current line of code is inside a new method, the debugger stops on the line of code immediately after the line that called the new method.

Examining the State of an Application

Several tools are available to you in Visual Web Developer for examining the state of an application when you're debugging. The following sections explore some of the more commonly used tools for debugging your application.

IntelliSense

Visual Web Developer 2008 provides IntelliSense features when debugging that are greatly enhanced from previous versions. For example, if you hover over an object in your code, you see a pop-up that can be drilled into so that you can examine everything about that object. Figure 27.7 shows the IntelliSense pop-up for a DropDownList control.

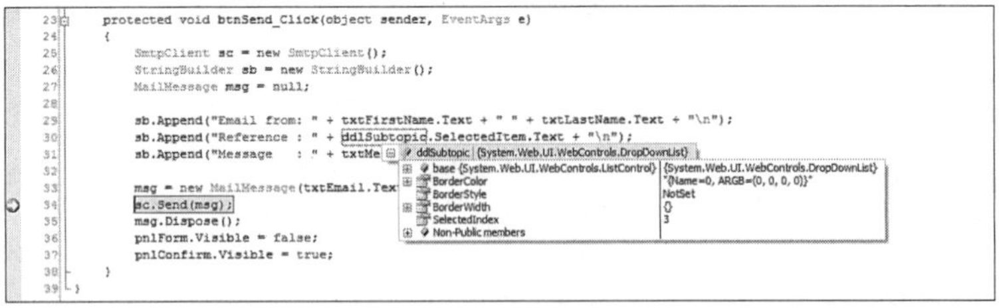

FIGURE 27.7
IntelliSense features when debugging enable you to drill down easily into an object.

IntelliSense also gives you detailed pop-ups when an error occurs in your code. When trying to send email, the pop-up shown in Figure 27.8 appears when an error occurs. When this error occurs, the debugger automatically stops execution and displays the pop-up informing you of the error and giving you options to assist you in correcting it.

FIGURE 27.8

Visual Web Developer's IntelliSense can make it easier to track down and correct errors in your application.

```
15 public partial class contactus : System.Web.UI.Page
16 {
17
18     protected void Page_Load(object sender, EventArgs e)
19     {
20         if (IsPostBack) System.Threading.Thread.Sleep(5000);
21     }
22
23     protected void btnSend_Cl
24     {
25         SmtpClient sc = new S
26         StringBuilder sb = ne
27         MailMessage msg = nul
28
29         sb.Append("Email from
30         sb.Append("Reference
31         sb.Append("Message
32
33         msg = new MailMessage
34         sc.Send(msg);
35         msg.Dispose();
36         pnlForm.Visible = fal
37         pnlConfirm.Visible = true;
38     }
39 }
```

SmtpException was unhandled by user code
Failure sending mail.
Troubleshooting tips:
Get general help for this exception.
InnerException: Check the Response property of the exception to determine why the request failed.
InnerException: Check the Status property of the exception to determine why the request failed.
Get general help for the inner exception.
Search for more Help Online...
Actions:
View Detail...
Copy exception detail to the clipboard

➜ For more information on handling errors in an ASP.NET application, **see** Chapter 28, "Handling Errors in an ASP.NET Application."

The Locals Window

You can open the Locals window by selecting Debug, Windows, Locals. Using the Locals window, you can drill into any *local variable* in the application. A local variable is one that is currently accessible by your application. For example, in the contactus.aspx page, the MailMessage instance called msg (seen previously in Figure 27.7) is accessible only in the btn_Send event where it is declared. As soon as the btn_Send event finishes executing, the msg variable is no longer available and is no longer displayed in the Locals window.

The Locals window (shown in Figure 27.9) shows each local variable with a plus sign next to it. By clicking the plus sign next to a variable, you can drill down into the object and examine its current state.

FIGURE 27.9

The Locals window is a powerful debugging tool for tracking down a variable's state.

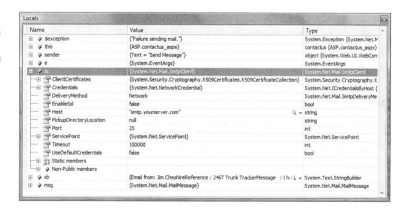

> **NOTE** Much of the capability provided by the Locals window has been incorporated into the new IntelliSense features discussed previously.

The Watch Window

The Watch window is a convenient way to watch the value of a variable or an expression as code executes. When the value of a watched variable or expression is changed during code execution, the new value is displayed in the Watch window, with red text serving as an indicator that the value has changed.

You can access the Watch window by selecting Debug, Windows, Watch. Figure 27.10 shows the Watch window with two watches defined.

FIGURE 27.10

The Watch window provides a powerful interface for watching the values of variables and expressions.

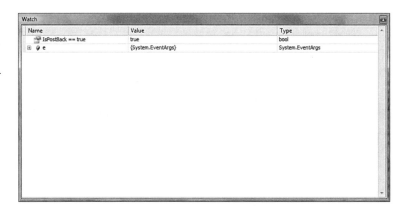

You can add new watches to the Watch window by typing directly inside the window, or by dragging a variable from your code and dropping it into the Watch window.

> **TIP** Application execution must be halted by the debugger when you add a watch.

The Immediate Window

You can display the Immediate window (shown in Figure 27.11) by selecting Debug, Windows, Immediate. The Immediate window enables you to enter expressions in free text that are evaluated immediately.

FIGURE 27.11

The Immediate window makes it easy to evaluate and modify variables and properties.

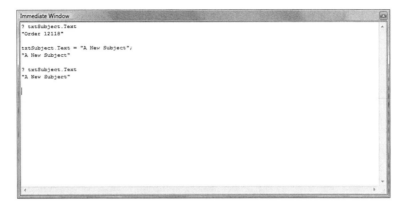

To display the value of a variable or property with the Immediate window, type the expression preceded by a question mark. For example, if you enter the following expression in the Immediate window, the value of the variable called MyValue is displayed:

```
? MyValue
```

You can also assign values to a property or variable in the Immediate window. To change the value of the MyValue variable to "Debugging Is Fun", enter the following expression into the Immediate window:

```
MyValue = "Debugging Is Fun";
```

TIP   In the previous example, the MyValue variable is assigned a value using C# syntax. If you are using a Visual Basic project, you need to enter code in the Immediate window with Visual Basic syntax.

You can also display details on an object by using the Immediate window. Figure 27.12 shows an example of evaluating the msg variable in the btnSend_Click event of the contact.aspx page.

By using the debugging tools available in Visual Web Developer, you can track down and correct problems in code much more easily than ever before.

FIGURE 27.12

The Immediate window can be used to evaluate an object.

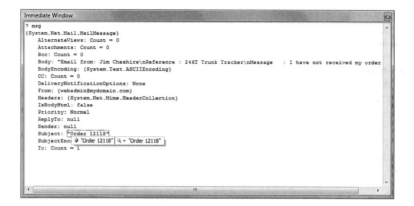

Debugging Client-Side Scripts

Many web applications consist of some combination of client-side scripts and server-side code. Visual Web Developer 2008 makes it easy to debug client-side code.

Before you can debug client-side scripts, you need to change your settings in Internet Explorer. By default, Internet Explorer disables the debugging of client-side scripts. Visual Web Developer 2008 can detect whether Internet Explorer has script debugging disabled and displays a warning, as shown in Figure 27.13.

FIGURE 27.13

Visual Web Developer detects when script debugging is disabled in the browser and tells you how to enable it.

To enable script debugging in Internet Explorer, open Internet Explorer and select Tools, Internet Options. Click the Advanced tab and uncheck the check box that says Disable Script Debugging (Internet Explorer), as shown in Figure 27.14.

After you enable script debugging, debugging a client-side script is as simple as setting a breakpoint in the script file and starting the debugging of your application, just as you do when debugging server-side code. Figure 27.15 shows a breakpoint in the ClientLibrary.js script file that you added in Chapter 26. Notice that Visual Web Developer's IntelliSense features allow for evaluation of client-side variables just as it does with server-side code.

FIGURE 27.14

Uncheck the Disable Script Debugging (Internet Explorer) check box to enable script debugging in Internet Explorer.

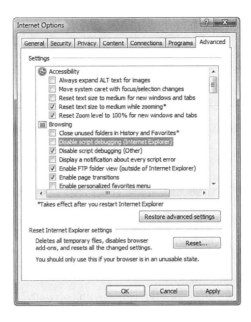

FIGURE 27.15

A breakpoint has been hit in client-side code. Note that IntelliSense provides the same powerful features that it does when debugging server-side code.

Using the Error List to Locate Application Errors

Not all errors are found while your code is running. Visual Web Developer can locate many problems for you before you start running your code. When it finds such problems, it displays them for you in the Error List, as shown in Figure 27.16.

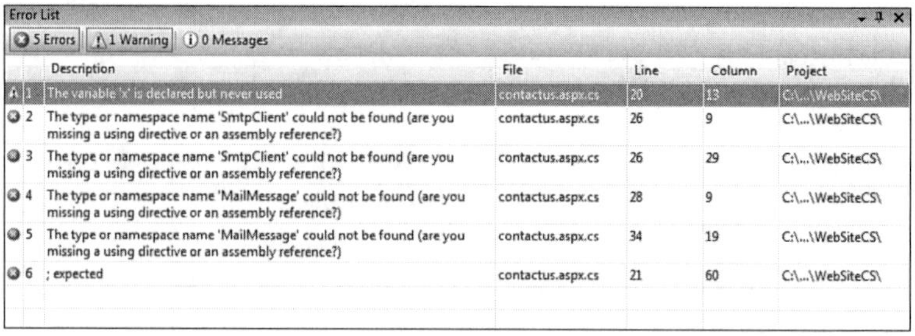

FIGURE 27.16

The Error List displays errors, warnings, and other information of interest to application developers.

The Error List displays problems with an application that are encountered when the application is compiled. To populate the Error List, you need to build your application by selecting Build, Build Web Site. You can also choose to build a single page or rebuild the application, a process by which cached files used by Visual Web Developer are deleted and re-created.

To locate the code for an item listed in the Error List, simply double-click on the item and Visual Web Developer takes you to the corresponding code. You can then correct the code yourself, or get assistance from Visual Web Developer with correcting the code. For example, double-clicking the first error in the Error List, seen previously in Figure 27.16, takes me to the code shown in Figure 27.17. As you can see, Visual Web Developer provides a Smart Tag that makes correcting the error a simple task.

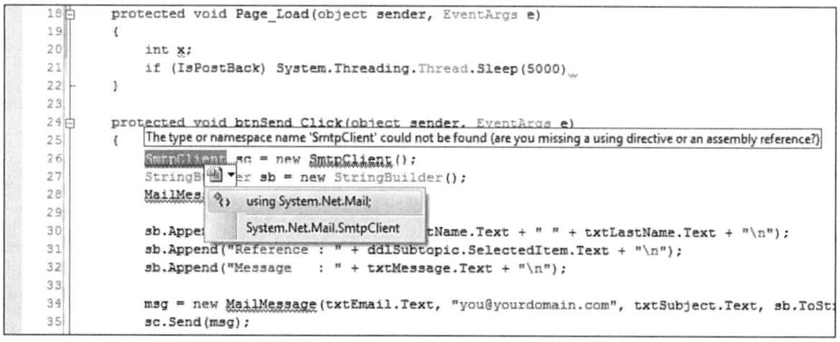

FIGURE 27.17

The code for the first error in the Error List is located in the code file for contactus.aspx. Notice that Visual Web Developer provides a Smart Tag for correcting the problem.

Visual Web Developer does not provide a Smart Tag for every code error. For example, the last error listed in the Error List shown previously in Figure 27.16, refers to a line of C# code with a missing semicolon at the end. Because the error message itself is enough to tell you what needs to be done to correct the issue, Visual Web Developer assumes that you will just add the semicolon to the line.

Some errors (such as the missing semicolon error) are underlined in the code with a red, wavy underline. These errors are ones that were located by a Visual Web Developer feature called *compile-on-demand*. Visual Web Developer marks these errors with a red, wavy underline as soon as you enter the incorrect code. It also removes these errors from the Error List immediately upon correcting the offending code.

Other errors are underlined in the code with a blue, wavy underline. These errors are compile-time errors and are found only when the application is built. These errors are removed from the Error List until the application is built without encountering the error.

The easiest way to become familiar with debugging applications is to set some breakpoints yourself and examine the application as you step through the code. You'll find that doing so with Visual Web Developer 2008 is intuitive and powerful. It's never been easier to track down and correct bugs in your applications.

Checkpoint

In this chapter, you learned how to debug ASP.NET applications and how to use the new features in Visual Web Developer 2008 to debug client-side scripts in your website. These skills will help you locate and correct problems in your ASP.NET application that would otherwise be difficult or impossible to track down.

In the next chapter, you'll learn how to handle errors that do occur in your application and how you can log information about errors so that they can be corrected if necessary.

CHAPTER 28

Handling Errors in an ASP.NET Application

IN THIS CHAPTER

Exceptions and the .NET Framework

In the previous chapter, we talked about the fact that computer code will always have bugs in it. In a best-case scenario, you can debug your code before your website goes live. Unfortunately, the best-case scenario never happens. Therefore, you're going to have to plan for errors when visitors use your website.

The .NET Framework uses a method known as *structured exception handling* to handle errors. Structured exception handling means that code that might generate an error is enclosed within a block of code called a *Try block* that can react to any errors that occur. If an error occurs, code execution jumps to another block of code that is designed to handle errors called the *Catch block*. Finally, code that is designed to clean up any objects that were created is placed in a block of code called the *Finally block*.

Exception-Handling Blocks

A typical exception-handling block of code might look like the following:

For C#

```
MailMessage msg;
try
{
  msg = new MailMessage();
  // code to initialize the MailMessage object would go here.
  SendEmail(msg);
}
catch(Exception ex)
{
  // do something to handle the exception
  throw;
}
finally
{
  if(msg) msg.Dispose();
}
```

For Visual Basic

```
Dim msg As MailMessage
Try
    msg = New MailMessage()
    ' code to initialize the MailMessage object would go here
    SendEmail(msg)
Catch (ex As Exception)
    ' do something to handle the exception
    Throw
Finally
    If Not msg Is Nothing Then msg.Dispose()
End Try
```

If an error occurs while the code that is within the Try block is being executed, execution of code immediately jumps to the code in the Catch block. After that code finishes, the code in the Finally block runs. If the code in the Try blocks runs without generating any errors, the code in the Finally block runs after the last line in the Try block is executed, and code in the Catch block is skipped.

> **NOTE** The Throw statement that you see in the previous code sample is explained in the "Bubbling Exceptions" section later in this chapter.

> **NOTE** The Finally block is optional.

When an exception is handled by a Catch block, the exception is said to have been *caught*. The code sample contains one Catch block that catches all exceptions that occur. However, many exception types are specific to certain situations. For example, if an error occurs when you are using the SmtpClient class to send an email, an `SmtpException` occurs. You can write code that reacts specifically to that type of exception, such as the code that follows:

```
try
{
    SendEmail();
}
catch (SmtpException smtpEx)
{
    // handle the exception
}
```

When this code runs, the code within the Catch block runs only if the specific exception that occurs is an `SmtpException`.

Bubbling Exceptions

Computer code runs in what is called a *stack*. As methods are called, they are placed onto the stack. Using this method, the computer always knows not only what code is currently executing, but also the code that got you to where you are now.

Consider the following code:

```
void FuncA()
{
    int x = 2;
    try
    {
        FuncB(x);
    }
```

```
  catch (SmtpException ex)
  {
    // handle it
  }
}

void FuncB(int y)
{
  int i;
  int x = 0;
  i = y / x;
}
```

If you call FuncA from the Page_Load event of Default.aspx, the call stack would look like the following, from top to bottom:

```
Default.Page_Load(object sender = {ASP.default_aspx},
➥System.EventArgs e = {System.EventArgs})
Default.FuncA()
Default.FuncB(int y = 2)
```

In this sample code, an exception is going to occur in FuncB because it is dividing a number by zero. However, the code that does that is not within a Try block, so FuncB will *throw* the exception back to the function that called it—in this case, FuncA. This is known as *bubbling* and developers often say that the exception *bubbles* up the call stack.

Up and Down the Call Stack

Many debuggers (including Visual Web Developer) show you the call stack from bottom to top, the reverse of what I showed you. However, the computer sees the call stack from top to bottom because of the way that the memory allocated to the call stack is laid out.

It's an advanced concept, so you'll just have to take my word for it, but knowing that helps to make sense of why we say that an exception that is unhandled *bubbles up* the call stack or is *thrown up* the call stack. If the stack were actually laid out the way that Visual Web Developer shows it to you, an exception would bubble down the stack, and that certainly doesn't make as much sense.

If FuncA isn't able to handle the exception that is thrown to it from FuncB, the exception bubbles up to the Page_Load event and the Page_Load event is given a chance to handle it. If it doesn't, the exception bubbles up again until it runs out of places where it can be handled. At that point, the exception stops the application from executing.

NOTE   If you don't handle an exception in your ASP.NET application, ASP.NET handles it for you and displays an error to the user. Customizing the appearance and behavior of ASP.NET's automatic error page is discussed in the "Using the <customErrors> Element" section, later in this chapter.

Implementing Structured Exception Handling

As you've read through this chapter so far, you might have realized that the code added to the contactus.aspx page doesn't have any exception-handling code. It's time to add some now.

Open the code file for the contactus.aspx page. The code that needs exception handling is in the btnSend_Click method. As written, the code displays an error to the user if something goes wrong, as shown in Figure 28.1.

FIGURE 28.1
Because there isn't any exception-handling code, ASP.NET handles the error and displays an error to the user.

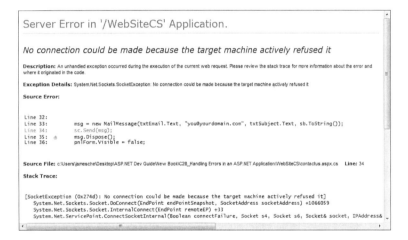

Server Error in '/WebSiteCS' Application.

No connection could be made because the target machine actively refused it

Description: An unhandled exception occurred during the execution of the current web request. Please review the stack trace for more information about the error and where it originated in the code.

Exception Details: System.Net.Sockets.SocketException: No connection could be made because the target machine actively refused it

Source Error:

```
Line 32:
Line 33:         msg = new MailMessage(txtEmail.Text, "you@yourdomain.com", txtSubject.Text, sb.ToString());
Line 34:         sc.Send(msg);
Line 35:         msg.Dispose();
Line 36:         pnlForm.Visible = false;
```

Source File: c:\Users\jamesche\Desktop\ASP.NET Dev Guide\New Book\C28_Handling Errors in an ASP.NET Application\WebSiteCS\contactus.aspx.cs   **Line:** 34

Stack Trace:

```
[SocketException (0x274d): No connection could be made because the target machine actively refused it]
   System.Net.Sockets.Socket.DoConnect(EndPoint endPointSnapshot, SocketAddress socketAddress) +1066059
   System.Net.Sockets.Socket.InternalConnect(EndPoint remoteEP) +33
   System.Net.ServicePoint.ConnectSocketInternal(Boolean connectFailure, Socket s4, Socket s6, Socket& socket, IPAddress&
```

Displaying a default error message, such as the one shown in Figure 28.1, is not an attractive way to inform a user that something's gone wrong. But that's not the only problem. It can also display details about the code that's running that might reveal information about your application that shouldn't be revealed. By implementing structured exception handling in your code, you control how and when problems are communicated to your users.

> **NOTE**
> You can control whether ASP.NET displays a stack trace when an error occurs by using the <customErrors> element. For more information on using the <customErrors> element, see "Using the <customErrors> Element" later in this chapter.

Modifying the btnSend_Click Method

To add exception handling to the Click event, you need to wrap several lines of code in a Try block and add a Catch block. Modify the code in the Click event so that it matches the following code:

For C#

```
SmtpClient sc = null;
StringBuilder sb = null;
MailMessage msg = null;

pnlForm.Visible = false;

try
{
    sc = new SmtpClient();
    sb = new StringBuilder();

    sb.Append("Email from: " + txtFirstName.Text + " " + txtLastName.Text
    ➥ + "\n");
    sb.Append("Reference : " + ddlSubtopic.SelectedItem.Text + "\n");
    sb.Append("Message    : " + txtMessage.Text + "\n");

    msg = new MailMessage(txtEmail.Text, "you@yourdomain.com",
    ➥txtSubject.Text, sb.ToString());
    sc.Send(msg);
    pnlConfirm.Visible = true;
}
catch (SmtpException)
{
    // code to handle the SmtpException here
    pnlError.Visible = true;
}
    catch (Exception)
{
    pnlError.Visible = true;
    throw;
}
finally
{
    if (msg != null) msg.Dispose();
}
```

For Visual Basic

```
Dim sc As SmtpClient = Nothing
Dim sb As StringBuilder = Nothing
Dim msg As MailMessage = Nothing

pnlForm.Visible = False

Try
    sc = New SmtpClient()
    sb = New StringBuilder()

    sb.Append("Email from: " + txtFirstName.Text + " " + txtLastName.Text
    ➥+ vbCrLf)
    sb.Append("Reference : " + ddlSubtopic.SelectedItem.Text + vbCrLf)
    sb.Append("Message    : " + txtMessage.Text + vbCrLf)
```

```
    msg = New MailMessage(txtEmail.Text, "you@yourdomain.com",
    ➥txtSubject.Text, sb.ToString())
    sc.Send(msg)
    pnlConfirm.Visible = True

Catch sEX As SmtpException
    ' code to handle the SmtpException here
    pnlError.Visible = True

Catch eX As Exception
    pnlError.Visible = True
    Throw

Finally
    If Not msg Is Nothing Then msg.Dispose()
End Try
```

If the code in the Try block completes successfully, the `pnlConfirm` Panel control displays a message telling the user that the message was successfully sent. However, if an error occurs while the code in the Try block is executed, execution moves to one of the Catch blocks.

The first Catch block catches a specific exception type: an `SmtpException`. I've placed a comment in the first Catch block to indicate that you would typically have code in the application to handle that specific type of exception. For example, you might want to log a message to the Event Viewer of the web server with details of the exception and a notice that SMTP credentials might need to be checked. After the exception has been handled, the `pnlError` panel is displayed so that the user knows that an error occurred.

> **N O T E** You will add the `pnlError` Panel in the next section.

If the exception that occurs is an exception type other than `SmtpException`, the code in the second Catch block executes. In that Catch block, the `pnlError` Panel is displayed and then the Throw method is called. When the Throw method is called, the exception is thrown up the call stack to be handled elsewhere. In this case, it could be handled by a global exception handler in your application or by ASP.NET itself.

In the Finally block, the Dispose method is called on the `MailMessage` object. However, first check to make sure that the `msg` variable actually contains a valid object. If an exception occurred in the Try block prior to the creation of a new `MailMessage` object, the `msg` variable is still null.

Adding a Panel to Display Errors

The last step to configuring exception handling for the contactus.aspx page is to add a Panel control to display an error message. Follow these steps to add the pnlError control referred to in the code you've added:

1. Add a new Panel control under the pnlConfirm Panel that is already on the page.

2. Enter some text into the Panel control that informs the user that an error has occurred when sending the email.

3. Change the Visible property of the new Panel to **False**.

4. Change the ID property of the new Panel to **pnlError**.

5. If you're using C#, click OK in the Verification Results dialog, as shown in Figure 28.2. This dialog is not displayed if you are using Visual Basic.

FIGURE 28.2

C# developers see the Verification Results dialog when adding the new Panel control.

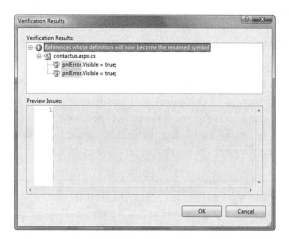

Throwing Exceptions

In the second Catch block in the btnSend_Click method, the Throw method is used to throw the exception. Some developers recommend that the exception object be passed as a parameter of the Throw method as follows:

```
throw eX;
```

In fact, passing the exception when you throw it is bad practice. Exception objects store the stack that led up to the exception. If you pass an exception object when you throw it, it can cause the stack to point to the wrong place. Consider the following code:

```
void FuncA()
{
    try
    {
```

```
      FuncB();
   }
   catch (Exception eX)
   {
      throw eX;
   }
}
```

When this code runs and an exception occurs, the stack trace for the exception points to the stack in FuncA and not the stack in FuncB where it should point. However, if you simply call the Throw method without passing the exception variable as a parameter, the stack trace points to the problem in FuncB as it should.

Adding a Global Exception Handler

You should always try to anticipate when an exception might occur and include a Catch block to handle it. However, you won't be able to predict all exceptions. For that reason, it's a good idea to implement a global exception handler.

ASP.NET applications have an application-level method called Application_Error that is in the global.asax file in your application. It is called anytime an exception happens that is not handled. You can use the Application_Error method to record details on any exception that isn't handled in your code.

→ For more information on the global.asax file, **see** "Application and Session Events," **p. 42**.

Visual Web Developer doesn't add a global.asax file to ASP.NET applications by default. To add a new global.asax file, right-click on the project in Solution Explorer and select Add New Item. Select the Global Application Class item in the Add New Item dialog and click Add.

The Application_Error method is automatically added to the global.asax file when you add it to your project. Any code that is placed into the Application_Error method automatically executes when an unhandled exception occurs in your application. For example, you might want to put code into the Application_Error method that sends an email to the website administrator or logs errors into an error log.

Using the `<customErrors>` Element

The <customErrors> element enables you to control what users see when an unhandled error occurs in your application. The <customErrors> element is defined in the web.config file. The following is a typical <customErrors> element:

```
<customErrors mode="RemoteOnly" defaultRedirect="~/error.aspx" />
```

The `defaultRedirect` attribute specifies a URL that is displayed when an unhandled error occurs. You can use this to display a customized error page to your users so that they don't see the generic ASP.NET error page, as shown previously in Figure 28.1.

> **TIP** The `defaultRedirect` attribute does not have to point to an ASP.NET page. It can be a plain `.html` page or any other kind of page that the web server can serve.

The `mode` attribute controls when the custom error settings take effect. The following values are available:

- **On**—Custom error settings apply to anyone browsing the website, whether locally or remotely.
- **RemoteOnly**—Custom errors apply only to users browsing the website from a remote client. Custom error settings are ignored for users browsing on the web server machine. This is the default setting.
- **Off**—Custom errors do not apply to any user. Users see the generic error page generated by ASP.NET.

`<error>` Elements

The `<customErrors>` element can also contain one or more `<error>` elements. These elements enable you to redirect a user to a specific page based upon the HTTP status code for the error. The following `<customErrors>` element contains an `<error>` element and redirects users to a page called notfound.htm when they request a page and get a status message of 404 (file not found).

```
<customErrors mode="RemoteOnly">
  <error statusCode="404" redirect="notfound.htm" />
</customErrors>
```

> **CAUTION** Custom error settings apply only to requests that are processed by ASP.NET. For example, if you browse to page.htm and the web server responds with a 404 status code, the custom error settings you've just seen do not redirect the user to the notfound.htm page because requests for `.htm` pages are not handled by ASP.NET by default.

Not all status codes can be handled by ASP.NET's `<error>` elements. For example, if a user requests a page and gets a 401 status back (indicating that the user is denied access to the page,) an error element with a `statusCode` attribute of 401 has no effect on the request. The web server returns 401 status codes before it hands off the request to ASP.NET, so ASP.NET doesn't even get a chance to handle it.

Checkpoint

In this chapter, you added structured exception handling to the contactus.aspx page. At this point, you have completely finished the ASP.NET application. All the functionality is in place and it is now a fully functional application.

I can't possibly anticipate all the features that readers would like to see added to the application, so if there's something that you'd like to know how to accomplish that I didn't cover, please contact me through my website at www.jimcobooks.com and suggest a tutorial. I'll gladly consider all requests that I receive and will produce new video tutorials as time permits.

CHAPTER 29

ASP.NET Tracing and Other Troubleshooting Techniques

IN THIS CHAPTER

ASP.NET Tracing

One of the ways that developers log information about the execution of an application is to write code into the application at various points that prints out specific information about the state of the application. For example, if I have a page that is consistently slow and I want to see how long functions within the page are taking to execute, I might add some server-side code to dump out the time when I enter a function and again when I exit a function.

Such a troubleshooting technique is perfectly fine, but it does have one major drawback; it requires that server-side code be changed to get data. ASP.NET provides a much better tool for obtaining statistics on such things, and it requires only modifying the web.config file. That tool is called ASP.NET tracing.

Enabling Tracing

To enable ASP.NET tracing, use the `<trace>` element in the web.config file. The following line of code shows how tracing is enabled in the web.config file:

```
<trace enabled="true" pageOutput="false" requestLimit="15"/>
```

The following attributes of the `<trace>` element are available for configuring how tracing works with your application:

- **enabled**—Specifies whether tracing is enabled. The default value is `false`.
- **localOnly**—Specifies whether trace output is restricted to the local console. The default is `true`.
- **requestLimit**—Specifies the number of requests that will be traced. The default is 10.
- **mostRecent**—If `true`, trace data for the most recent requests will be saved up to the number specified by the `requestLimit` attribute. If `false` (the default value), when the number of requests specified by the `requestLimit` attribute is reached, no more requests are traced.
- **pageOutput**—If this attribute is `true`, trace output gets added at the bottom of each page. If it's false (the default), trace output is available only if you use the trace.axd handler.

> **NOTE** Use of the trace.axd handler is covered later in this chapter.

- **traceMode**—Specifies whether trace information is sorted by time (a value of `SortByTime`) or by a category defined by the user (`SortByCategory`.) `SortByTime` is the default. Unless you have defined trace categories, there is no difference in the two settings.

- **writeToDiagnosticsTrace**—If true, trace messages are forwarded to System.Diagnostics tracing, where any trace listener can intercept it. This is an advanced topic that not covered in this book.

Tracing can also be enabled at the page level with the `trace` attribute of the `@ Page` directive. The following `@ Page` directive enables tracing for the page:

```
<%@ Page Language="C#" CodeFile="Default.aspx.cs" Inherits="_Default"
➥Trace="true" %>
```

Analyzing Trace Output

ASP.NET tracing can output a lot of data. There are several sections in trace output.

Request Details

The Request Details section is shown in Figure 29.1.

FIGURE 29.1
The Request Details section of trace output displays information about the HTTP request.

Request Details			
Session Id:	4aimmk45vcsbotnrubyx5o55	Request Type:	GET
Time of Request:	7/29/2007 5:48:25 PM	Status Code:	200
Request Encoding:	Unicode (UTF-8)	Response Encoding:	Unicode (UTF-8)

The following information is available in the Request Details section:

- **Session ID**—The ASP.NET Session ID if one was sent with the request.
- **Request Type**—The HTTP verb for the request. This is usually either GET or POST.
- **Time of Request**—The date and time of the request.
- **Status Code**—The HTTP status code of the request.
- **Request Encoding**—The encoding of the request.
- **Response Encoding**—The encoding of the response.

Trace Information

The Trace Information section is shown in Figure 29.2.

FIGURE 29.2

The Trace Information section provides valuable information on how long each phase of the page takes to complete.

Trace Information

Category	Message	From First(s)	From Last(s)
aspx.page	Begin PreInit		
aspx.page	End PreInit	8.52063600262044E-05	0.000085
aspx.page	Begin Init	0.000127390492367047	0.000042
aspx.page	End Init	0.000161473036377528	0.000034
aspx.page	Begin InitComplete	0.00018892065891056	0.000027
aspx.page	End InitComplete	0.000215180979705521	0.000026
aspx.page	Begin PreLoad	0.00024095241549513	0.000026
aspx.page	End PreLoad	0.000266514319557374	0.000026
aspx.page	Begin Load	0.000293263529303305	0.000027
aspx.page	End Load	0.000818330262645113	0.000525
aspx.page	Begin LoadComplete	0.000880349318139596	0.000062
aspx.page	End LoadComplete	0.000989581078042042	0.000109
aspx.page	Begin PreRender	0.00101800647847701	0.000028
aspx.page	End PreRender	0.00104873664110941	0.000031
aspx.page	Begin PreRenderComplete	0.00107569537469148	0.000027
aspx.page	End PreRenderComplete	0.00110886998207873	0.000033
aspx.page	Begin SaveState	0.00132467953329264	0.000216
aspx.page	End SaveState	0.00835127090174869	0.007027
aspx.page	Begin SaveStateComplete	0.00840567725786378	0.000054
aspx.page	End SaveStateComplete	0.00843340424551165	0.000028
aspx.page	Begin Render	0.00845896615351951	0.000026
aspx.page	End Render	0.00921283291591529	0.000754

The Trace Information section displays each phase of the page's lifecycle and how long each phase takes. The times that appear in the From First(s) column represent the amount of time that has elapsed since the page's lifecycle began. The number in the From Last(s) column shows the amount of time since the prior event.

TIP An application can write information to the Trace output as well. Any information written to Trace output by an application appears in the Trace Information section as well.

The Trace Information section is an excellent tool to determine whether a particular portion of a page's lifecycle is contributing to a page's slowness.

→ For more information on the ASP.NET page lifecycle, **see** "Page Events and the Page Lifecycle," **p. 44**.

Control Tree

The Control Tree section is shown in Figure 29.3.

FIGURE 29.3

The Control Tree section contains details on every control in the page.

Control Tree

Control UniqueID	Type	Render Size Bytes (including children)	ViewState Size Bytes (excluding children)	ControlState Size Bytes (excluding children)
_Page	ASP.default_aspx	501	0	0
ctl02	System.Web.UI.LiteralControl	174	0	0
ctl00	System.Web.UI.HtmlControls.HtmlHead	46	0	0
ctl01	System.Web.UI.HtmlControls.HtmlTitle	33	0	0
ctl03	System.Web.UI.LiteralControl	14	0	0
form1	System.Web.UI.HtmlControls.HtmlForm	247	0	0
ctl04	System.Web.UI.LiteralControl	35	0	0
ctl05	System.Web.UI.LiteralControl	20	0	0

The Control Tree section details every control on the page (which can include controls that ASP.NET adds automatically when it builds the page before sending it to the browser) and the size of each control in bytes. The size of Viewstate and Control State is also listed for each control.

The Control Tree section can be invaluable if you determine that a page is large and is taking too long to download to the browser. For example, you might realize as you use other troubleshooting steps that a page takes a long time to download because of a very large Viewstate. By using the Control Tree section of ASP.NET tracing, you can determine which controls on the page are contributing to Viewstate so that you can target specific controls in an attempt to reduce the size.

→ For more information on ASP.NET Viewstate and Control State, **see** "ASP.NET Viewstate and Control State," **p. 62**.

Session State

The Session State section (shown in Figure 29.4) shows each Session variable and its value.

FIGURE 29.4

The Session State section lists the Session variables for the ASP.NET Session.

Session State		
Session Key	**Type**	**Value**
IsUserMember	System.String	true

Figure 29.4 shows only one Session variable, called IsUserMember, with a value of true.

→ For more information on ASP.NET Session state, **see** "Understanding Session Variables," **p. 55**.

Application State

The Application State section (shown in Figure 29.5) shows all the application variables defined in the application.

FIGURE 29.5

Application variables are displayed in the Application State section.

Application State		
Application Key	**Type**	**Value**
DatabaseName	System.String	DB01
WSURL	System.String	http://www.mysite.com/webservice.asmx
InProd	System.Boolean	True

Request Cookies Collection

The Request Cookies Collection (shown in Figure 29.6) section shows you all the cookies that were included with the request.

FIGURE 29.6

The Request Cookies
Collection shows you
all cookies sent with
the request, includ-
ing the ASP.NET
Session cookie.

Request Cookies Collection		
Name	Value	Size
ASP.NET_SessionId	4aimmk45vcsbotnrubyx5o55	42

Response Cookies Collection

The Response Cookies Collection section shows the same information shown in the Request Cookies Collection, but cookies listed here are cookies sent to the browser in the response from the web server.

Headers Collection

The Headers Collection section (shown in Figure 29.7) displays all the HTTP headers associated with the request.

FIGURE 29.7

The Headers
Collection section
shows all the HTTP
headers associated
with the request.

Headers Collection	
Name	Value
Connection	Keep-Alive
Accept	*/*
Accept-Encoding	gzip, deflate
Accept-Language	en-us
Cookie	ASP.NET_SessionId=4aimmk45vcsbotnrubyx5o55
Host	localhost:64309
User-Agent	Mozilla/4.0 (compatible; MSIE 7.0; Windows NT 6.0; SLCC1; .NET CLR 2.0.50727; Media Center PC 5.0; .NET CLR RTC LM 8)
UA-CPU	x86

Response Headers Collection

The Response Headers Collection section (shown in Figure 29.8) shows all the headers returned by the web server.

FIGURE 29.8

The Response
Headers Collection
section shows the
headers returned by
the server.

Response Headers Collection	
Name	Value
X-AspNet-Version	2.0.50727
Cache-Control	private
Content-Type	text/html

Form Collection

The Form Collection section (shown in Figure 29.9) contains an entry for each form field that was submitted. It's populated only when the request being traced is the POST of a form.

FIGURE 29.9

The Form Collection section shows all the form fields and values.

Form Collection	
Name	**Value**
__VIEWSTATE	/wEPDwULLTExNTc2NTI3OTlkZDbklZlQnwOk8XJEH7s+NE8P3uO7
txtName	Jim
txtEmail	me@mydomain.com
btnSend	Send
__EVENTVALIDATION	/wEWBAKjqpPoCQLEhISFCwKE8/26DAKFzrr8AcUijpRJyHZqh96pESMg6XgTBECr

As shown in Figure 29.9, the form fields shown here include the Viewstate form field and other invisible form fields used by ASP.NET.

Querystring Collection

The Querystring Collection section (shown in Figure 29.10) shows all the querystring parameters passed in the URL of the request.

FIGURE 29.10

The Querystring Collection section shows the querystring parameters from the request.

Querystring Collection	
Name	**Value**
id	1103
user	jc22
auth	true

Server Variables

The Server Variables section contains all the server variables from the web server. Figure 29.11 shows a truncated list.

FIGURE 29.11

The Server Variables section shows all the server variables from the web server.

Server Variables	
Name	**Value**
ALL_HTTP	HTTP_CONNECTION:Keep-Alive HTTP_ACCEPT:image/gif, image/x-xbitmap, image/jpeg, image/pjpeg powerpoint, application/x-ms-application, application/vnd.ms-xpsdocument, application/xaml+xml, a HTTP_ACCEPT_LANGUAGE:en-us HTTP_COOKIE:ASP.NET_SessionId=4aimmk45vcsbotnrubyx5o55 HT HTTP_USER_AGENT:Mozilla/4.0 (compatible; MSIE 7.0; Windows NT 6.0; SLCC1; .NET CLR 2.0.5072 RTC LM 8) HTTP_UA_CPU:x86
ALL_RAW	Connection: Keep-Alive Accept: image/gif, image/x-xbitmap, image/jpeg, image/pjpeg, application/x powerpoint, application/x-ms-application, application/vnd.ms-xpsdocument, application/xaml+xml, a Language: en-us Cookie: ASP.NET_SessionId=4aimmk45vcsbotnrubyx5o55 Host: localhost:64309 Us Agent: Mozilla/4.0 (compatible; MSIE 7.0; Windows NT 6.0; SLCC1; .NET CLR 2.0.50727; Media Cen UA-CPU: x86
APPL_MD_PATH	
APPL_PHYSICAL_PATH	C:\Users\jamesche\Desktop\Exceptions\

ASP.NET Health Monitoring

ASP.NET has powerful features for monitoring the health of an application that you can employ by making small modifications to your web.config file. One of the most common problems that developers encounter with ASP.NET applications is the loss of Session state due to the application recycling. Determining why an application is recycling is often difficult, but by using ASP.NET's health monitoring features, you can easily log detailed information when your application recycles.

Configuring the Application for Health Monitoring

To configure your application so that application restarts are logged in the Event Viewer, add the code in Listing 29.1 to your `web.config` file directly under the opening `<system.web>` element.

Listing 29.1   Application Lifetime Event Code

```
<healthMonitoring enabled="true" heartbeatInterval="0">
  <rules>
    <add name="Application Events" eventName="Application Lifetime Events"
      provider="EventLogProvider" minInterval="00:00:30" />
  </rules>
</healthMonitoring>
```

The first line of this code enables health monitoring with a `heartbeatInterval` of 0. The `heartbeatInterval` attribute acts as a timer for health monitoring, and if you wanted to have your application's health checked at a regular interval, you could control that by using this attribute. However, in this case, you want to log an event that the application itself is going to cause when it's recycled, so specify a `heartbeatInterval` of 0.

The next few lines add a new health monitoring rule. The name of the rule is Application Events, but you can name it anything you want. The `eventName` attribute specifies the name of the event you want to monitor. In this case, you want to monitor the Application Lifetime Events. You can monitor other events as well in the `System.Web.Management` namespace, but this is the only one covered here.

ASP.NET offers some preconfigured providers for logging health monitoring events. In this case, the `EventLogProvider` is used, which means that the event will be logged in the Windows Application log visible with the Event Viewer.

Finally, specify a `minInterval` attribute of 30 seconds. The `minInterval` attribute specifies the minimum interval between events that are logged. The reason you specify 30 seconds is because you don't want a large number of events logged and filling up the Application log. In some cases, a misbehaving process might make changes to a file in your application many times a second, and when changes are made to certain files, the application recycles. If you log every one of those changes, it could fill up your Application log.

Viewing Health Monitoring Logs

After you've added the health monitoring code to your `web.config` file, browse to any page in your application. After the page has loaded in your web browser, add a new empty line to the `web.config` file and save it. Then, open your `global.asax` file (if there is one in your application), add an empty line to it, and save it. After that is done, you can view the events that were logged with the Event Viewer, located in Administrative Tools in Windows.

Figure 29.12 shows the event that was logged when the `web.config` file was modified, and Figure 29.13 shows the event that was logged when the `global.asax` file was modified.

Monitoring the Network with Fiddler

ASP.NET applications rely on the integrity of data passed over the network between the web server and the browser. If there's a breakdown in that process, you can suffer from problems such as loss of session state, failure for users to authenticate, numerous types of errors, and so on. Monitoring that goes on over the network is a powerful tool for troubleshooting ASP.NET applications, and Fiddler (www.fiddlertool.com) is a great (and free) tool for doing that.

Fiddler is an *HTTP proxy*. That means that it inserts itself between your browser and the network and monitors the traffic. You can use it to track the entire conversation between your browser and the web server without worrying about capturing other network traffic on your computer.

Figure 29.14 shows Fiddler displaying the headers from a request to a secure website.

FIGURE 29.14

Using Fiddler, you can easily monitor the network traffic between the browser and the web server.

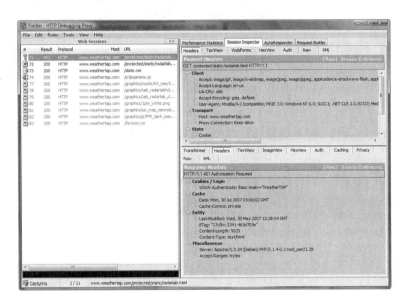

Eric Lawrence, the developer of Fiddler, is a program manager on the Internet Explorer team at Microsoft. He has written excellent documentation and recorded walkthrough videos that illustrate how you can use Fiddler to troubleshoot web applications. You can access this information by browsing to www.fiddler2.com/fiddler/help/.

Checkpoint

As you've seen in this chapter, many tools are available to you that aid in troubleshooting your ASP.NET application. Using these tools, you should be able to keep an eye on your application's health and fix problems when they arise.

PART XI

Deploying ASP.NET Applications

CHAPTER 30

Publishing an ASP.NET Application

IN THIS CHAPTER

Using the Copy Web Site Tool

After you've finished development and testing of your application, you're ready to copy it to your production web server. If you use Visual Web Developer to deploy your website, you'll likely be using the Copy Web Site tool shown in Figure 30.1.

FIGURE 30.1

The Copy Web Site tool allows you to copy your website from one location to another.

The Copy Web Site tool is accessible if you select Website, Copy Web Site from the menu in Visual Web Developer. However, it's more convenient to simply click the Copy Web Site button at the top of Solution Explorer as shown in Figure 30.2.

Copy Web Site Button

FIGURE 30.2

The Copy Web Site button in Solution Explorer provides fast access to the Copy Web Site tool.

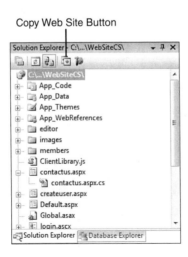

Let's review the process of deploying a website with the Copy Web Site tool of Visual Web Developer.

Connecting to a Remote Site

When the Copy Web Site tool is first launched for a project, you need to connect to the remote website to copy the application. To do that, click the Connect button at the top of the Copy Web Site tool, as shown previously in Figure 30.1.

Not Necessarily Remote

The terminology used in Visual Web Developer is a little bit misleading. The currently open website is called the Source Web Site and the destination website is called the Remote Web Site. However, the destination website need not be remote. In fact, the Source Web Site might be located on a remote server and the site that Visual Web Developer refers to as the Remote Web Site might be located on your local machine.

Just remember that the website displayed in the left pane is the source website and the website displayed in the right pane is the destination website.

When you click the Connect button, you see the Open Web Site dialog, where you'll need to specify a destination location for the website you are copying as shown in Figure 30.3.

FIGURE 30.3
The Open Web Site dialog box is used to specify the location for the destination website when publishing.

NOTE
This dialog box, and the options available to you here, are identical to the Choose Location dialog discussed in Chapter 8, "Creating Websites." If you need a refresher on the options available for creating a new website, refer to the information in Chapter 8.

After you've connected to a remote website with the Open Web Site dialog, that connection persists between sessions with Visual Web Developer. In other words, the next time you open the same application, the Copy Web Site tool will still be connected to the website you have selected as the destination.

Copying Websites with the Copy Web Site Feature

After you've selected a destination path, the easiest method of copying a website from the source location to the destination is to right-click in the pane displaying the source website and select Copy Site to Remote, as shown in Figure 30.3.

FIGURE 30.4

To copy the source website to the destination location, right-click on the source website and select Copy Site to Remote.

If a file has changed since the last time the website was copied, an arrow appears next to the filename. The arrow always points in the direction that the file is to be copied when the source and destination websites are synchronized. In Figure 30.5, two files in the source website are newer than files in the destination website. One file (login.ascx) in the destination website also is newer than the corresponding file in the source website.

To synchronize the two websites so that they are identical to each other, right-click in either pane and choose Synchronize Site. If you'd prefer, you can select the files that you'd like to synchronize and then click the Synchronize button. The Synchronize button is the button between the two panes with an icon showing two arrows pointing in opposite directions.

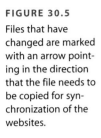

FIGURE 30.5
Files that have changed are marked with an arrow pointing in the direction that the file needs to be copied for synchronization of the websites.

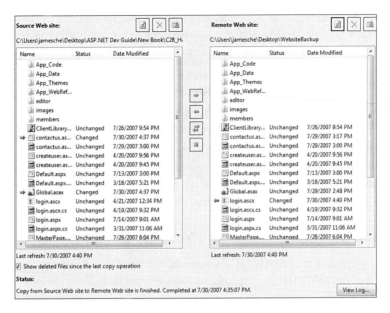

TIP	You can also drag and drop files between the source and the destination websites.	

CAUTION	If a file is edited outside the Visual Web Developer environment, Visual Web Developer can lose track of the file's status. To ensure that you are always looking at the latest status, click the Refresh button at the top of the website's pane in the Copy Web Site tool.	

When you use the Copy Web Site tool to copy files, all files in the website are copied, including your source code. If you'd prefer to deploy your website without copying source code, publishing the website might be more appealing to you.

→ For more information on publishing websites in Visual Web Developer, **see** Chapter 3, "ASP.NET Compilation Models."

Special Considerations for Membership Websites

When you added uses to the web application's membership database in Chapter 13, the membership database for the website was updated with that membership information. In addition to storing information about the user, ASP.NET stores the name of the ASP.NET application in the database. If the user attempts to log in to the website and the application name doesn't match the application listed for the user, he or she is denied access.

This is one of the most common problems that ASP.NET developers encounter when publishing an ASP.NET application. Users are added to the database on the developer's local machine and the local application name is added to the database. Then, when the website is published, the application name changes and the user can no longer log in.

Fortunately, there's an easy solution to this problem. If you add membership information into the web.config file that specifies an explicit application name that matches the application name in your membership database, you can ensure that users will always be able to successfully log in, regardless of where the website gets copied.

Obtaining the Application Name from the Database

To ensure that the web.config file specifies the correct application name, you need to open the membership database after adding one or more users and check the application name that was added.

Double-click the aspnetdb.mdf file in the App_Data directory in your website to open the database in the Database Explorer, as shown in Figure 30.6.

FIGURE 30.6

The Database Explorer provides a convenient interface for exploring SQL Server Express databases.

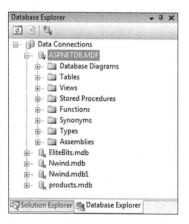

Click the plus sign next to the Tables node to view the tables in the database. The table that contains the application name is the aspnet_Applications table. Right-click on that table and select Show Table Data, as shown in Figure 30.7.

FIGURE 30.7

To see the data in a table, right-click on the table and select Show Table Data.

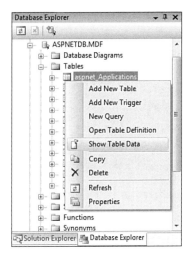

The first column in the table shows the application name. In this case, the application name is /, as shown in Figure 30.8. That's the value that you'll want to specify in the web.config file.

FIGURE 30.8

The application name appears in the first column of the table.

Editing the web.config File

To ensure that users can log in after you publish your website, you need to add membership to the web.config file and explicitly specify the application name. Add the following code to your web.config file directly under the opening <system.web> element.

> **TIP** Remember to click the Solution Explorer tab to switch back to a view of the files and folders in your website.

```
<membership>
  <providers>
    <clear/>
    <add name="AspNetSqlMembershipProvider"
        type="System.Web.Security.SqlMembershipProvider, System.Web,
➥Version=2.0.0.0, Culture=neutral, PublicKeyToken=b03f5f7f11d50a3a"
        connectionStringName="LocalSqlServer"
        enablePasswordRetrieval="false"
        enablePasswordReset="true"
        requiresQuestionAndAnswer="true"
        requiresUniqueEmail="false"
        passwordFormat="Hashed"
        maxInvalidPasswordAttempts="5"
        minRequiredPasswordLength="7"
        minRequiredNonalphanumericCharacters="1"
        passwordAttemptWindow="10"
        passwordStrengthRegularExpression=""
        applicationName="/" />
  </providers>
</membership>
```

That seems like a lot of code just to specify the application name. You have to add so much code because you have to clear the existing membership settings (using the <clear /> element), and then add the membership settings back with the desired configuration. In this case, only the applicationName attribute was changed.

> **NOTE** Many other attributes specified here enable you to control features of ASP.NET membership. Feel free to experiment with them if you want to modify membership requirements.

After you've made that modification to your web.config file, you can publish your membership site to your remote server and, assuming the remote server supports the use of SQL Server Express Edition, you can use all the membership features that you used locally.

Wrapping Up

You've now completed a full-featured ASP.NET website complete with data features, email features, membership features, and more! I hope that you've learned a lot about how to take advantage of ASP.NET and the powerful features provided by Visual Web Developer 2008.

I'd like to leave you with this thought: Don't think of this as the end of your ASP.NET journey! Instead, use this as a starting point to your exploration into this exciting technology. ASP.NET is a powerful and user-friendly development environment.

I wish you the best of luck in all your web application development endeavors!

APPENDIX A

Application Settings in Visual Web Developer

IN THIS APPENDIX

Accessing Application Settings

Application settings in Visual Web Developer enable you to configure many different options that affect the entire application. To access the VWD application settings, select Tools, Options from the main menu to display the Options dialog shown in Figure A.1.

FIGURE A.1

The Options dialog in Visual Web Developer contains a wide array of settings that control the application.

TIP

> When the Options dialog is first displayed, only four categories are listed. To see all categories, check the Show All Settings check box.

Let's start by discussing the settings that are available in the Options dialog.

Environment Settings

Environment settings contain configuration options for the Visual Web Developer user interface and that control how particular elements of the interface operate. There are several subsections in the Environment settings section.

General Settings

The general settings (shown previously in Figure A.1) contain settings that affect the Visual Web Developer environment. The following settings are available:

- **Window Layout**—You can choose between a tabbed-document layout or a multiple-document interface. Tabbed-document is the default and matches the Expression Web interface.

- **Items Shown in Window Menu**—If more than one window is open, a list of opened windows appears on the Windows menu. You can specify how many items are shown in the Windows menu by entering a value between 1 and 24.

- **Items Shown in Recently Used Lists**—The File menu contains a menu of recent files and recent projects. This setting configures how many items appear in each list.
- **Show Status Bar**—When this check box is checked, Visual Web Developer displays a status bar at the bottom of the interface.
- **Close Button Affects Active Tool Window Only**—Visual Web Developer allows for multiple tool windows to be displayed in a single pane, as shown in Figure A.2. When this check box is checked, clicking the Close button on the pane closes only the active tool. If this check box is unchecked, all tools in the pane close. It is checked by default.

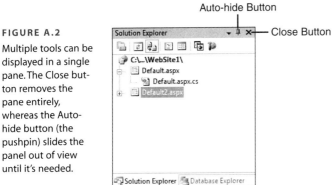

FIGURE A.2

Multiple tools can be displayed in a single pane. The Close button removes the pane entirely, whereas the Auto-hide button (the pushpin) slides the panel out of view until it's needed.

- **Auto-Hide Button Affects Active Tool Window Only**—When this check box is checked, clicking the Auto-hide button (shown previously in Figure A.2) hides only the active tool. If it's unchecked, the entire pane is hidden. It is unchecked by default.
- **Animate Environment Tools**—When you click the Auto-hide button, the pane slides off to the side if this check box is checked. The speed of that animation can be controlled by the slider. This check box is checked by default.
- **Restore File Associations**—Clicking this button restores any file associations that were originally configured for Visual Web Developer. This is useful in cases where some other product has taken over a particular file type.

AutoRecover

This section (shown in Figure A.3) contains settings that configure whether or not Visual Web Developer saves backups of files in situations where it closes unexpectedly. You can choose the time interval between saves of backup files and also how many days of backups Visual Web Developer will save.

FIGURE A.3

Visual Web
Developer can auto-
matically save files at
a preset interval.
These backed up files
can be recovered if
Visual Web
Developer shuts
down unexpectedly.

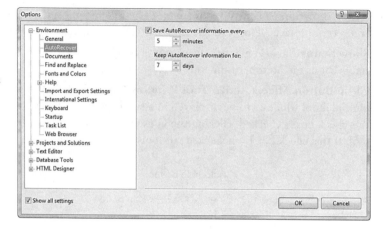

Backup files are saved to the Visual Studio 2005\Backup Files\<Project_Name> folder in
the user's Documents directory (where Project_Name is the actual filename for the project).
Files appear in this directory only if Visual Web Developer shuts down unexpectedly.

Documents

This section contains settings for how Visual Web Developer deals with documents that are
being edited. The following settings are available, as shown in Figure A.4:

- **Reuse Current Document Window, If Saved**—When you open or create a new document, the default behavior is to open a new tab or window for the document being
  opened or created. However, if this check box is checked and the document in the current window has been saved, Visual Web Developer opens a new document inside the
  current document window, replacing the current document with the new one. This
  option is unchecked by default.

FIGURE A.4

Many settings are
available for docu-
ments that are being
edited.

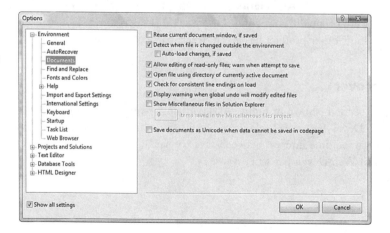

- **Detect When File Is Changed Outside the Environment**—When this check box is checked, if a currently opened file is changed outside of Visual Web Developer, a notification dialog is displayed when Visual Web Developer is activated that the file has been modified, as shown in Figure A.5. This check box is checked by default.

FIGURE A.5

Visual Web Developer can detect when changes are made to a file outside the Visual Web Developer interface.

- **Auto-load Changes, If Saved**—If this check box is checked, any changes made outside Visual Web Developer are automatically made to the document inside Visual Web Developer, provided the document has been saved inside Visual Web Developer. If unsaved changes have been made to the document inside Visual Web Developer, the document is not updated. This check box is available only if the Detect When File Is Changed Outside the Environment check box is checked. This box is unchecked by default.

TIP

If you're working with both Expression Web and Visual Web Developer, you may find it convenient to check this check box so that any changes made in Expression Web are made available automatically in Visual Web Developer.

- **Allow Editing of Read-only Files; Warn When Attempt to Save**—When this check box is checked, Visual Web Developer allows you to edit read-only files, but you'll be warned when you attempt to save the file. This check box is checked by default.

CAUTION

If you enable document check-in and check-out in Expression Web, all files that are not checked out in Expression Web are marked as read-only. When this box is checked in Visual Web Developer, you can edit those read-only files.

- **Open File Using Directory of Currently Active Document**—When this check box is checked, the Open dialog used when opening files displays the directory of the currently active document. If this check box is unchecked, the Open dialog displays the last used directory. This check box is checked by default.

- **Check for Consistent Line Endings On Load**—Because Web forms and code files are text files, it's possible that a third-party editor might use inconsistent methods of inserting line breaks. When this check box is checked, Visual Web Developer warns you if a file uses inconsistent line break characters. This option is checked by default.

- **Display Warning When Global Undo Will Modify Edited Files**—One of the more advanced programming features of Visual Web Developer is called *refactoring*. When Visual Web Developer refactors code, it can cause changes to multiple code files. When this check box is checked, Visual Web Developer warns you when an undo operation will change any edited files due to refactoring.

> **NOTE** I don't go into how refactoring works in this book, but you can find information on refactoring at www.informit.com.

- **Show Miscellaneous Files in Solution Explorer**—If you have a solution open in Visual Web Developer and then select File, Open File to open a file that is outside of the project folder, the file is not displayed in Solution Explorer by default. If this check box is checked, a Miscellaneous Files folder is created in Solution Explorer when a file is opened from outside of the solution, and that file is added to the folder. This check box is not checked by default.

- **Items Saved in Miscellaneous Folder**—Enter a number between 0 and 256 in this text box to specify how many external files are displayed in the Miscellaneous Folder in Solution Explorer.

- **Save Documents As Unicode When Data Cannot Be Saved in Codepage**—When this check box is checked, Visual Web Developer saves files as Unicode if they cannot be saved in the codepage that is configured for the page. The `CodePage` attribute of the `@ Page` directive is used to configure the codepage. This option is unchecked by default.

Find and Replace

The Find and Replace section (shown in Figure A.6) contains the following settings:

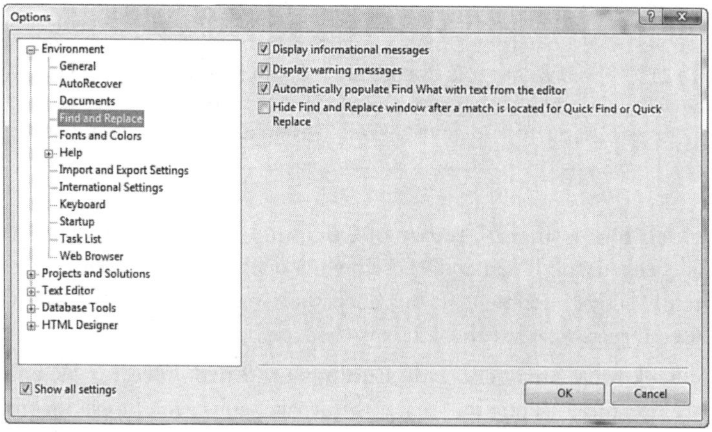

FIGURE A.6

Find and Replace settings are located in the Environment section.

- **Display Informational Messages**—When this check box is checked, Visual Web Developer displays an informational dialog during Find and Replace. Only dialogs that have an Always Show This Message check box (as shown in Figure A.7) are affected by this setting. This check box is checked by default.

FIGURE A.7

If a Find and Replace dialog has an Always Show This Message check box, it is affected by the Display Informational Messages setting.

- **Display Warning Messages**—When this check box is checked, Visual Web Developer displays warning messages during Find and Replace operations when applicable. Only dialogs with an Always Show This Message check box, as shown previously in Figure A.7, are affected by this setting. This check box is checked by default.

> **TIP**
>
> Both the Display Informational Messages and the Display Warning Messages check boxes are three-state check boxes. They can be checked, unchecked, or filled. If you uncheck any of the Always Show This Message check boxes in a warning or informational message, the corresponding options check box will be filled instead of checked.

- **Automatically Populate Find What with Text from the Editor**—If this check box is checked, any selected text in the editor will be automatically added to the Find What text box in Find and Replace dialogs. This check box is checked by default.
- **Hide Find and Replace Window After a Match Is Located for Quick Find or Quick Replace**—When this check box is checked, the Find and Replace dialog is hidden after a match is found when using Quick Find or Quick Replace as shown in Figure A.8. Otherwise, the Find and Replace dialog remains visible during the Find process. This check box is unchecked by default.

Fonts and Colors

The Fonts and Colors section of the Options dialog (shown in Figure A.9) allows you to configure the colors and fonts that are used in different user interface elements in Visual Web Developer.

FIGURE A.8

By default, the Find and Replace dialog remains visible after a match is found using Quick Find or Quick Replace.

FIGURE A.9

The Fonts and Colors section contains settings for over 20 user interface elements in Visual Web Developer.

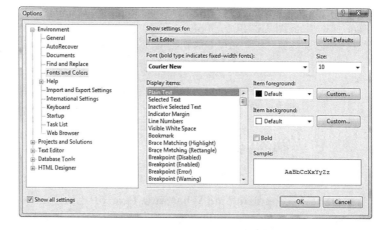

Select the user interface element you'd like to configure in the Show Settings For dropdown. You can then change the font and color settings as per your preference. If you'd like to revert to default settings, click the Use Defaults button.

TIP   The Use Defaults button applies to only the selected user interface element.

Help—General

The General Help settings (shown in Figure A.10) contain settings that affect the Help window in Visual Web Developer.

FIGURE A.10

General Help settings control the appearance of the Help window in Visual Web Developer.

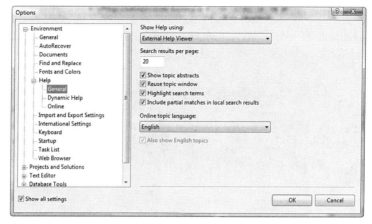

- **Show Help Using**—This drop-down enables you to configure whether Help is displayed within the Visual Web Developer interface or as an external window.

- **Search Results Per Page**—Enables you to configure how many results are shown on each page when searching in Help.

- **Show Topic Abstracts**—Specifies whether or not a brief excerpt of each Help topic is shown in the search results. This check box is checked by default.

- **Reuse Topic Window**—When this check box is checked, each new topic is opened in the same window. When the check box is unchecked, a new window is opened for each topic. This box is checked by default.

- **Highlight Search Terms**—When this check box is checked, search terms are highlighted in each search results topic. This box is checked by default.

- **Include Partial Matches in Local Search Results**—When this check box is checked, search results are found when any of the searched words are found. If the box is unchecked, only topics that match all your search terms are displayed. This check box is checked by default, but it's often preferable to uncheck it so that you don't get irrelevant search results.

- **Online Topic Language**—Specifies the language that is used for online Help sources.

- **Also Show English Topics**—If this check box is checked, English topics are shown in addition to the language that is selected in the Online Topic Language drop-down. This check box is checked by default.

> **TIP** Some online Help sources may not offer content in all languages, so if you choose a language other than English, you may want to also leave the Also Show English Topics check box checked.

Help—Dynamic Help

The Dynamic Help options (shown in Figure A.11) configure how Dynamic Help works in Visual Web Developer.

FIGURE A.11

The Dynamic Help options control what categories and topics are considered when Visual Web Developer is displaying Dynamic Help.

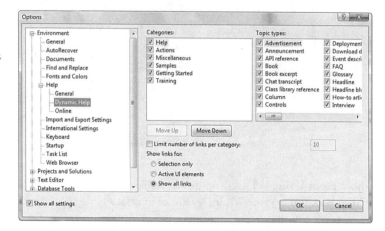

Dynamic Help is a help system that displays context-sensitive help links based upon the code that is being entered or edited. It also displays relative help links for ASP.NET controls as you work in Design view. Dynamic Help is displayed in the Dynamic Help panel shown in Figure A.12.

FIGURE A.12

Dynamic Help displays links that are relevant to the code or control you are currently editing.

> **TIP**
>
> On a slower machine, Dynamic Help can dramatically reduce performance in Visual Web Developer. If you experience performance problems when using Dynamic Help, you can reduce the amount of content it displays by using the options available in the Options dialog.

Help—Online

Visual Web Developer can use online Help so that your documentation is always up to date. It can also search other help sources besides MSDN, such as popular ASP.NET development sites and other topic-sensitive resources.

The Online section of Help settings (shown in Figure A.13) enables you to configure when Visual Web Developer uses online help and what online help systems are used.

FIGURE A.13

The Online Help settings configure which online sources Visual Web Developer uses and when.

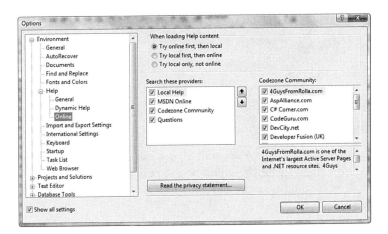

Import and Export Settings

As you've no doubt realized, many configuration settings are available in Visual Web Developer. It's likely that you may tweak many of these settings to your liking. Visual Web Developer saves all of your settings into a file located at `<Profile_Documents_Folder>\Visual Studio 2005\Settings\VWD Express\CurrentSettings.vssettings` by default.

> **TIP**
>
> The settings file also saves the layout of windows in Visual Web Developer.

Using the Import and Export Settings options shown in Figure A.14, you can direct the location of the settings file to any directory you choose. You also have the option of specifying a UNC path or local drive for a team settings file. The team settings file enables you to share settings with a team of users. When a change is made to the team settings file, Visual Web Developer automatically applies those changes to every developer using that file.

FIGURE A.14

Visual Web Developer uses a settings file that you can easily back up if you need to save your settings. You can also use a team settings file so that multiple users can share settings.

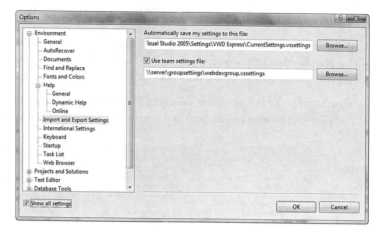

International Settings

Using the International Settings options, you can choose to have Visual Web Developer use the localized language for the application (depending upon which language version you installed) or use the language configured in Windows.

Keyboard

The Keyboard options make it simple to configure keyboard shortcuts in Visual Web Developer. You can either remove existing shortcuts or create your own shortcuts, as shown in Figure A.15.

FIGURE A.15

Visual Web Developer keyboard shortcuts can be configured in the Keyboard settings section of the Options dialog.

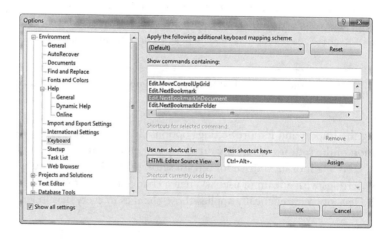

Keyboard shortcuts can be configured so that they apply to only certain areas of Visual Web Developer. In Figure A.15, a keyboard shortcut that moves to the next document bookmark is being created and that shortcut will apply in only HTML source view.

Startup

By default, Visual Web Developer opens with the Start Page visible. The Start Page displays news and information on ASP.NET development. Content on the Start Page is updated dynamically once an hour so that it always contains fresh and relevant information.

You can configure whether or not the Start Page is displayed, the URL used for the Start Page, and the update interval in the Startup section. These settings are shown in Figure A.16.

FIGURE A.16

The Startup section enables you to configure the startup behavior, the URL for the Start Page, and the update interval.

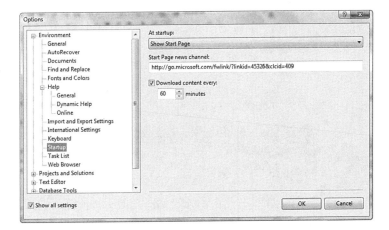

TIP

Ajax is used to update the Start Page, which means that when a refresh of content occurs, the page doesn't blank out and refresh. Any updated content automatically changes inline instead.

Task List

The Task List settings (shown in Figure A.17) make it easy to configure specifics words (called *tokens*) that can be used to generate file-specific tasks automatically.

If you are entering ASP.NET code into a file and you enter a comment that begins with TODO, Visual Web Developer automatically creates a task in the Task List as shown in Figure A.18. You can configure your own tokens to create tasks automatically as well.

FIGURE A.17

The Task List settings provide a great way to improve workflow and efficiency.

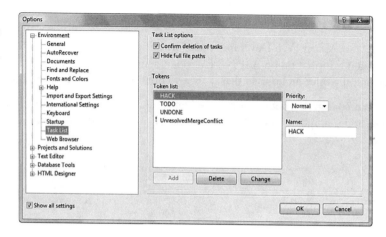

TODO Comment

FIGURE A.18

The TODO comment shown here causes a task to be created automatically for the comment that is entered.

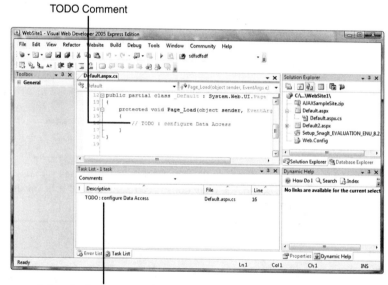

Automatically Generated Task

Web Browser

The options in the Web Browser section (shown in Figure A.19) affect Visual Web Developer's internal web browser.

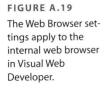

FIGURE A.19
The Web Browser settings apply to the internal web browser in Visual Web Developer.

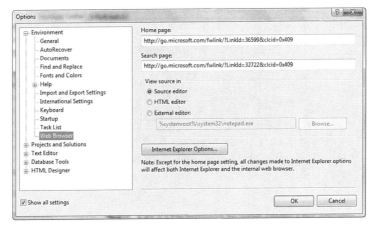

| TIP | To access the internal web browser, select View, Other Windows, Web Browser. |

The Web Browser section also provides settings for configuring how HTML source is viewed in the internal web browser. You can choose between Visual Web Developer's source editor, Visual Web Developer's HTML editor, and an external editor.

Projects and Solutions Settings

The Projects and Solutions section controls how Visual Web Developer deals with projects and solutions and what happens when projects are built and run.

General

The General section of the Projects and Solutions section provides settings for project files and solution files. As shown in Figure A.20, you can configure locations for projects, project templates, and user item templates.

There is also a series of check boxes.

- **Always Show Error List if Build Finishes with Errors**—By default, Visual Web Developer displays a list of errors if a build fails. If this box is unchecked, the Error List is not automatically displayed. This box is checked by default.

→ For more information on the Error List, **see** "Using the Error List to Locate Application Errors," **p. 393**.

FIGURE A.20

Project and solution settings are configured in the Projects and Solutions section.

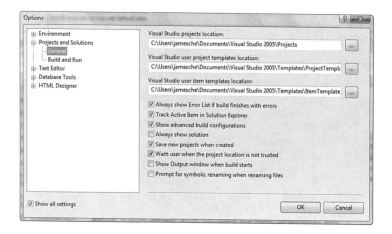

- **Track Active Item in Solution Explorer**—If this box is checked, Visual Web Developer expands folders as necessary in Solution Explorer so that the active item is selected. This box is checked by default.

- **Show Advanced Build Configurations**—Build configurations are build settings that can be customized per application. When Visual Web Developer was first released, it was necessary to check the Show Advanced Build Configurations box to have access to build configurations. With the latest service packs installed, this box is no longer functional.

- **Always Show Solution**—By default, Visual Web Developer does not show a solution in Solution Explorer. Instead, the top-level object is the project itself. If this box is checked, the solution is also displayed in Solution Explorer.

- **Save New Projects When Created**—This box has no effect.

- **Warn User When the Project Location Is Not Trusted**—By default, when you create a new project on a remote path such as a UNC path or an HTTP path, Visual Web Developer warns you that the project location is not trusted. Uncheck this box to suppress that warning.

- **Show Output Window When Build Starts**—By default, when a project is built, the status bar in Visual Web Developer is the only indicator of what's going on. If this box is checked, the Output Window is displayed when your project is built so that you can see details on the build process. This box is checked by default.

- **Prompt for Symbolic Renaming When Renaming Files**—Most developers name their code files with the same naming convention used in code. For example, a file that defines a class called WebMenu might be called `WebMenu.cs` or `WebMenu.vb`. When this box is checked, Visual Web Developer asks whether you'd like to change code references when such a file is renamed. This box is unchecked by default.

Build and Run

The Build and Run section (shown in Figure A.21) contains settings that relate to building and running your web application.

All the options regarding building and running your web application are available in the Build and Run section.

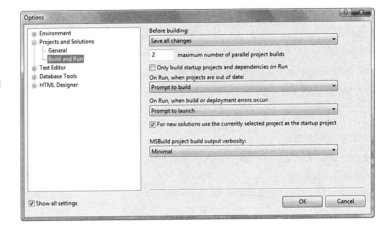

Text Editor Settings

The Text Editor section contains settings to configure how code is handled in Visual Web Developer's text editor and code editors. This section includes many settings because Visual Web Developer enables you to configure separate settings or specific languages. We'll cover the settings that apply to all languages in this section.

General

The General section of the Text Editor section (shown in Figure A.22) applies to any file type being edited in Code view or Source view.

The General section in the Text Editor section applies to all files.

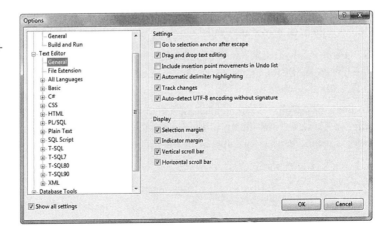

The following check boxes are available in the Settings section of the dialog:

- **Go to Selection Anchor After Escape**—When this box is checked, pressing the Esc key on your keyboard moves the insertion point to the beginning of the selection. This box is unchecked by default.

- **Drag and Drop Text Editing**—When this box is checked, you can edit text by selecting it and dragging and dropping it to another location in the current document or into another open document. This box is checked by default.

- **Include Insertion Point Movements In Undo List**—When this box is checked, movements of the insertion point are included in the Undo List. Therefore, if you click inside a document to move the insertion point to another location and then press Ctrl+Z to undo, the insertion point moves back to its original location. This box is unchecked by default.

- **Automatic Delimiter Highlighting**—By default, Visual Web Developer highlights block element delimiters so that when one is selected, the matching delimiter is also selected. For example, if you click an opening `<div>` tag, both the opening and closing `<div>` tag are bolded in Visual Web Developer. If you uncheck this box, that behavior is disabled.

- **Track Changes**—When code is changed, Visual Web Developer displays a yellow vertical line on the left edge of changed code and a green vertical line on the left edge of unchanged code. If this box is unchecked, that behavior is disabled.

- **Auto-detect UTF-8 Encoding Without Signature**—By default, Visual Web Developer uses byte order marks, charset tags, and scanning of byte sequences to determine whether a document is saved with UTF-8 encoding. If this box is unchecked, this behavior is disabled.

> **NOTE**
>
> A discussion of character encoding and other localization topics is outside the scope of this book. For more information on that topic, the InformIT network is a great resource at www.informit.com.

The following check boxes are available in the Display section of the dialog.

- **Selection Margin**—When this option is checked, a selection margin is displayed on the left edge of code as shown in Figure A.23. You can click in the selection margin to select a line of code or click and drag to select multiple lines.

- **Indicator Margin**—When checked, a margin for code indicators appears along the left edge in Code view as shown in Figure A.24. For example, breakpoint indicators and bookmark indicators both appear in the indicator margin.

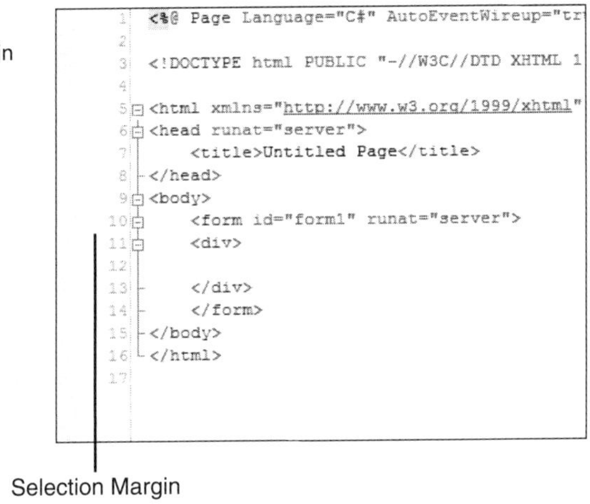

FIGURE A.23

The selection margin makes it easy to select code.

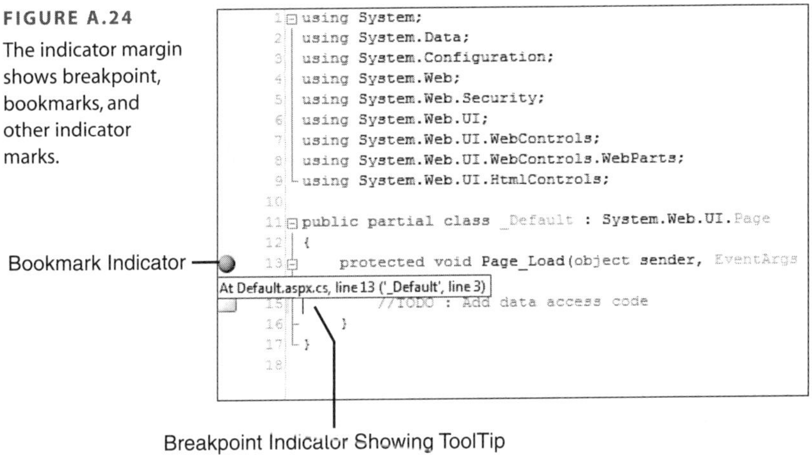

```
1  <%@ Page Language="C#" AutoEventWireup="tr
2
3  <!DOCTYPE html PUBLIC "-//W3C//DTD XHTML 1
4
5  <html xmlns="http://www.w3.org/1999/xhtml"
6  <head runat="server">
7      <title>Untitled Page</title>
8  </head>
9  <body>
10     <form id="form1" runat="server">
11     <div>
12
13     </div>
14     </form>
15  </body>
16  </html>
17
```

Selection Margin

FIGURE A.24

The indicator margin shows breakpoint, bookmarks, and other indicator marks.

```
1  using System;
2  using System.Data;
3  using System.Configuration;
4  using System.Web;
5  using System.Web.Security;
6  using System.Web.UI;
7  using System.Web.UI.WebControls;
8  using System.Web.UI.WebControls.WebParts;
9  using System.Web.UI.HtmlControls;
10
11 public partial class _Default : System.Web.UI.Page
12 {
13     protected void Page_Load(object sender, EventArgs
```
At Default.aspx.cs, line 13 ('_Default', line 3)
```
15                 //TODO : Add data access code
16     }
17 }
18
```

Bookmark Indicator

Breakpoint Indicator Showing ToolTip

- **Vertical Scroll Bar**—When checked, a vertical scroll bar is available so that you can easily scroll up and down to view code that falls outside the viewable area. If unchecked, the keyboard is used to scroll up and down.
- **Horizontal Scroll Bar**—When checked, a horizontal scroll bar is available so that you can scroll left and right to view code that falls outside the viewable area. If unchecked, the keyboard is used to scroll left and right.

File Extension

The File Extension section of the Text Editor section is used to configure file extensions recognized by Visual Web Developer. One use of this is to configure common file extensions not recognized by Visual Web Developer for a particular editing environment. In Figure A.25, the PHP file extension is configured for editing in the source code editor.

FIGURE A.25

The File Extension section can be used to tell Visual Web Developer how to deal with unknown file extensions.

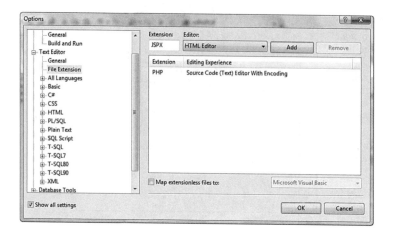

This feature is also convenient when you create your own handlers for your own file extensions. ASP.NET enables you to create HttpHandlers that enable you to have your own custom file extension processed by ASP.NET. Using the File Extension section, you can make sure that your custom file extension is handled appropriately in Visual Web Developer.

> **NOTE** HttpHandlers are an advanced topic not covered in this book. If you'd like more information on how to develop and use HttpHandlers, see the InformIT network at www.informit.com.

> **NOTE** Keep in mind that the File Extension section is not for mapping file extensions to external applications. It is meant only to configure which environment within Visual Web Developer is used to handle particular file types.

All Languages—General

The General section for All Languages (shown in Figure A.26) contains settings for code view for all languages.

The following check boxes are available, all of which can be checked, filled, or unchecked. When filled, it indicates that some languages have the item checked, whereas others do not.

- **Auto List Members**—Enables IntelliSense when checked. This option is checked by default.
- **Hide Advanced Members**—When checked, hides advanced members in IntelliSense. This option is partially selected by default, meaning that it's checked for some languages and unchecked for others.

FIGURE A.26

The General section of the All Languages section configures how code is displayed for all languages.

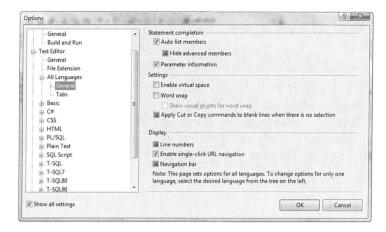

- **Parameter Information**—When checked, displays parameter information when entering methods and so forth. This option is checked by default.

- **Enable Virtual Space**—When checked, you can click outside of code in the code editor and enter text such as comments. This is useful if you like to add comments in a block outside your code area. This item and the Word Wrap item are mutually exclusive. This option is unchecked by default.

- **Word Wrap**—When checked, enables word wrap in code view. This option is unchecked by default.

- **Show Visual Glyphs for Word Wrap**—When checked, Visual Web Developer displays visual indicators when a line is wrapped, as shown in Figure A.27. This option is available only when Word Wrap is checked and is unchecked by default.

FIGURE A.27

Visual glyphs for word wrap appear as small arrows at the right edge of a line.

```
10
11    public partial class _Default : System.Web.
      UI.Page
12    {
13        protected void Page_Load(object sender,
      EventArgs e)
14        {
15            //TODO : Add data access code
16        }
17    }
18
```

- **Apply Cut or Copy Commands to Blank Lines When There Is No Selection**—When checked, enables you to copy or cut blank lines to the clipboard to be pasted elsewhere. This option is checked by default.

- **Line Numbers**—When checked, Visual Web Developer displays line numbers in the left margin of code view. This option is checked by default.

- **Enable Single-click URL Navigation**—When checked, Visual Web Developer creates hyperlinks in code view when other files or pages are referenced. You can click those links to navigate to the file or page. This option is checked by default.

- **Navigation Bar**—When checked, Visual Web Developer displays two drop-downs in code view so that objects or classes can be selected, as well as events or methods. This option is partially selected by default, meaning that it is checked for some languages and unchecked for others.

All Languages—Tabs

The Tabs section controls how indentation and tabs work in your code files in Visual Web Developer. The following indentation settings are available as shown in Figure A.28.

FIGURE A.28
Tab and indentation settings are configured in the Tabs section.

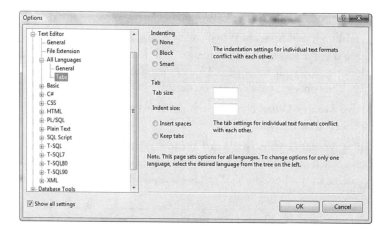

- **None**—No automatic indentation is performed.

- **Block**—New lines are started at the same starting point as the previous line. This is the default selection.

- **Smart**—Visual Web Developer attempts to indent lines properly, based on the context.

You can also configure the tab size, the indent size, and whether Visual Web Developer should use spaces for indentations or keep the tab characters.

> **NOTE** The next section in the Options dialog is Database Tools. Settings in this section are for advanced database administration and are outside of the scope of this book. For details on the Database Tools settings in Visual Web Developer, see the documentation included with Visual Web Developer.

HTML Designer Settings

The HTML Designer settings enable you to configure how Visual Web Developer works in Design view.

General

In the General section of the HTML Designer section (shown in Figure A.29) you configure in which view pages are opened, whether IDs are applied to tables, and the automatic keyboard switching settings and vertical switching settings.

FIGURE A.29

The General section in HTML Designer controls how pages appear in the designer.

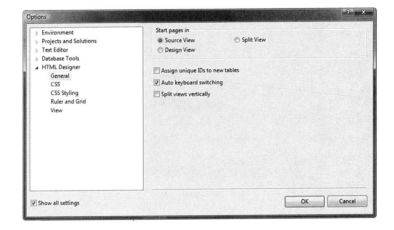

By default, Visual Web Developer will not add an ID attribute to tables that you add to your pages. However, if you check the Assign Unique IDs to New Tables check box shown previously in Figure A.29, a unique ID attribute is added to all new tables that are inserted into your page.

> **TIP** Table IDs are not added to tables that already exist on the page. If the Assign Unique IDs to New Tables check box is checked, only tables added thereafter have a unique ID assigned.

The Auto Keyboard Switching check box (which is checked by default) controls whether Visual Web Developer automatically switches the keyboard to the language you are currently using in Visual Web Developer. The keyboard for that language must be installed on your machine for this feature to work.

> **NOTE** For information about adding a keyboard setting to your particular version of Windows, see the Windows Help files.

By default, Visual Web Developer displays split screen view with a horizontal split. If you check the Split Views Vertically check box, split views are displayed with a vertical split instead, as shown in Figure A.30.

FIGURE A.30

Checking the Split Views Vertically check box causes Split view to be displayed with a vertical split instead of a horizontal one.

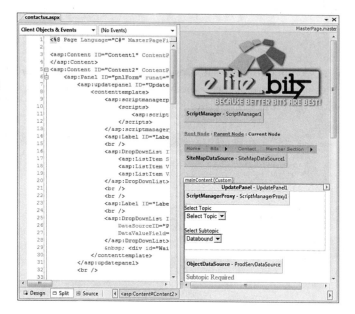

CSS

The CSS section (shown in Figure A.31) controls how different properties are applied to page elements as they are formatted in Design view. By default, CSS (Classes) is selected for all elements. By changing the value to CSS (Inline Styles) for an element, you can force Visual Web Developer to use inline styles instead for formatting.

FIGURE A.31

The CSS section provides settings to control how Visual Web Developer automatically applies CSS to your page.

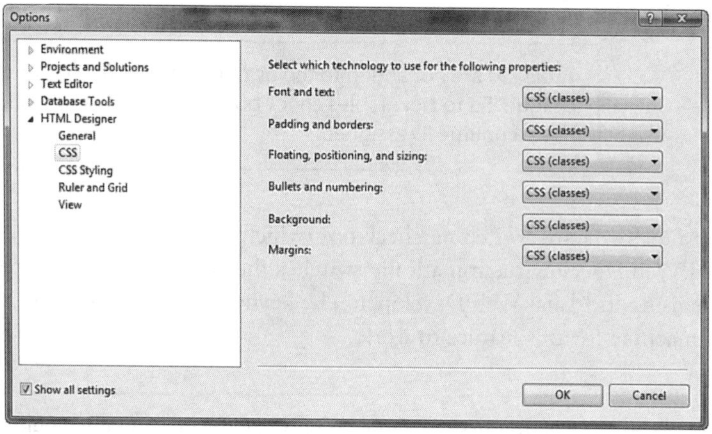

CAUTION

Be careful when selecting inline styles. An inline style will always override other CSS styling, so you might not get the results you intend when using the CSS (Inline Styles) option.

CSS Styling

The CSS Styling section (shown in Figure A.32) provides control over the application of CSS to your page. These options are used in conjunction with the Style Application toolbar.

FIGURE A.32

The CSS Styling section helps you configure the formatting of CSS and is used in conjunction with the Style Application toolbar.

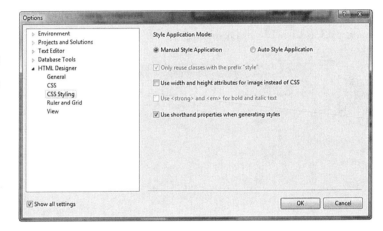

→ For more information on the Style Application toolbar, **see** "Using the Style Application Toolbar," **p. 251**.

The Style Application Mode setting configures whether Visual Web Developer applies styles based on the rules you specify or based on predefined rules. Four check boxes are available to provide more granular control over style application.

- **Only Reuse Classes with the Prefix "style"**—This check box is available only when Auto Style Application is selected. When it's checked (the default setting) and you make a formatting modification to an element that is already styled using one of the automatically created CSS classes (that is, style1, style2, and so on), Visual Web Developer will modify the existing style instead of creating a new one.

- **Use Width and Height Attributes for Image Instead of CSS**—When this box is checked, Visual Web Developer will use the width and height attributes on images instead of CSS styling. Note that the width and height attributes are deprecated and CSS is preferred. This check box is unchecked by default.

- **Use <strong> and <em> for Bold and Italic Text**—When this box is checked, Visual Web Developer will use the <strong> and <em> HTML elements to apply bold and italic formatting to text instead of using CSS. These elements are deprecated, and CSS is the preferred method. This box is also unchecked by default.

- **Use Shorthand Properties when Generating Styles**—When this box is checked, Visual Web Developer will use CSS shorthand properties when generating CSS styles. This box is unchecked by default.

> **NOTE** For more information on shorthand properties in CSS, see www.informit.com/discussion/index.asp?postid=7b7afc64-69cd-4c1f-a201-0c39723cc17d.

Ruler and Grid

The Ruler and Grid section (shown in Figure A.33) configures the units and behavior of the ruler and grid in Visual Web Developer.

FIGURE A.33

The Ruler and Grid section provides basic settings for the ruler and grid in Visual Web Developer.

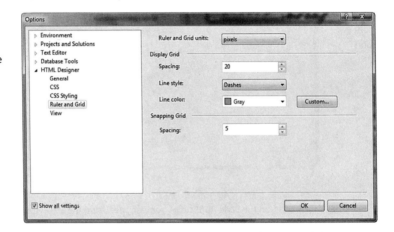

View

The View section (shown in Figure A.34) enables you to configure the foreground and background color for many page elements that you can insert using Visual Web Developer.

Click the Custom button to specify a custom color using the standard Windows color picker.

FIGURE A.34

The View section controls the colors that are used to display page elements in Visual Web Developer.

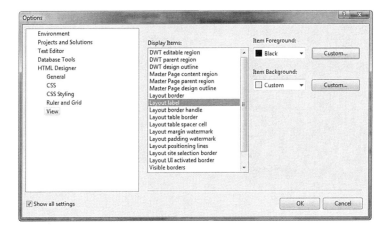

Restoring and Backing Up Settings

As you've seen, a lot of settings are available in Visual Web Developer. This appendix has really only touched the surface of the ways you can configure Visual Web Developer to work for you. As you work in Visual Web Developer, you'll arrange windows the way you want them, configure your toolbox and your menus, and so on. If you ever have to rebuild your computer (or if you get a new computer), it would be quite time-consuming to have to configure everything all over again. Fortunately, Visual Web Developer makes it very easy to back up and restore your settings.

Backing Up Settings

To back up your settings in Visual Web Developer, follow these steps:

1. Select Tools, Import and Export Settings.
2. Select the Export Selected Environment Settings, as shown in Figure A.35, and click Next.
3. Select the settings you want to back up, as shown in Figure A.36, and click Next.

CAUTION

> If a setting has a yellow triangle with a black exclamation point next to it, it indicates that the setting could contain personal information about you or your computer that will be exported. If you are sharing your backup with someone else, you should be aware that personal information might be available to that person.

FIGURE A.35

You have the option of exporting settings, importing settings, or resetting settings to the defaults.

FIGURE A.36

You can select many settings for your backup.

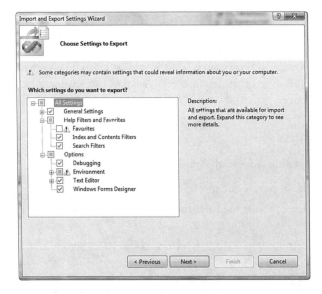

4. Enter the name for your new settings file and the location where you want it stored, as shown in Figure A.37, and click Finish to complete the export.

FIGURE A.37

You can choose a name for your backup file as well as the location where it will be saved.

Restoring Settings

To restore your settings using an existing settings file, follow these steps:

1. Select Tools, Import and Export Settings.

2. Select the Import Selected Environment Settings option, as previously shown in Figure A.35.

3. Select Yes, Save My Current Settings to save your current settings before importing the new settings. Otherwise, select the radio button to import the new settings, as shown in Figure A.38.

FIGURE A.38

You can choose to back up your existing settings before importing new settings if you choose.

4. Select the settings file to use or click Browse to select an unlisted settings file, as shown in Figure A.39.

5. Select the settings to import, using the list as previously shown in Figure A.36, and then click Finish to import your settings.

Restoring Settings to the Default Settings

In cases where you'd like to revert to the default settings, you can do so by selecting the Reset All Settings radio button in the Import and Export Settings Wizard, as shown previously in Figure A.35. When you do, you'll be given the opportunity to save your current settings.

FIGURE A.39
If the desired settings file is not listed, you can use an unlisted one by clicking Browse.

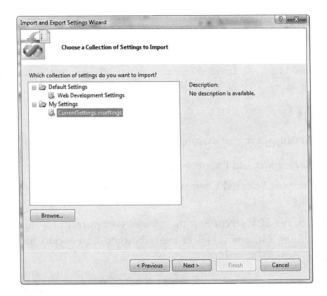

CAUTION	Keep in mind that resetting Visual Web Developer to the default settings may remove custom controls added to the Toolbox as well as other changes made to the Visual Web Developer interface.

Authentication tab (Internet Information Services MMC), 88

authorization, 98-99

ASP.NET Configuration Settings dialog, 108-109

IIS Manager, 110

<authorization> element, application configuration files, 67

Authorization tab (Internet Information Services MMC), 87

Auto Format dialog (Visual Web Developer, Design view), 151

Auto Style Application option (CSS Styling section), 453

AutoDetect Cookieless Mode option (Internet Information Services MMC, State Management tab), 92

AutoDetect value (cookieless authentication), 108

AutoEventWireup attribute, page lifecycles, 49

autoformatting master pages, 152

automating aspnet_compiler.exe, Visual Web Developer Express Edition, 37-39

AutoPostBack property, processing ASP.NET forms, 220

AutoRecover section (Visual Web Developer), 431

B - C

backups, Visual Web Developer application settings, 455

bin folders (websites), 116

bold text, 84, 453

breakpoints

debugging server-side code, 386-388

page lifecycles, 48

broken image placeholders, fixing, 209-210

Browser File file type (Visual Web Developer), 132

btnSend_Click method, enabling exception-handling, 401-403

bubbling exceptions, 399-400

Build and Run section (Visual Web Developer, Projects and Solutions section), 445

Button control, processing ASP.NET forms, 220

C# code

btnSend_Click method, modifying for exception handling, 401-402

exception-handling blocks, 398

sending email, 337

web form configuration, 366

cache API, 59-60

cache scavenging, 61

caching

@ OutputCache directive, 58

cache API, 59-60

cache scavenging, 61

control caching, 58

fragment caching, 58-59

page output caching, 57

post-cache substitution, 59

retrieving items, 61-62

call stacks, 400

Choose Location dialog (Visual Web Developer)

File System button, 121

FTP Site button, 123

Local IIS button, 122

Remote Site button, 124

Class file type (Visual Web Developer), 131

E

F

Fiddler, 417-418

File Extension section (Visual Web Developer, Text Editor section), 447-448

File Not Found error messages, troubleshooting, 79

File System button (Choose Location dialog), 121

filtering data (data source configuration), 304-306

Find and Replace section (Visual Web Developer), 434-435

finding application errors via Error List, 393-395

Fonts and Colors section (Visual Web Developer), 435-436

Form Collection section (ASP.NET tracing), 414

form validation

CompareValidator control, 230

CustomValidator control, 230

necessity of, 226

RangeValidator control, 227

RegularExpressionValidator control, 228-229

RequiredFieldValidator control, 227

Validation control

adding to, 234-236

configuring, 234-236

ControlToValidate property, 233

Display property, 231

EnableClientScript property, 233

ErrorMessage property, 232

SetFocusOnError property, 233

Text property, 231

ValidationGroup property, 233-234

ValidationSummary control, 230

formatting

ASP.NET skin file control codes, 274-276

CSS styles, applying via Style Application toolbar (Visual Web Developer), 251-254

master pages, 150-155

forms

ASP.NET forms versus HTML forms, 214

contact forms example

adding controls, 215-217

configuring Topics DropDownList control, 217-219

required elements, 215

CSS

applying to, 260-262

removing from, 262

displaying confirmations, 221

adding confirmation messages, 222-223

adding server-side code, 223-224

Panel control, 222

HTML forms versus ASP.NET forms, 214

processing, 219

AutoPostBack property, 220

Button control, 220

IsPostBack property, 220-221

sending results to email

adding server-side code, 336-338

attachments, 340-341

HTML email, 339

reviewing contact forms, 336

Forms authentication, 102, 186

configuring

ASP.NET Configuration Settings dialog, 104

ASP.NET Website Administration Tool, 103

IIS Manager, 104-105

Cookie Protection option, 106

I

IDs, CSS, 244-247, 262

IIS (Internet Information Services), 8

anonymous browsing, disabling for Windows authentication, 99-101

ASP.NET configuration

IIS 5.1, 10-11, 82-92

IIS 6.0, 10-11, 82-92

IIS 7, 12-14, 93

troubleshooting, 15

ASP.NET 2.0 application pools, 17-19

missing ASP.NET tabs, 16

IIS 5 connections strings, configuring for membership databases, 179

IIS 6 connections strings, configuring for membership databases, 179

IIS 7 connections strings, configuring for membership databases, 181-183

IIS Manager, configuring

authorization, 110

Forms authentication, 104-105

images

broken placeholders, fixing, 209-210

master pages, adding to, 149

Immediate window (IntelliSense), 390-391

Import and Export Settings section (Visual Web Developer), 439

inline code files, web form creation, 136

inline CSS styles, 243

inline server-side code, 24-25

moving code-behind server-side code to, 27-28

moving to code-behind server-side code, 29

InProc Session state mode (Internet Information Services MMC, State Management tab), 91

InsertItemTemplate (FormView control), 324

IntelliSense, 388

Immediate window, 390-391

Locals window, 389

Watch window, 390

International Settings section (Visual Web Developer), 440

Internet Information Services MMC (Windows XP/Windows Server 2003), 82

Application tab, 88-90

ASP.NET tab, 83-84

Authentication tab, 88

Authorization tab, 87

Custom Errors tab, 86-87

General tab, 84-85

Locations tab, 92

State Management tab, 90-91

IsPostBack property, processing ASP.NET forms, 220-221

italicized text, 84, 453

J - K - L

JIT (just-in-time) compilation, 32

JPEG files, adding to master pages, 149

JScript File file type (Visual Web Developer), 131

Kerberos authentication, 112

Keyboard section (Visual Web Developer), 440

M

N - O

P

Q - R

adding DetailsView control, 313-314

configuring DetailsView control, 313-314

configuring GridView control, 310

paging in, 309

sorting in, 309

records, editing interfaces

adding to, 319-322

deleting from, 323

editing in, 323

references, adding to Web services, 359

RegularExpressionValidator control, form validation, 228-229

Remote Site button (Choose Location dialog), 124

remote site connections, Copy Website tool, 423-424

RemoteOnly setting (Internet Information Services MMC, Custom Errors tab), 87

removing CSS from web forms, 262

Repeater control (ASP.NET), 297

Request Cookies Collection section (ASP.NET tracing), 413

Request Details section (ASP.NET tracing), 411

Request Execution Timeout setting (Internet Information Services MMC, Application tab), 89

Require SSL option (Forms authentication), 106

RequiredFieldValidator control, form validation, 227

resetting passwords, 205-209

Response Cookies Collection section (ASP.NET tracing), 414

Response Headers Collection section (ASP.NET tracing), 414

restoring Visual Web Developer application settings, 457-458

<roleManager> element, machine configuration files, 67

roles, 186

adding users to, 192-193

creating, 191

definitions, ASP.NET configuration, 72

enabling, 190-191, 195

Ruler and Grid section (Visual Web Developer, HTML Designer section), 454

rules (CSS), 240-241

S

saving email configuration files, 334

scavenging (cache), 61

ScriptManager control (ASP.NET AJAX Extensions), 371-373

ScriptManagerProxy control (ASP.NET AJAX Extensions), 371

scroll position (web pages), maintaining, 314

security

authentication, 98

Forms authentication, 102-107

Windows authentication, 99-101

authorization, 98-99

configuring via ASP.NET Configuration Settings dialog, 108-109

configuring via IIS Manager, 110

Security Setup Wizard (Website Administration Tool), 70

Security tab (Website Administration Tool), 69

access method selection, 70

data storage, 71

new access rule additions, 74-75

web form creation, 130

code-behind files, 134-135

inline code files, 136

web pages, 137

creating, 130

testing, 138

website creation, 119-136, 136-139

Visual Web Developer Express Edition, automating aspnet_compiler.exe, 37-39

W

Watch window (IntelliSense), 390

web application compilation model, 32

Web Browser section (Visual Web Developer), 442

web.config files

ASP.NET email configuration, 332

membership websites, editing for, 427-428

page lifecycles, 49-50

web.config.comments files, ASP.NET configuration, 67

web.config.default files, ASP.NET configuration, 67

Web Configuration File file type, 132-133

web design

Expression Web, 137

Visual Web Developer, 137

Web form code

design-time code, 23

directives, 22-23

Web Form file type (Visual Web Developer), 131

web forms

AJAX, adding to, 372

AJAX Library client libraries, 376-377

AJAX Library client scripts, adding to ScriptManagerProxy, 377-378

AJAX Library controls, 375

ScriptManager control (ASP.NET AJAX Extensions), 373

UpdatePanel control (ASP.NET AJAX Extensions), 374

applying

ASP.NET themes to, 277

CSS to, 260-262

creating, 130

code-behind files, 134-135

inline code files, 136

master/detail views, 310

configuring DetailsView control, 312-314

configuring GridView control, 310

paging, 309

removing CSS from, 262

sorting, 309

user controls versus, 164

Web services, using in

adding data sources, 362-363

adding references, 359

configuring, 364-366

web methods, 346, 349

web pages. *See also* **master pages**

creating (Visual Web Developer), 137

Expression Web, creating via, 132-133

master pages, connecting to, 159-161

previewing

Expression Web, 137

Visual Web Developer, 137

scroll position, maintaining, 314

testing, Visual Web Developer, 138

user controls

adding to, 166-167

converting to, 168-169

Visual Web Developer, creating in, 130

Windows authentication. *See* **NTML authentication**

anonymous browsing, disabling in IIS, 99-101

Kerberos authentication, 112

Windows mode (Internet Information Services MMC, Authentication tab), 88

Windows Server 2003, Internet Information Services MMC, 82

Application tab, 88-90

ASP.NET tab, 83-84

Authentication tab, 88

Authorization tab, 87

Custom Errors tab, 86-87

General tab, 84-85

Locations tab, 92

State Management tab, 90-91

Windows Vista, IIS 7 ASP.NET configuration, 93

Windows XP, Internet Information Services MMC, 82

Application tab, 88-90

ASP.NET tab, 83-84

Authentication tab, 88

Authorization tab, 87

Custom Errors tab, 86-87

General tab, 84-85

Locations tab, 92

State Management tab, 90-91

wizards

CreateUserWizard (Website Administration Tool), 74

Security Setup Wizard (Website Administration Tool), 70

WSDL (Web Services Description Language) documents, 347

X - Y - Z

XmlDataSource control (ASP.NET), 289

XMLHttp, 370